THE SCOTT AND LAURIE OKI SERIES
IN ASIAN AMERICAN STUDIES

CONTEMPORARY ASIAN AMERICAN ACTIVISM

Building Movements for Liberation

EDITED BY

DIANE C. FUJINO AND
ROBYN MAGALIT RODRIGUEZ

UNIVERSITY OF WASHINGTON PRESS
Seattle

Contemporary Asian American Activism: Building Movements for Liberation is published with the assistance of a grant from the Scott and Laurie Oki Endowed Fund for publications in Asian American Studies.

Design by Katrina Noble
Composed in Charis SIL, typeface designed by SIL International

26 25 24 23 22   5 4 3 2 1

Printed and bound in the United States of America

All royalties from this book will be split between the Yuri Kochiyama Fund and a nonprofit established in Amado Khaya's name in support of justice and liberation struggles broadly represented by this book.

UNIVERSITY OF WASHINGTON PRESS
uwapress.uw.edu

LIBRARY OF CONGRESS CATALOGING-IN-PUBLICATION DATA
Names: Fujino, Diane Carol, editor. | Rodriguez, Robyn Magalit, editor.
Title: Contemporary Asian American activism : building movements for liberation / edited by Diane C. Fujino and Robyn Magalit Rodriquez.
Description: Seattle : University of Washington Press, [2022] | Includes bibliographical references and index.
Identifiers: LCCN 2021015714 (print) | LCCN 2021015715 (ebook) | ISBN 9780295749792 (hardcover) | ISBN 9780295749808 (paperback) | ISBN 9780295749815 (ebook)
Subjects: LCSH: Asian Americans—Politics and government. | Asian Americans—Civil rights—History. | Asian American political activists. | Asian Americans—Social conditions. | Social movements—United States—History. | United States—Race relations—History. | United States—Social conditions—1980–
Classification: LCC E184.A75 C68 2022 (print) | LCC E184.A75 (ebook) | DDC 305.895/073—dc23
LC record available at https://lccn.loc.gov/2021015714
LC ebook record available at https://lccn.loc.gov/2021015715

♾ This paper meets the requirements of ANSI/NISO Z39.48-1992 (Permanence of Paper).

For Amado and Ezio
For Kano and Seku
Working toward abolitionist and cooperative futures

CONTENTS

ACKNOWLEDGMENTS

Just as social movements are inherently collective, the process for envisioning and developing a book that centers organizing and movement building knowledge has been deeply collective. Many thanks are due to many people, both those directly involved in creating this book and those whose contributions to Asian American liberation struggles have greatly influenced our thinking and praxis. There are too many to name, and we intend to keep this brief. To the many who we have not named on these pages, we ask your forgiveness.

For their support in helping to coordinate the 2019 conference at the University of California, Santa Barbara (UCSB), that began the process of conceptualizing this anthology, we extend gratitude to the participants of the symposium and this anthology: Jessica Antonio, Nikole Cababa, Angelica Cabande, Ga Young Chung, May C. Fu, Wayne Jopanda, Soya Jung, Katherine H. Lee, Pam Tau Lee, Katherine Nasol, Alex Tom, Eddy Zheng. Special thanks to Karen Umemoto for her collaboration in conceptualizing the symposium. We wish to thank the staff members and students at our respective campuses. At UCSB we thank Cora Danielson and Arlene Phillips of the Department of Asian American Studies and Rosa Pinter of the Center for Black Studies Research. At the University of California, Davis, we thank Kirby Araullo of the Department of Asian American Studies. Katherine H. Lee, a graduate student at UCSB at the time, and Wayne Jopanda, a graduate student at UC Davis, offered vital support at all stages of the project. Robyn's students Angela Alejandro, Annelle Garcia, and Anna Pak offered important feedback on the introduction to help Robyn and Diane better attend to the perspectives and concerns of a new generation of aspiring Asian American activists.

We thank the University of California's Humanities Research Institute for a grant in support of the symposium and this book as well as the generous funding support from various units and programs in support of the symposium, including, at UC Davis, the Department of Asian American Studies and the Bulosan Center for Filipinx Studies;

at UCLA, the Asian American Studies Center; and at UC Santa Barbara, the Department of Asian American Studies; the Center for Black Studies Research, the Office of the Dean of Social Sciences, the Office of the Associate Vice Chancellor for Diversity, Equity and Inclusion, the MultiCultural Center, and the Global Environmental Justice Project. We thank Kahlil Kochiyama, Ericka Kodama, David Leong, and Kim Chao, all UCSB students at the time, and the many talented artists and budding artists who participated in the "Declaring Visibility" spoken word program at UCSB that generated support for the symposium.

For the development of this anthology, special thanks go to May Fu for her collaboration and support; to Matef Harmachis for review and editing; and to Kano Fujino-Harmachis for research assistance. We thank the amazing people at the University of Washington Press, which has long advanced scholarship and writings in Asian American studies: Jason Alley, Julie A. Fergus, Kait Heacock, and Joeth Zucco as well as our copyeditor, Elizabeth Gratch, and indexer, Chris Dodge, and especially Mike Baccam, an exceptionally gifted editor with sharp intellect and an enthusiastic supporter from our first conversation with him.

Robyn is thankful to Diane and her family and most especially to her husband, Joshua Vang, not only for their support in getting the book manuscript to the finish line but for their emotional support during an incredibly trying time. Robyn lost her beloved son, Amado, in the final stages of the project. This book could not have been completed in the time frame that it was without their patience and love. For his role in her political education including a deeper understanding of the National Democratic movement of the Philippines, Robyn wishes to thank the late Vic Clemente who died just days before Amado. Vic has not yet been given the honor he deserves for his organizing work. There are too many other people to whom Robyn owes a deep debt of gratitude (*utang na loob*) for her political formation, and she hopes this does them justice.

Diane extends her profound gratitude to a great many in the movement and the communities that surround her for sustenance and for critical ideas and praxis, of which there are too many to name. Let me attempt a short list. I wish to recognize my elders, May and Yasuo Fujino, Mathilda Barker, Linbrook and Marcia Barker, Yuri Kochiyama, Mo Nishida, Mitsuye Yamada, Michael Yasutake, Fred

Ho, Gloria Liggett, Marcus V. Lopez, and Elizabeth Robinson for your guiding light; to Sara Bazan, Lia Grippo, Nenaji Jackson, Zaveeni Khan-Marcus, Raquel Lopez, Marisela Marquez, and Marcelino Sepulveda for your tremendous support and astute minds.; and to Robyn, Don, Wendy, Sandee, Arnel, Lori, Mark, Bev, Jaden, Azriel, Janet, Elaine, and Karina for creating a loving family. Special thanks to Robyn, a powerhouse who has deeply shaped my life over many years, and to her family, who has shown us how to bring in a community to share in the grieving process. My deepest love and appreciation to Matef, Kano, and Seku for their unflinching support as I continue to generate an avalanche of work and for the humor, lightness, joy, and hopefulness they bring into my life.

This book also emerged through a great many setbacks, both of a collective nature in the extraordinary year of 2020 and of a deeply personal nature. We thank the many for their patience as we struggled through teaching assistant strikes, the pandemic, economic and environmental precarity, and movements for Black lives, struggles against anti-Asian violence, and much more.

All of our contributors are committed to ensuring that this book contributes as a primer for all generations of Asian American activists, from Asian American Movement veterans to "yelders" and Millennials to Gen Z and beyond. We have created a website, at https://asianamericanactivism.org, to provide additional resources and to post announcements about lectures, workshops, and other book-related activities.

CONTEMPORARY ASIAN AMERICAN ACTIVISM

INTRODUCTION

BUILDING AN ARCHIVE OF ASIAN AMERICAN ORGANIZING PRAXIS

ROBYN MAGALIT RODRIGUEZ AND DIANE C. FUJINO

IN THE MIDST OF 2020—AN EXTRAORDINARY YEAR OF GLOBAL pandemic, sheltering-in-place, and rising anti-Asian racism, extreme economic inequities, unrelenting police and state violence against Black communities, ongoing environmental catastrophe, and a tyrannical executive government—and most especially after the killings of six Asian women in Atlanta, Georgia, on March 16, 2021, there has been unprecedented mainstream attention to anti-Asian racism and Asian American protest. Until this moment, the considerable Asian American activism that's taken place over many decades has been rendered conspicuously invisible. And yet Asian Americans have been organizing against anti-Asian racism and violence and participating in the uprisings for justice from the antiwar movement to Occupy to Black Lives Matter and the Movement for Black Lives to Standing Rock and Mauna Kea to the environmental justice movement to women and queer liberation to undocumented immigrant rights to cost-of-living adjustments on campuses and more. These current struggles build on a history of Asian American activism, heightened in the Asian American Movement (AAM) of the 1960s and 1970s but occurring before that as well.

Through this volume we bring attention to contemporary Asian American struggles such that the work of today's activists becomes part of the archive of the theories and practices of Asian American Movement building across the decades. The intergenerational lessons gleaned from Asian American activists and activism can serve as a guide and inspiration to today's organizers as they take up the ongoing and multifaceted work of liberation. As Alex T. Tom, a contributor to this anthology, states, "We need a 'movement of movements' to win the hearts and minds of millions." While the Asian American studies (AAS), and ethnic studies more broadly, has critiqued the nature of various structures of power and domination and diagnosed the social ills they produce, we believe that movement organizers offer vital perspectives on how we must go about dismantling those structures toward building a liberatory society.

This book is, to our knowledge, the first anthology examining contemporary Asian American activism. It is also one of the few that centers on the praxis—the application of theories of liberation in practice—of Asian American activists and organizers. There is a growing body of literature, both scholarly and more personal accounts, on Asian American activism, but most of it focuses on the prominent period of the AAM of the 1960s and 1970s.[1] With notable exceptions, there is little by way of sustained attention to the study and narration of current-day Asian American activism.[2] This is the case despite the plethora of Asian American organizations working on the ground at the local, state, and national levels and the online presence of Asian American grassroots organizations and AAM documents.[3] In the struggles around policing and prisons, affordable housing, cooperative economics, and much more, Asian American activists show up, speak out, and help build movements and organizations.

Yet the Asian American Right has seemingly out-organized the Asian American Left, at least in terms of gaining mainstream visibility. By utilizing WeChat and other social media platforms and duplicitously misappropriating the language of the Black civil rights struggles, "Chinese Tea Party" organizers generated some of the largest Asian American mobilizations in the pre-pandemic period centered on two issues: eliminating affirmative action in admissions to Harvard University and organizing in support for Chinese American New York police officer Peter Liang, who in 2014 shot and killed Akai Gurley, an unarmed young Black father. In both cases they misappropriated the civil rights movement's language around equal treatment, arguing that all Harvard applicants should be treated equally without regard to factors such as race and that Liang should be subject to the same consequences as white police officers.[4] In doing so, right-wing activists appeal to the model minority trope that presents Asian Americans as exceptional minorities in their ability to overcome discrimination through hard work, education, delayed gratification, and self-reliance—and, ostensibly, without any need for activist struggles.

Asian American studies scholars and activists have long critiqued the model minority concept for its collusion with anti-Blackness in ways that fail to account for structural racism and harm coalitional politics as well as for its erasure of anti-Asian racism and social problems impacting Asian American communities. This anthology provides a challenge and partial corrective to the model minority myth and its logic erasing unruly resistance, aligned with what Soya Jung, a contributor to this anthology, calls "model minority mutiny."[5] It also aims to equip newer generations of Asian American activists and organizers with the kinds of insights and capacity necessary for deeply transformational, radical societal change. Here we distinguish between activists and organizers. Activists work for social justice in a myriad of ways, including short-term, one-off, or supporting actions. Organizers do the deep and sustaining work to develop campaigns with long-term objectives and grapple with strategies that can achieve a more equitable distribution of power and resources, the building of social movements, and ultimately, a liberatory society. We hope that learning from the knowledge of the organizers and activist-scholars in this anthology can help to inspire people to deepen their critical thinking and activist practice and can help to transform activists into organizers. Because we believe that social transformation arises through praxis, or the unity of theory and practice, we believe that both study and struggle are necessary and intertwined components in our collective work toward creating emancipatory futures.

The book emerges from a symposium on contemporary Asian American activism, organized by the coeditors of the volume and held January 24–26, 2019, at the University of California, Santa Barbara, to coincide with the fiftieth anniversary of the founding of Asian American studies and in recognition of the field's birth through student strikes and community activism. We especially hoped to amplify the knowledge of Asian American organizers. Though activists and organizers helped bring about and shape Asian American studies in its early years, they have become much more marginal to theory building and education over the last few decades. It is not the writings or experiences of Asian American organizers that form the core of Asian

American studies publications and curriculum but, rather, the work of full-time, professionally trained academics. We recognize the importance of scholarly knowledge production in the field of Asian American studies. We also value the knowledge that emerges from activist praxis and wanted our symposium—and now this book—to re-center political movement knowledge production. The symposium consisted of public presentations and, most meaningfully to us, closed-door discussions that provided valuable and uncommon opportunities to engage with other organizer-intellectuals and scholar-activists to analyze our long-standing organizing work and the state of Asian American Movement building.[6] In this introduction we reflect not only on the chapters in this anthology but also on the dialogues we had before, during, and since the symposium and closed-door discussion that brought us all together.

FIGURE I.1. This book emerges from a symposium on contemporary Asian American activism, held January 24–26, 2019, at the University of California, Santa Barbara, to coincide with the fiftieth anniversary of the founding of Asian American studies. Several of the symposium organizers and speakers are pictured here. *Left to right*: Alex Tom, Wayne Jopanda, Katherine Lee, Diane Fujino, Karen Umemoto, Ben Lee, Pam Tau Lee, Mo Nishida, Robyn Rodriguez, Ga Young Chung, and Eddy Zheng. Photo courtesy of Wayne Jopanda.

THE ASIAN AMERICAN MOVEMENT, 1960s–1970s: RADICALISM, INTERNATIONALISM, SOLIDARITY

This anthology narrates and analyzes contemporary Asian American activism while locating this struggle in its roots in the AAM of the late 1960s and 1970s, which itself was part of a longer genealogy of Chinese, Japanese, Filipino, Korean, South Asian, and other activist histories.[7] The AAM represents the most prominent and significant expression of Asian American activism in US history. So, while it no longer exists as it did fifty years ago, the afterlife of the AAM continues on to the present in many important ways.

In the late 1960s activists, primarily young but also spanning generations, created a nationwide social movement that, for the first time, centered large-scale pan-Asian organizing across multiple cities and regions. Activist struggles took place on college campuses; in urban Chinatowns, Little Tokyos, and Manilatowns; and in rural communities. The very term *Asian American* originated in the AAM. It was, as Yen Le Espiritu posits, a political strategy to resist anti-Asian racism, rather than a framework to unify diverse cultures, histories, languages, and religions. While the AAM shaped a social consciousness as "Asian Americans," the concept and movement simultaneously embraced pan-Asian and Third World political formations.[8] As Roy Nakano, Miriam Ching Louie, Fred Ho, Steve Louie, Glenn Omatsu, Diane Fujino, Laura Pulido, Daryl Maeda, Judy Wu, Karen Ishizuka, the KDP collective, and others contend, the AAM was inseparable from its political milieu and strongly influenced by Black Power nationally and Third World anticolonialism internationally.[9]

The AAM originated in the struggle for Third World studies (soon called "ethnic studies") in the late 1960s at San Francisco State College, UC Berkeley, and elsewhere as well as in the growing antiwar movement against US intervention in Vietnam. These two movements point to the domestic and global Third World influences that shaped the early AAM and gave rise to an Asian American politics and identity strongly rooted in Third World radicalism and anticolonial struggles. As Daryl Maeda describes, "Asian Americans were uniquely positioned by the war in Vietnam, for unlike every other racial group, they were conflated with the enemy."[10]

Yet AAM activists were not simply critical of the war or the ways it aggravated the racialization of Asian Americans as outsiders; they also believed that the Vietnam war "was an imperialist effort by the United States to further its geopolitical dominance through conquest."[11] AAM organizations such as the San Francisco Bay Area Coalition Against the War and the New York–based Asian Americans for Action connected US militarism and imperialism in Southeast Asia with US bombings of Hiroshima and Nagasaki, Kanaka Maoli (Native Hawaiian) land theft, the ongoing US control of Philippine politics and economy, and other offenses. When a Japanese American anti-gentrification activist in Los Angeles's Little Tokyo stated, "The people of Vietnam are laying down their lives to protect their lands—we as a community need the same type of spirit," he was drawing a line from Vietnam to Little Tokyo that demanded liberation, premised not in the politics of liberal democracy, integration, and narrow civil rights but on the return of land to Indigenous peoples, the political sovereignty of nations and peoples, community control of institutions, and ultimately, self-determination.[12] Filipino activists were drawn to the National Democracy movement for liberation in the Philippines, taking up the high-risk struggle of opposing the Marcos dictatorship as well as opposing US neocolonialism in their own or their parents' homeland while also, for some, working on Filipino American issues.[13] This framework for critiquing imperialism and racial capitalism can be seen in the contemporary Asian American struggles discussed in this anthology.

In the period of the late 1960s and 1970s, the politics of revolutionary nationalism combined with internationalism among Black, Puerto Rican, Chicana/o, Indigenous, and Asian American radicals such that activist struggles for the liberation for one's own community could coexist with the decolonial demand for liberation for all oppressed people.[14] The AAM, seemingly more than any other movement of the period, intertwined freedom for Asian Americans with freedom for all peoples and therefore extended a particularly strong solidarity with other communities.[15] The Asian American Political Alliance (AAPA), started at Berkeley in May 1968 and expanded nationwide, issued a document that claimed self-determination for Asian Americans and all oppressed people that reflected the Black Panther Party and Black Power's call for self-determination. Some of the most iconic images of the AAM show the influence of Black Power on Asian American politics. This includes the *Life* magazine photograph of Yuri Kochiyama trying to comfort the slain Malcolm X on the stage of the Audubon ballroom; the militant image of Richard Aoki, an early Japanese American member of the Black Panther Party, wearing beret, sunglasses, and AAPA button; and images of Asian American activists with signs reading, "Yellow Peril Supports Black Power." The farmworker struggle and the famous 1965 grape strike in Delano, California, led by Mexican labor leaders Cesar Chavez and Delores Huerta and started by Filipino laborers and labor leaders Larry Itliong and Philip Vera Cruz, brought together Mexican and Filipino agricultural workers, students, and farmworkers, urban and rural, as another important site of solidarity making. One of the most central struggles of the AAM involved the decade-long battle to prevent evictions of elderly Filipino and Chinese men living in the low-income International Hotel while also fighting the gentrification of San Francisco.[16]

While Asian Americans' experiences of racism were significant in driving many to join the AAM, they were also working through intersectional identities and practices addressing a multitude of interconnected issues, local and international. Asian American activists, particularly women, found inspiration in Mao's statement "Women hold up half the sky," and they worked to challenge the patriarchy in US society and Asian American communities as well. One distinctive feature of the AAM was its focus on collective leadership, an approach to leadership informed by feminist understandings. Perhaps more than any other movement, the AAM seemed to lack the singular charismatic leaders who created other kinds of problems—a model strongly critiqued by Ella Baker.[17] The collective leadership structure of many AAM organizations further expanded opportunities for Asian American women's leadership. As AAPA activist Lillian Fabros noted: "Asian women were at least half, if not more, of the Asian students involved in supporting the TWLF [Third World Liberation Front] Strike. This was a sharp contrast to the Black and Chicano student groups, where women were far fewer."[18] Despite the struggles around sexism and other internal problems, the AAM asserted an intentional practice of developing humane social relations and paying attention to process as well as outcome. AAM activists often strove to reject the development of the charismatic icon that plagued other movements and instead developed structures and ways of organizing that allowed many to become leaders while largely rejecting the hierarchies of conventional leadership. The practice, of course, was always more contradictory than the strivings, but such intentions did enable women and others marginalized by power to take on leadership roles.

Today's organizers build on the knowledge and material changes gained in the 1960s and 1970s as well as in the lesser-known Asian American struggles of the 1980s, 1990s, and 2000s. In this anthology we consciously highlight an intergenerational temporality to amplify the ways the present builds on the AAM's core principles and organizing practices of the past and continues to inform visions and strategies for the future.

INTERGENERATIONAL TEMPORALITY, TAKING TIME, AND BUILDING SOCIAL RELATIONSHIPS

Asian American activism today cannot be understood without tracing its roots to the Asian American Movement. Intergenerational continuity is not necessarily a given. Most AAM activists in the late 1960s were isolated from the earlier genealogy of Filipino American, Korean American, Chinese American, and Japanese American struggles.[19] These histories had been nearly erased for the AAM generation through World War II constraints on earlier Japanese immigrant radicalism, the Cold War repression of the Chinese immigrant Left, the early Cold War repositioning of Asian Americans into integrated workplaces and suburbs, and the postwar creation of the model minority trope that concealed Asian American radicalism and anti-Asian racism.[20] But through their organizing, AAM activists came to learn about earlier Asian American struggles. When they fought the International Hotel evictions of the Filipino and Chinese elderly tenants, they learned from the *manong* (elder) residents about a history of Filipino farmworkers organizing.[21] Through their organizing in Chinatowns as well as to dismantle Title II of the 1950 McCarran Act (which allowed for the detention of anyone deemed subversive without the need for evidence), AAM activists learned about the McCarthy-era repression of the Chinese Left.[22] When Karen Ishizuka, author of *Serve the People*, and other West Coast Sanseis visited Yuri Kochiyama and Kazu Iijima in New York or when Mo Nishida and other youth met Paul Kochi while organizing in Little Tokyo, Los Angeles, they learned about a radical Nisei past.[23] This was tremendously important. It allowed AAM activists to recuperate intergenerational knowledge and connections to their past in ways that shaped their own identities and political struggles.

Compared to the still rather limited knowledge of pre-1960s Asian American activism, especially outside of labor and citizenship struggles, the AAM has been much better studied and circulated in large part because of the establishment of Asian American studies, itself a victory of the AAM. As a result of the ongoing work of scholars, activists, and artists, Asian American young people today often know something—even if in a cursory way—about AAM icons such as Yuri Kochiyama, Grace Lee Boggs, and Philip Vera Cruz or about struggles around ethnic studies, the International Hotel, and Vincent Chin or possibly of AAM organizations such as the Asian American Political Alliance, Asian Americans for Action, and Katipunan ng Demokratikong Pilipino (KDP).[24]

Movement elders have played a critical role in transferring knowledge and mentoring younger generations of activists. "Yelders," a term Alex T. Tom introduced to us, referring to "younger elders" whose activism began in the 1980s and 1990s, have also been important activist mentors to young people today and are serving to bridge knowledge and organizing practices across the three most active periods of Asian American activism: the 1960s and 1970s; the 1990s; and the present. This is evidenced in the lives of the contributors to this book. Tom, for example, came of age politically in the 1990s, influenced by Pam Tau Lee, an AAM veteran. Robyn Rodriguez, who also became conscientized in the 1990s, was influenced by Diane Fujino, who in turn was mentored by AAM elders such as Yuri Kochiyama, Mo Nishida, and Fred Ho. Mentorship is bidirectional, and younger activists also teach valuable knowledge and new perspectives to older activists. Though the organizations of decades past may no longer exist, and indeed in some cases the dissolution of some organizations was rather dramatic and traumatic, the AAM was not necessarily demobilized. These organizations instead took new forms, and their ideas inspired new generations of organizers. An intergenerational lens can create and circulate knowledge and inspire hope in new generations. The beauty and promise of the AAM has not died, even if it seems to yield far less influence than in the past.

We also center an intergenerational perspective because in today's culture there is a tendency toward a "presentist" perspective, as noted by Scot Nakagawa, a seasoned organizer and artist with decades of experience fighting against vigilante white supremacist groups and authoritarian evangelical political movements. That is, in the age of

Instagram and the instantaneous posting, commenting, and sharing that come with social media, we tend to always think in the present tense. Things that are not now seem to be easily dismissed as old and irrelevant.

An intergenerational perspective privileges the importance of time, not just the wisdom from elders who have lived longer and have more experiences in and of the world but also the importance of taking time and spending time in the process of social movement building. Thus, to effectively organize is to be present, though not presentist. This approach is nicely captured in the story that opens Filipina American scholar-activist Karin Aguilar-San Juan's *The State of Asian America*:

> One hot summer weekend in July 1992, I took the train from Boston to New York City to meet Yuri Kochiyama and Bill Kochiyama, an elder Japanese American couple with a long history of activism on a wide range of issues—including notable personal and political alliances with the African American community . . . I felt moved by the Kochiyamas' commitment to struggles of liberation for all peoples. . . . Moreover they made me feel at home, though I was a perfect stranger. . . . My visit with the Kochiyamas was brief, only long enough to give me a glimpse of the significance of their lives and work, of the continuing need for Asian American activism, and the need to make our stories known among Asians and non-Asians alike.[25]

This story highlights the importance of intergenerationality in activism, both the transfer of knowledge from generation to generation and also the importance of taking time, making time, and being present in helping grow activist work. Moreover, as one of Robyn's undergraduate students, Nelle Garcia, observes, today's "cancel culture," because it flourishes in the virtual world, does not give people a chance to grow and learn. Growth requires time.

Organizing movements is ultimately about relationship building and the intimate connections between people that deepen in the context of activism and struggle. When we stop doing the work of building relationships, the forward motion of mass movement building stalls. Relationships require encountering one another as people, developing shared experiences together, sharing knowledge with one another. Though "friends," "connections," or "followers" are possible on social media, relationships as we describe them here may not be fully possible in the same way through social media platforms.

Black scholar-activist Alisa Bierria uses the idea of "radical care" to discuss the intimacies and relationships forged through activist struggle.[26] In the current political moment of callout and cancel culture, an intergenerational approach centered on relationship building and radical care is so vital. Activism built through relationships requires activists to engage with each other face to face, to get to know each other and commit to each other through their mutual work in organizations and campaigns. In relationships built over time and with care, it is much more difficult to simply call out and cancel people. To be fair, in previous historical moments a version of callout culture did exist; it might have been described as dogmatism and sectarianism. We recognize that some of the issues that we are plagued by in today's activist struggles are not entirely new, and there is much to be gleaned from the mistakes, growth, and wisdom of our elders and yelders.

Intergenerational knowledge is multidirectional. It is not just about wisdom passed down from elders but also about knowledge transfers from the youth to older people. As Robyn's students Anna Pak and Angela Alejandro observe, it is a reciprocal relationship, a giving and a taking. In fact, *listening* and *horizontal listening* are key to organizing. The scholar-activist George Lipsitz, a significant mentor for Diane, regularly says, *Too often we pick up a microphone (or megaphone) when we actually need hearing aids.* The movement provides opportunities to "learn to listen" and to "listen to learn."[27] Such thinking builds with intentionality on the ideas of Paulo Freire, who offers the concept of "problem posing" learning that requires multiple people, with multiple perspectives, and especially those most impacted by a problem, to participate in creating the solutions for social problems. This expands the democratic participation that's indispensable to transformative social change while also rejecting the hierarchy of authority and lessening the burden on any single individual to figure it all out. Giving one person that much power is, in fact, an impossible task and one that has led to repeatedly terrible and authoritarian outcomes, including the present moment of fascism/neofascism in the making in this country and globally. Horizontal listening and collective work must necessarily be present in a liberatory society and in the development of egalitarian, productive, and democratic social institutions.[28]

Asian American activism, and the pan-ethnic formations on which it centers, is sustained intergenerationally. The connection made between Filipina American Karin Aguilar–San Juan and Japanese American Yuri Kochiyama was one that bridged ethnic divides. Robyn and Diane share a similar dynamic. Both are deeply rooted in their ethnic histories as Filipino American and Japanese American, respectively, but came together around a shared political identity as Asian Americans *and* a shared vision of liberation.

CONTEMPORARY ASIAN AMERICAN ACTIVISM: LESSONS FROM THE ASIAN AMERICAN MOVEMENT

Asian Americans have and continue to be involved in a range of struggles. The activism of Asian Americans today is continuous in many ways with the AAM. Asian American activists have sustained a commitment to exposing and opposing forms of US imperialism abroad (as evidenced in campaigns opposing US militarization in Asia) as well as a commitment to cross-racial solidarity (evident, for instance, in immigrant rights, workers' rights, Black Lives Matter, and environmental justice campaigns), forms of activism that defined the AAM. Moreover, Asian American activists continued to mobilize around a pan-ethnic Asian American political identity across numerous issue areas. In addition, contemporary activists have addressed issues that may have been absent or only on the margins in the 1960s and 1970s. For example, if LGBTQI issues were sidelined in the AAM, in some cases causing LGBTQI activists to feel actively shunned within AAM organizations, we have seen a flourishing of LGBTQI organizing in more recent years within Asian American communities and the broader society. If a collective Asian American identity was a defining feature of the AAM, with the changing demographics of the Asian American communities in the United States, ethnic-based and diasporic activism has increased and sometimes eclipse more pan-ethnic activism. Notably, if Asian American activism in the 1960s and 1970s gravitated toward more left-leaning analyses of society and supported progressive causes, this continues today alongside a rise of right-wing activism as well.

This anthology centers the knowledge produced by organizers and activist-scholars about organizing strategies and tactics as methods informed by radical analyses of structural problems. We note that it is beyond the scope of this introduction to provide an overview of important radical theorizing emanating from Asian American studies and ethnic studies scholars and Asian American Movements with respect to neoliberal globalization, racial capitalism, settler colonialism, empire, the carceral state, hetero-patriarchy, and other ideas, though organizers and activists on the ground are often informed by such theorizing. It is also beyond the scope of this introduction to provide a comprehensive review of Asian American activism since the AAM, but this is available elsewhere.[29] We do explore various approaches to dismantling structures of domination *and* to building alternative institutions and abolitionist futures that move us toward a society in which people's needs are met, participatory democracy and community care matters, and our radical imaginations are set free.[30] All of the contributors have spent most of their lives working in and alongside grassroots groups, nonprofit organizations, or other activist formations. They have identified especially important lessons from the AAM that continue to be relevant for Asian American organizing today—political education; radical love, relationship and community building, and collective leadership; and radicalism, cross-racial solidarity, and internationalism—as well as new challenges for activists given today's dynamics.

POLITICAL EDUCATION THROUGH ASIAN AMERICAN STUDIES

If an important milestone of the AAM was the creation of Asian American studies, the field has continued to impact generations of Asian American activists. Nearly all of the contributors to this anthology identify AAS, or ethnic studies broadly, as an especially important catalyst for their activism, whether studied in college or outside of it. AAS offered them a framework and a language to make sense of their personal experiences of injustice and marginalization. When asked during the symposium's closed-door sessions about the origins of their activism, almost everyone started with stories of personal and intergenerational traumas, including experiences of racism, growing up poor, or living in a household with differently abled family members. These experiences of marginalization, disadvantage, and oppression were experiences that many could not fully explain and therefore could not fully act upon until AAS offered an analytic framework for understanding and naming the causes of those experiences, a sense of community that comes with understanding that one's experiences are not something one goes through alone, and a sense of inspiration that transformation is possible.[31]

Meanwhile, community organizations are providing political education beyond college and university campuses rooted in AAS or ethnic studies and expanding the growing field of Indigenous studies. This is evident across nearly every contribution to this book, from the juvenile justice diversion program in Hawai'i grounded in Kanaka Maoli epistemologies (Karen Umemoto), to ethnic studies taking place in prisons (Eddy Zheng), to programs being done for youth in women and queer-led Southeast Asian and South Asian organizations (May Fu), and more. These are examples of the long afterlife of the AAM. Though AAS has become highly institutionalized and is unrecognizable in certain ways to those who fought for its establishment, there remain elements of AAS deeply rooted in liberation struggles, community organizing, and activist-scholarship that have profoundly impacted Asian American activist theorizing and practice. If what activists wanted was to transform colleges and universities to help facilitate political education that would inspire learners to engage in movements for far-reaching, systemic change, they succeeded in many ways—that is, alongside an ongoing critique of the institution of the university, including Asian American studies.[32]

RADICAL LOVE TODAY OR DISASTER TOMORROW

We need "radicalization today," or it will be "disaster tomorrow." These were the words of Pam Tau Lee in her keynote address before the Contemporary Asian American Activism symposium at UC Santa Barbara. She believes in the importance of "embracing or reconnecting to the Asian radical tradition," a belief shared by all contributors to this volume. We define *radicalism* as the development of an understanding of the root causes of dispossession, marginalization, exploitation, and genocide. *Radical*, after all, is defined as forming at the root. We agree that those committed to liberation must analyze settler colonialism, racial capitalism, hetero-patriarchy, and other structures of domination. Hence, we value the work that critical scholars do in that regard. However, equally important is the development of visions—grounded in practice—for solutions to the root causes of domination in large-scale structural change. Without radical praxis, humanity and the planet will surely face disastrous consequences. We recognize that the term *radical* has many negative connotations, but for us, radicalism and radical politics are deeply connected to the term *love*. We subscribe to the vision of "radical love" that Pam Tau Lee so eloquently describes.[33] For us the institutional and cultural changes we want in the world are rooted in love: love for each other and love for the Earth.

In our discussions we underscored the importance of the notion of radical love and care as an alternative to dominant notions of self-care that are circulating popularly and even in activist spaces. We note that self-care is something that many activists are touting as a means of addressing some of the very real issues of disillusionment and burn-out that plague many in our ranks. Many campaigns take years to achieve, such as the fight for the DREAM Act (Ga Young Chung's chapter), tenant struggles against real estate developers (Angelica Cabande's chapter), or taxi drivers' struggle for fair wages in the expanding gig economy (as discussed by Javaid Tariq). Moreover, many of us engage in organizing work that is over and above the work we do for pay. Thus, the issue of ensuring longevity and sustainability of organizing in the fight for liberation worldwide is vital. We cannot afford to lose our most committed and energetic social justice fighters. The decline in our ranks is yet another disaster that Pam Tau Lee references. Yet many of the contributors to this volume worry that the call for self-care is sometimes mistakenly understood as a need to retreat from or to cease activist work in favor of more inwardly and individually focused mental health. In our discussions, however, we considered how self-care might be better understood as *collective self-care* when we support and strengthen others as we renew ourselves for the work of long-haul movement building. We further discussed how political education that sharpens our radical analysis can be a form of collective self-care. When we get too caught up in the here and now, it can tax and drain us, but political education helps us see the bigger picture. Political education, furthermore, allows us to see that regardless of what path we choose in our lives, whether we work in a nonprofit organization, as educators, or in other spaces that do not seem to be straightforwardly connected to social justice work, we can organize, as Lee notes, "wherever our feet land" (Katherine Lee's chapter).

SOLIDARITY, RADICALISM, AND INTERNATIONALISM

What is distinctive about the AAM, according to activists and scholars alike, is its politics of solidarity. AAM activist Steve Louie states,

"One of the hallmarks of the Asian American Movement was to 'unite all who can be united,' whether that was within the Asian community or with other communities, especially people of color."[34] According to scholar Laura Pulido, a distinctive feature of the AAM was that activists "were more likely to join organizations associated with *other* racial/ethnic groups, especially African Americans. . . . Asian Americans joined such organizations out of solidarity, an awakening identity as people of color." She further notes, "In contrast, Chicanas/os and African Americans were much more likely to focus on their own communities."[35] Asian American cross-racial solidarity politics is especially evident in what many consider the inaugural moment of the AAM—the struggle for ethnic studies at San Francisco State University and UC Berkeley in 1968 and 1969 and in Asian American support for the Black Panther Party. Black liberation was seen as a necessary prerequisite to the liberation of Asian Americans and all other racialized groups. Several chapters in this book touch on cross-racial solidarity, including Tau Lee's focus on Asian-Indigenous solidarities, Chung's on undocumented Korean immigrant organizing, and Rodriguez's on student organizing in the University of California system in the 1990s.

Moreover, building on the Asian-African conference in Bandung, Indonesia, in 1955, antiracism and anti-imperialism became a core orientation among AAM activists. Among the foremost Asian American activists are those who exemplified strong practices of Third World radicalism and solidarity, including Richard Aoki, Grace Lee Boggs, Philip Vera Cruz, Alex Hing, Fred Ho, David Hyun, Yuri Kochiyama, Nobuko Miyamoto, and Michael Yasutake. AAM organizations such as AAPA, the Storefront, the Red Guard Party, I Wor Kuen, Wei Min She, along with publications like *Gidra*, all promoted Third World solidarity rooted in anti-imperialist politics. AAPA's platform states, "We Asian Americans support all oppressed peoples and their struggles for Liberation and believe that Third World People must have complete control over the political, economic, and educational institutions within their communities."[36] This statement and the longer platform from which it comes, show a politic that intertwined Asian American liberation with the liberation of all oppressed peoples of the world. Third World politics continue to inform Asian American activism today as suggested in the conversation with Javaid Tariq and the chapter by Pam Tau Lee. Meanwhile, Jessica Antonio's chapter on BAYAN USA illustrates how Third World movements actively engage their diasporas abroad.

FIVE ORGANIZING CHALLENGES IN BUILDING MOVEMENTS FOR LIBERATION

We recognize that the path toward emancipation is rocky and perilous. This is particularly true if we are seeking to build long-haul movements for liberation and working beyond the low-hanging fruit, or the more easily doable actions, on the road to justice. So even as we experience profound joy and meaning in our activism, we offer five challenges facing organizers. Some are reiterations of earlier struggles, and all present serious concerns in the present moment.

IDENTITY POLITICS

Glenn Omatsu, in an influential essay published in *Amerasia Journal* in 1989, offered a contrast between his current milieu and the politics and ideology of the 1960s and 1970s. He wrote: "The birth of the Asian American movement coincided not with the initial campaign for civil rights but with the later demand for black liberation . . . that the focus of a generation of Asian American activists was not on asserting racial pride, but reclaiming a tradition of struggle by earlier generations; that the movement was not centered on the aura of racial identity but embraced fundamental questions of oppression and power . . . and that the main thrust was not one of seeking legitimacy and representation within American society but the larger goal of liberation."[37]

Omatsu was writing in the late 1980s, at a time when identity politics were strong and also being strongly critiqued.[38] Activist-intellectuals such as Omatsu were wary that identity politics had veered too far from an analysis of structures of white supremacy, capitalism, and empire that had been at the core of the AAM. Instead, many espoused an Asian American identity more invested in politics of representation, such as gaining more Asian American elected officials or increasing visibility in the media and popular culture. Such aspirations and goals were very different from the liberationist ideology and demands that animated the AAM.

In the pan-Asian and Third World formation of the AAM, politics necessarily intertwined with identity formation. In Gary Okihiro's framing of identities as social formations, he emphasizes a US Third

World concept that was necessarily about racial and national identities *and* about a politic of liberation intertwined with a radical vision of a new society free from, or working to be free from, the vestiges of colonialism, racial capitalism, and patriarchy.[39] We, too, contend that *identities formed from politics* can and have enabled activists to work for liberation across differences. This often occurred through the creation of new and fluid formations such as the collective Asian American identity rooted in antiracism that allows for overlapping pan-Asian, ethnic-specific, and Third World identities and for both revolutionary nationalism and internationalism. By contrast, *politics formed from identity* can and too often do lead to the problematic practices of narrow or skin nationalism that work against the idea of liberation for all and coalitional justice. This type of crude identity politics masks the fact that there may be many who look like us but think nothing like us. In short, racial identities can be a source of healthy cultural pride and a recognition of the rich ways of knowing and ways of being that reside within our communities. But we raise a caution about the trapping of identity politics in our struggles today that lead to seek "legitimacy and representation," rather than critiques of "fundamental questions of oppression and power" and the dismantling of systems of domination widely.

SOLIDARITY VERSUS ALLYSHIP WITH BLACK LIBERATION

Asian Americans have made notable efforts in working in solidarity with the Black struggle by actively opposing anti-Blackness within Asian American communities and rejecting the model minority trope for its rootedness in anti-Blackness.[40] Soya Jung, a contributor to this book, describes the model minority as "the racial invitation that white elites offered to Asian Americans [that] went something like this: 'If you come here and assimilate into this anti-black settler state, if you behave properly, we will let you hustle for your prosperity. You won't be white, but you might get close, and at least you won't be black. You'll be the poster child of the American Dream, and together we will squash the insurgency underfoot that threatens our collective fortunes.'" (In smaller print she adds: "We might occasionally spy on you, round you up, and detain you; and some of you will have to stay in crappy jobs and housing. But it's all to keep the Dream alive.")[41] She urges Asian Americans to commit "model minority mutiny" and to recognize that "our liberation depends on black freedom."[42]

Soya Jung, like Glenn Omatsu before her, is working within the genealogy of AAM Third World solidarity that is different from the allyship model of today. The solidarity model she puts forward recognizes that Black liberation is vital to the liberation of all people while also recognizing that Asian Americans experience complex sets of struggles that they must directly confront, wrestle with, and resist. Allyship, as it is generally defined, is a process whereby those with relative privilege are called to grapple with and question the various ways structures of power have positioned them vis-à-vis those who are underprivileged or marginalized—think white allyship to people of color or straight allyship to queer folks.[43]

Increasingly, Asian Americans are engaging allyship work with Blacks that does not necessarily advance a solidarity for liberation. In such a framework of allyship, Asian Americans recognize their positioning as model minorities in relation to Blacks. However, emancipatory solidarity goes deeper than that. Sung Yeon Choimorrow posits, "We should not replicate white allyship," and instead encourages "AAPIs to think about standing in solidarity with Black Lives Matter and other racial justice movements as partners in struggle rather than as allies."[44] Yet allyship—as opposed to solidarity—is how many Asian Americans situate their politics vis-à-vis the Black struggle today. According to Soya Jung, solidarity means that "we can embrace an authentic Asian American politics that is rooted in history, shaped by current conditions and unapologetically antiracist. We can make more visible *our own* stories of exploitation, vigorously refuse the complicities of excess, and set fire to the last 75 years of model minority myth making. Some of us were part of making that myth. Now all of us who call ourselves Asian American must work to undo it."[45] In brief, to engage in liberatory solidarity is to walk alongside other peoples of color in dismantling white supremacy as it shapes *all* of our lives. Even if some folks of color are allowed positions of relative privilege, white supremacy is a system meant to dominate and subjugate all communities of color. We must all stand together to resist anti-Black racism, white supremacy, and colonialism in all its forms.

CANCEL CULTURE

It seems as if the long-standing charges of oppression by Black people, Indigenous people, people of color, women, and queer people are finally being heard and addressed today in movements such as Black

Lives Matter, Standing Rock, #MeToo, and many more. But the dangers of identity politics remain. Having one's complex, intersectional identities and experiences finally acknowledged has led some to demand punishment for any and every instance of written, spoken, or acted-out harm. This response is creating an atmosphere in which a charge becomes a conviction, without the benefit of any investigation or due process and without processes of restorative justice that are necessary if we are to create abolitionist futures.[46] People who have worked for years against oppression are being "canceled" for a mistake they made or for an erroneous interpretation of their thoughts or actions in social media and elsewhere. For example, if someone doesn't offer a land acknowledgment, they might be accused of being implicated in settler colonial, native erasure. Or if a person misgenders another individual, they may be accused of upholding heteropatriarchy. Or if a non-Black person of color speaks out against white supremacy and anti-Blackness, they might be accused of misappropriating the Black struggle.

We worry that liberation is being viewed as a set of mechanical things to do, rather than a critical engagement with the work of movement building for liberation, which requires us to think strategically about how to bring along people, from where they are, to create emancipatory communities. We worry that cancel culture makes people excessively focused on being politically correct in ways that impede our abilities to work with boldness and courage, even as we strive to be humane and caring with our words and actions. We worry about the ways cancel culture harms individuals and our movements for justice.

Only in the most recent period have we been hearing people, young as well as older, critique cancel culture and make appeals for "calling in" rather than "calling out" people so that racism and other forms of oppression enacted by individuals are challenged while also creating greater understanding and compassion. This requires situating individuals in their larger context and recognizing how even those of us who are committed to dismantling structures of power continue to grapple with the ways those structures shape our thoughts, actions, and everyday lives. This approach echoes Martin Luther King Jr.'s appeal to target "the forces of evil" rather than "persons who are caught in those forces," without dismissing the responsibility of those who inflict harm and to address violence of the spirit as well as physical violence.⁴⁷ Such a call-in culture seeks to challenge power and oppression while holding individuals accountable in ways that do not merely reenact the most crude forms of identity politics. Redressing individual cases of racism, sexism, ableism, or other injuries is important but can also conceal the larger structural racism and structural oppression at work. Calling in can better engage larger critiques of racial capitalism, patriarchy, and colonialism beyond the individual and create transformative social institutions.

Liberation requires the building of what Pam Tau Lee calls the "greater we." It is a form of intersectionality that allows Asian Americans to draw lines of connection to each other, to other communities of color in the United States, and to other oppressed peoples around the world. Intersectionality through an AAM lens is not only about acknowledging the complexity of individuals' intersecting identities but about building solidarities across multiple forms of difference and recognizing how power impacts all of our lives. The challenge is about how to build unity while also recognizing how racialization and racism impacts us differently, as we continue to deal with the long aftereffects of Trumpism.

WORKING WITHIN OR OUTSIDE INSTITUTIONS

Many of the contributors to this book struggle with working within the contradictions of institutions, whether we work in higher education or nonprofit organizations. We have to contend with working within, even as we work against, the state. We often depend on both the government and private foundations for funding. Grassroots organizations may experience a degree of autonomy from the state or foundations but also struggle in sustaining their work because of a dependence on volunteer labor or dues from members. Even those who volunteer for or pay dues to grassroots groups usually depend on wages earned within the context of global racial capitalism.

This dilemma leads to critical questions: Can we work within institutions, including governments, nonprofits, and universities, to create liberatory change? In what ways do institutions impose constraining mechanisms, including punishment and disciplinary restraint as well as a reward system that encourages small, achievable actions, that limit our work to reformist change? In the latter formation we work to create some change, and perhaps mostly the appearance of change, but fail to even seek the far-reaching transformations that will, by necessity, threaten the institution, systems of domination, and relations of power themselves. These are questions that Barbara Tomlinson and George Lipsitz pose about how the neoliberal audit system and the corporatization of the university shape the production of knowledge and broader work of scholars. How might we create "insubordinate spaces" within larger institutions that contest the neoliberal logic that "works to delegitimize and eradicate *any* alternatives to market time and market space" and creates "a place of market competition and market subjects"?[48] Stefano Harney and Fred Moten offer the concepts of "fugitivity" and of "marronage" to be "always at a war, always in hiding" in the "undercommons" as a possible way "to be in but not of" the university.[49] We do not offer a prescriptive solution. But instead we raise these questions that, to us, require collective study and collective struggle—or in Robin D. G. Kelley's words, "love, study, struggle"—so that we do not, on one hand, abandon spaces that offer crucial resources and opportunities for critical thinking and engagement and, on the other, lose sight of other models of change, including cooperatives, that have the potential to create humane and self-sustaining political economies and social relations.[50]

REFORMISM VERSUS RADICAL TRANSFORMATION

Inasmuch as the contributors of this book are committed to radical transformation, a challenge that emerged in our closed-door session is what can be characterized as the perennial debate between more reformist or short-term change and long-term, deeply transformative, structural change. For scholar-activists like us, as well as Karen Umemoto, May Fu, and Ga Young Chung, the concern is how to respond to the issues rapidly transpiring around us, which on-the-ground activists must immediately address while still doing the sometimes very slow work of reflecting and analyzing issues as scholars and researchers to better illuminate how daily crises are connected to larger structures of power. Organizers such as Angelica Cabande, who is at the front lines of fighting the incessant and pernicious spread of gentrification in San Francisco as driven by Silicon Valley elites, expressed how she and other organizers sometimes find themselves so caught up in the urgency of day-to-day struggles that it becomes difficult to take a step back to strategize on how to grow and sustain movements over time.

We believe that building movements for liberation necessitates working for reformist actions but not by making reformism our end goal. The contributors to this volume use radical analysis of imperialism, white supremacy, racial capitalism, hetero-patriarchy, ableism, and more to guide their praxis, striving to create smaller objectives and strategies that collectively build toward emancipatory futures. We believe it is important to celebrate and claim seemingly small victories, however incremental. It is in small victories that people are able to, as organizer Steven Dy, profiled in May Fu's chapter, states, "practice, practice, practice" the liberation they, and we, want for the world. But the point is to work for smaller goals as part of a larger, long-term strategy for transforming institutions and ideologies, communities and economies, and ourselves and our social relations as well. This collection of "radical love stories," as Pam Tau Lee describes the chapters in this book, is meant to offer a sense of hope to readers and to activate their commitment to propelling justice forward.

Our contributors include activists and intellectuals who have collectively, over the course of their lives, worked on an array of issues facing Asian American and the Asian diasporic communities from immigrant rights, ethnic studies, environmental justice, prison abolition, political prisoner support, anti-militarization, cross-racial solidarity, workers' rights, youth organizing, housing justice, gendered violence, anticolonial internationalism, and more. They've organized around these issues in grassroots organizations and movements, universities, nonprofit organizations, and even LLCs. Our contributors are also scholar-activists whose research and teaching are driven by their commitments to and participation in the same movements. Reflecting the pan-ethnicity of the AAM, our contributors focus their chapters on organizing in Chinese, Filipino, Korean, Native Hawaiian, Southeast Asian, South Asian, and pan-Asian communities. Many of our contributors center activist struggles in California, while others write about activism in Hawai'i, the Pacific Northwest, and the East Coast. We came together in large part because we had already forged deep relationships in the context of shared struggle. Some of us have marched in the streets together, participated in the same campaigns, or occupy overlapping activist ecologies. It is because of these relationships that we have a level of trust with one another so that we could engage in discussing hard questions related to activism and movement building. In their individual contributions, the voices collected here shed light on the key continuities with and lessons of the AAM that we collectively identified: radicalism, cross-racial solidarity, internationalism and local activism, political education, radical love and collective care, collective leadership, and movement building.

Just as this introduction reflects collective discussions, the chapters of this book were not done in isolation. Numerous contributors shared with us that the process of collective dialogue and feedback shaped their ideas in important ways that would not have been possible if they were working alone. The generative and interconnected collaboration in authoring this volume reflects the ethos of Asian American activism.

Part 1 focuses on the displacements of prisons and gentrification. Eddy Zheng discusses his campaign for ethnic studies education in the San Quentin State Prison in Northern California. Though punished for such struggles, he learned he could survive and, moreover, that there were "beautiful and unanticipated thing([s] that came out of it: people started having meetings and building up activism from the outside." Scholar-activist Karen Umemoto reflects on her collaborative research project to develop an alternative pathway out of the juvenile justice system in Hawai'i. Located in settler colonial structures, where Native Hawaiians are disproportionately imprisoned in their own lands, the program sought to "flip a system of surveillance and punishment to one embedded in practices and ethics of healing and restoration" rooted in Kanaka Maoli values and epistemologies. She further wrestled with the challenges of working through institutions and grassroots mobilizations. Continuing in the lineage of the cross-racial solidarity and housing rights work of the I-Hotel campaign, organizer Angelica Cabande discusses the anti-gentrification and housing justice struggles in San Francisco today.

Part 2 examines local struggles situated within internationalist frameworks. Activist-scholar Ga Young Chung studies the undocumented immigration activism of Korean Americans working against the erasures of the model minority trope. In an industry almost exclusively comprised of immigrant workers, Javaid Tariq, a founding member of the New York Taxi Workers Alliance (NYTWA), in an interview with Diane Fujino, illuminates the innovative strategies and persistent organizing of the NYTWA to resist the impacts of the neo-liberal gig economy and now the coronavirus pandemic on taxi and app-based drivers, the majority of whom are South Asian. Activist Jessica Antonio's chapter on the radical activism of BAYAN USA examines this long-standing and broad-based organization that offers a model for engaging Filipino Americans in anti-imperialist homeland struggles.

Part 3 examines the political education and radical pedagogy developed by community organizations and in university settings. These efforts connect the origins of Asian American studies and the AAM with today's struggles for educational transformation. Activist-scholar May Fu examines the role of political education in newer activist organizations—a Southeast Asian youth and queer organization in Providence, Rhode Island; a Vietnamese American organization in Orange County, California; and a Nepalese women's organization in Queens, New York. While Eddy Zheng, in his piece on prison activism, sought ethnic studies as a way to develop critical knowledge, scholar Katherine Lee examines the role of writing and writing instruction at the university to sharpen our thinking and actions. She states, "Writing, as practiced and conceptualized in the legacy of Asian American activism . . . has the potential to always be a collective, collaborative process in innovation." Soya Jung offers a critical reflection on her work with ChangeLab in Portland, Oregon, which offers a pivot from the intensive day-to-day work of organizers to read, analyze, and write about critical issues facing Asian American communities.

Part 4 focuses on Asian American Movement building across the generations. Alex T. Tom provides lessons on Asian American Movement building and ways to deepen our organizing praxis based on his years of experience and reflection with the Chinese Progressive Association. Activist-scholar Robyn Rodriguez, reflecting on her own political engagements, discusses student activism in the 1990s. She provides a lens into the AAM's afterlife while reflecting on the distinctive ways students, past and present, can contribute toward social justice movement building. Pam Tau Lee reflects on her life's work in the Asian American Left and environmental justice movements across five decades and provides a vision of what an Asian American radicalism might look like for the future. Finally, this volume ends with a spotlight on a young Afro-Filipino activist, Amado Khaya Canham Rodriguez, whose life connected struggles and communities from

California to New Jersey, from South Africa to the rural Philippines, where his life ended while doing the liberation work of utmost importance to him.

It is our hope that this book will not only illuminate contemporary Asian American activism, rooted in Asian American struggles of the past, but also serve as a catalyst for change in these most urgent times.

NOTES

1   For literature reviews of AAM studies, see Diane Fujino, "Who Studies the Asian American Movement? A Historiographical Analysis," *Journal of Asian American Studies* 11 (2008): 127–69, 10.1353/jaas.0.0003; and Adalberto Aguirre Jr. and Shoon Lio, "Spaces of Mobilization: The Asian American / Pacific Islander Struggle for Social Justice," *Social Justice* 35 (2008): 1–17. Excellent introductions to the AAM include Daryl Joji Maeda, *Rethinking the Asian American Movement* (New York: Routledge, 2012); Karen L. Ishizuka, *Serve the People: Making Asian America in the Long Sixties* (London: Verso, 2016); Michael Liu, Kim Geron, and Tracy Lai, *Snake Dance of Asian American Activism: Community, Vision, and Power* (Lanham, MD: Lexington, 2008); Fred Ho, ed., with Carolyn Antonio, Diane Fujino, and Steve Yip, *Legacy to Liberation: Politics and Culture of Revolutionary Asian/Pacific America* (Chico, CA: AK Press, 2000); and Steve Louie and Glenn K. Omatsu, *Asian Americans: The Movement and the Moment* (Los Angeles: UCLA Asian American Studies Center, 2001).

2   See, for example, the *Amerasia Journal* special issue on Asian American activism studies, edited by Diane C. Fujino and Robyn M. Rodriguez (2019) that includes, on current-day organizing, undocumented Korean activism (Elizabeth Rubio), Hmong queer organizing (Kong Pheng Pha), Khmer girls' activism (Monisha Das Gupta), and Afro-Asian solidarity (Jeanelle K. Hope); Loan Thi Dao, *Generation Rising: A New Politics of Southeast Asian American Activism* (Berkeley: Eastwind Books of Berkeley, 2020). We look forward to the publication of Diane Wong and Mark Tseng-Putterman's anthology on contemporary Asian American activism.

3   The Asian American Racial Justice Toolkit, https://www.asianamtoolkit .org, provides a great entry to online sources on Asian American justice organizations.

4   Yuanyuan Feng and Mark Tseng-Putterman, "'Scattered like Sand': WeChat Warriors in the Trial of Peter Liang," *Amerasia Journal* 45 (2019): 238–52; Shireen Roshanravan, "Weaponizing Our (In)Visibility: Asian American Feminist Ruptures of the Model-Minority Optic," in *Asian American Feminisms and Women of Color Politics*, ed. Lynn Fujiwara and Shireen Roshanravan (Seattle: University of Washington

Press, 2018), 261–81; Anemona Hartocollis and Ted Siefer, "On Eve of Harvard Bias Trial, Dueling Rallies Show Rifts among Asian-Americans," *New York Times*, October 14, 2018.

5 Soya Jung, "The Racial Justice Movement Needs a Model Minority Mutiny," *Race Files*, October 13, 2014, https://www.racefiles.com/2014/10/13/model-minority-mutiny.

6 Contemporary Asian American Activism & Intergenerational Perspectives: An Activist-Scholar Symposium, University of California, Santa Barbara, January 24–26, 2019, https://www.asamst.ucsb.edu/community/activism.

7 While *Asian Pacific Islander* is widely used as a term of inclusion, we chose *Asian American* to recognize the ways that the API rubric too often conflates complex histories and erasures of indigeneity and settler colonialism. Our introduction discusses the literature on Asian American activism studies.

8 Yen Le Espiritu, *Asian American Panethnicity: Bridging Institutions and Identities* (Philadelphia: Temple University Press, 1992).

9 Roy Nakano, "Marxist-Leninist Organizing in the Asian American Community of Los Angeles, 1969–79," MS, 1984 (available at the UCLA Asian American Studies Reading Room); Miriam Ching Louie, "'Yellow, Brown & Red': Towards an Appraisal of the Marxist Influences on the Asian American Movement," MS, 1991; Ho, with Antonio, Fujino, and Yip, *Legacy to Liberation*; Louie and Omatsu, *Asian Americans*; Diane C. Fujino, *Heartbeat of Struggle: The Revolutionary Life of Yuri Kochiyama* (Minneapolis: University of Minnesota Press, 2005); Laura Pulido, *Black, Brown, Yellow, and Left: Radical Activism in Los Angeles* (Berkeley: University of California Press, 2006); Daryl J. Maeda, *Chains of Babylon: The Rise of Asian America* (Minneapolis: University of Minnesota Press, 2009); Judy Tzu-Chun Wu, *Radicals on the Road: Internationalism, Orientalism, and Feminism during the Vietnam Era* (Ithaca: Cornell University Press, 2013); Ishizuka, *Serve the People*; Rene Ciria Cruz, Cindy Domingo, and Bruce Occena, eds., *A Time to Rise: Collective Memoirs of the Union of Democratic Filipinos (KDP)* (Seattle: University of Washington Press, 2017).

10 Maeda, *Chains of Babylon*, 99.

11 Maeda, *Chains of Babylon*, 98.

12 Diane C. Fujino, "The Indivisibility of Freedom: The Nisei Progressives, Deep Solidarities, and Cold War Alternatives," *Journal of Asian American Studies* 21 (2018): 197.

13 James Zarsadiaz, "Raising Hell in the Heartland: Filipino Chicago and the Anti–Martial Law Movement, 1972–1986," *American Studies* 55 (2017): 141–232; Karen Buenavista Hanna, "When Mothers Lead: Revolutionary Adaptability in a Filipina/o American Diasporic Community Theater Organization," *Amerasia Journal* 45 (2019): 188–206; Robyn Magalit Rodriguez, *Filipino American Transnational*

Activism: Diasporic Politic among the Second Generation (Leiden, Netherlands: Brill, 2019).

14 Activist and academic writings by and about 1960s and 1970s radicals of color have grappled with the tensions between nationalism and internationalism and theorize revolutionary nationalism and anti-imperialism, including Robin D. G. Kelley, *Freedom Dreams: The Black Radical Imagination* (Boston: Beacon Press, 2002); Max Elbaum, *Revolution in the Air: Sixties Radicals Turn to Lenin, Mao, and Che* (New York: Verso, 2002); Fred Ho, *Wicked Theory, Naked Practice: A Fred Ho Reader*, ed. Diane C. Fujino (Minneapolis: University of Minnesota Press, 2009).

15 Pulido, *Black, Brown, Yellow, and Left.*

16 Harvey C. Dong, "The Origins and Trajectory of Asian American Political Activism in the San Francisco Bay Area, 1968–1978" (PhD diss., University of California, Berkeley, 2002); Diane C. Fujino, "Grassroots Leadership and Afro-Asian Solidarities: Yuri Kochiyama's Humanizing Radicalism," in *Want to Start a Revolution? Radical Women in the Black Freedom Struggle*, ed. Dayo F. Gore, Jeanne Theoharis, and Komozi Woodard (New York: New York University Press, 2009), 294–316; Diane C. Fujino, *Samurai among Panthers: Richard Aoki on Race, Resistance, and a Paradoxical Life* (Minneapolis: University of Minnesota Press, 2012); Lilia Villanueva and Craig Scharlin, *Philip Vera Cruz: A Personal History of Filipino Immigrants and the Farmworkers Movement* (Los Angeles: UCLA Labor Center, Institute of Industrial Relations and UCLA Asian American Studies Center, 1992); *The Delano Manongs: Forgotten Heroes of the United Farm Workers*, documentary, directed by Marissa Aroy (New York: Media Factory, 2014); Nobuko Miyamoto, *Not Yo' Butterfly: My Long Song of Relocation, Race, Love, and Revolution*, ed. Deborah Wong (Berkeley: University of California Press, 2021).

17 Barbara Ransby, *Ella Baker and the Black Freedom Movement: A Radical Democratic Vision* (Chapel Hill: University of North Carolina Press, 2003).

18 Lillian Fabros, "Stand Fast and Don't Go Quietly into the Night," in *Mountain Movers: Student Activism and the Emergence of Asian American Studies*, ed. Russell Jeung, Karen Umemoto, Harvey Dong, Eric Mar, Lisa Hirai Tsuchitani, and Arnold Pan (Los Angeles: UCLA Asian American Studies Center, 2019), 149.

19 Fujino, "Who Studies the Asian American Movement," 127–69; Maeda, *Rethinking the Asian American Movement.*

20 Robert G. Lee, *Orientals: Asian Americans in Popular Culture* (Philadelphia: Temple University Press, 1999); Cindy I-Fen Cheng, *Citizens of Asian America: Democracy and Race during the Cold War* (New York: New York University Press, 2013); Ellen D. Wu, *Color of Success: Asian Americans and the Origins of the Model Minority* (Princeton: Princeton

University Press, 2014); Diane C. Fujino, "Cold War Activism and Japanese American Exceptionalism: Contested Solidarities and Decolonial Alternatives to Freedom," *Pacific Historical Review* 87 (2018): 264–304.

21 *The Fall of the I-Hotel*, documentary, directed by Curtis Choy (San Francisco: Chonk Moonhunter Productions, 1983); Estella Habal, *San Francisco's International Hotel: Mobilizing the Filipino American Community in the Anti-Eviction Movement* (Philadelphia: Temple University Press, 2007).

22 H. M. Lai, "A Historical Survey of Organizations of the Left among the Chinese in America," *Bulletin of Concerned Asian Scholars* 4 (1972): 10–20; Masumi Izumi, *The Rise and Fall of America's Concentration Camp Law: Civil Liberties Debates from the Internment to McCarthyism and the Radical 1960s* (Philadelphia: Temple University Press, 2019).

23 Ishizuka, *Serve the People*; Fujino, "Indivisibility of Freedom." On contesting the dominant narrative of Nisei (second-generation Japanese Americans) assimilationism, see Diane C. Fujino, *Nisei Radicals: The Feminist Poetics and Transformative Ministry of Mitsuye Yamada and Michael Yasutake* (Seattle: University of Washington Press, 2020).

24 See, for example, Yuri Kochiyama, with Marjorie Lee, Akemi Kochiyama-Shardinha, and Audee Kochiyama-Holman, *Passing It On: A Memoir* (Los Angeles: UCLA Asian American Studies Center, 2004); Grace Lee Boggs, *Living for Change: An Autobiography* (Minneapolis: University of Minnesota Press, 1998); Craig Scharlin and Lilia V. Villanueva, *Philip Vera Cruz: A Personal History of Filipino Immigrants and the Farmworkers Movement* 3rd ed. (Seattle: University of Washington Press, 2000); *Who Killed Vincent Chin?*, documentary, directed by Christine Choy and Renee Tajima-Pena (New York: Film News Now, 1987); Paula Yoo, *From a Whisper to a Rallying Cry: The Killing of Vincent Chin and the Trial That Galvanized the Asian American Movement* (New York: Norton Young Readers, 2021); Cruz, Domingo, and Occena, *Time to Rise*.

25 Karin Aguilar-San Juan, ed., *The State of Asian America: Activism and Resistance in the 1990s* (Boston: South End Press, 1994), 2.

26 Dean Spade and Roberto Sirvent, "BAR Abolition & Mutual Aid Spotlight: Alisa Bierria," *Black Agenda Report*, May 13, 2020, https://www.blackagendareport.com/bar-abolition-mutual-aid-spotlight-alisa-bierria.

27 George Lipsitz, "Listening to Learn and Learning to Listen: Popular Culture, Cultural Theory, and American Studies," *American Quarterly* 42 (1990): 615–36.

28 Paulo Freire, *Pedagogy of the Oppressed* (1970; reprint, New York: Continuum International Publishing Group, 2007).

29 For such a review, see Diane C. Fujino and Robyn M. Rodriguez, "The Legibility of Asian American Activism Studies," *Amerasia Journal* 45 (2019): 113, 111–36.

30 Charmaine Chua, "Abolition Is a Constant Struggle: Five Lessons from Minneapolis," *Theory & Event* 23 (2020): 127–47.

31 We recognize, of course, that venues beyond AAS serve to awaken a political consciousness. Angelica Cabande narrated at our symposium how she came to political awareness through conscious hip-hop, suggesting perhaps that AAS has a lesser impact for working-class people who do not have the opportunity to pursue higher education.

32 Gary Y. Okihiro, *Third World Studies: Theorizing Liberation* (Durham, NC: Duke University Press, 2016).

33 Pam Tau Lee's chapter in this book is a revised version of her keynote address at the opening of the Contemporary Asian American Activism symposium, January 24–26, 2019, UC Santa Barbara.

34 Louie and Omatsu, *Asian Americans*, xv.

35 Pulido, *Black, Brown, Yellow, and Left*, 106.

36 "AAPA Perspectives," *Asian American Political Alliance* newspaper, October 1969.

37 Glenn Omatsu, "The 'Four Prisons' and the Movements for Liberation," *Amerasia Journal* 15 (1989): xvi.

38 George Lipsitz, *The Possessive Investment in Whiteness: How White People Profit from Identity Politics* (Philadelphia: Temple University Press, 1998).

39 Okihiro, *Third World Studies*.

40 On Afro-Asian solidarity today, see, for example, May Fu, Simmy Makhijani, Anh-Thu Pham, Meejin Richart, Joanne Tien, and Diane Wong, "#Asians4BlackLives: Notes from the Ground," *Amerasia Journal* 45 (2019): 253–70; Alex T. Tom, "The Chinese Progressive Association and the 'Red Door,'" in *Black Power Afterlives: The Enduring Significance of the Black Panther Party*, ed. Diane C. Fujino and Matef Harmachis (Chicago: Haymarket Press, 2020), 289–300; "Black and Asian-American Feminist Solidarities: A Reading List," https://www.blackwomen radicals.com/blog-feed/black-and-asian-feminist-solidarities-a-reading -list?fbclid=IwAR2HaqGCe4b5ng6QmKOFdptGceeyU4SBaOPQsVtpN9o UzubAOfOz2-WI02I, accessed May 29, 2020; "Black/Asian Solidarity," https://crossculturalsolidarity.com/black-asian-solidarity, accessed June 22, 2020.

41 Jung, "Model Minority Mutiny."

42 Jung, "Model Minority Mutiny"; see also Mari Matsuda, "We Will Not Be Used," reprinted in *Asian American Studies Now: A Critical Reader*, ed. Jean Yu-wen Shen Wu and Thomas C. Chen, 558–64 (New Brunswick, NJ: Rutgers University Press, 2010).

43 Frances E. Kendall, "How to Be an Ally if You Are a Person with Privilege," 2003, http://www.scn.org/friends/ally.html.

44 Sung Yeon Choimorrow, "Solidarity Not Allyship: A Call to the AAPI Community," *Colorlines*, June 22, 2020.

45 Jung, "Model Minority Mutiny," emphasis added.

46 Diane C. Fujino, "A Spiritual Practice for Sustaining Social Justice Activism: An Interview with Ericka Huggins," in Fujino and Harmachis, *Black Power Afterlives*, 79–88.

47 Martin Luther King Jr., "Nonviolence and Racial Justice," in *A Testament of Hope: The Essential Writings of Martin Luther King, Jr.*, ed. James M. Washington (San Francisco: Harper & Row, 1986), 5–9.

48 Barbara Tomlinson and George Lipsitz, "Insubordinate Spaces for Intemperate Times: Countering the Pedagogies of Neoliberalism," *Review of Education, Pedagogy, and Cultural Studies* 35 (2013): 14; see also Barbara Tomlinson and George Lipsitz, "American Studies as Accompaniment," *American Quarterly* 65 (2013): 1–30.

49 Stefano Harney and Fred Moten, *The Undercommons: Fugitive Planning and Black Study* (Brooklyn, NY: Autonomedia, 2103), 26, 30.

50 Robin D. G. Kelley, "Transformative Scholarship, Freedom Dreams, and the Future of Black Studies," Center for Black Studies Research, UC Santa Barbara, February 6, 2017.

PART 1

INCARCERATIONS, DISPLACEMENTS, AND TRANSFORMATIONS

CHAPTER 1

PRISON-TO-LEADERSHIP PIPELINE

Asian American Prisoner Activism

EDDY ZHENG

HISTORICAL CONTEXT ABOUT ASIAN AMERICANS, MASS INCARCERATION, AND ACTIVISM IN PRISONS

THE CONNECTION BETWEEN ASIAN AMERICANS (AAs) AND mass incarceration has not been highlighted in literature or in the media, and known histories of activism around AA incarceration are even more scarce.[1] To my knowledge, the three most notable cases of activism involving incarcerated AAs are Japanese American internment and draft resisters Chol Soo Lee, Yu Kikumura, and David Wong.[2] The Vincent Chin case of 1982, which did not involve an AA who went to prison, is also relevant because the men who murdered Vincent Chin did not do any time and were not convicted for the murder because they were white. Each of these cases inspired vibrant activism and grassroots movements among many AAs across the country who fought for justice in response to the wrongful incarceration of AAs. Through their work, including the Bay Area support of Chol Soo Lee and the David Wong Support Committee led by Yuri Kochiyama in New York, these community-led movements and their successes demonstrate the importance of AA activism in relation to criminal justice.

Each of these examples mainly focuses on activism happening *outside* of the prison industrial complex. With the exception of Japanese internment, draft resistance, and Yu Kikumura's persistent

FIGURE 1.1. Eddy Zheng speaking at a rally. He notes: "Once I was able to tap into my CHI—Culture, History and Identity—I become a critical thinker and changemaker." Photo courtesy of Eddy Zheng.

self-advocacy and filing of lawsuits, there are no specific examples of activism *inside* the prison system led by AAs, and if there have been any, these cases are not very widely known. The silence around AAs, incarceration, and activism needs to be understood in the context of the unique issues that AAs face compared to other people of color in the penal system—namely, the small percentage of AAs in the prison compared to the overrepresentation of people of color and the model minority myth. Once in prison, we become a minority among minorities. We are not considered as significant when it comes to providing culturally competent services, programs, and resources. Thus, resistance in the prison space is in direct relation to survival for the AA population because we are categorized as "other" in the prison system.[3] Part of this survival and process of building solidarity among each other regardless of our ethnicity when we are all categorized together as other entails that we resist the system and the inhumane treatment that people have to experience inside. But there are no well-known examples of AA activism in the prison system. The lack is mostly due to the model minority myth, which has worked to create the perception that AAs are not impacted by mass incarceration and deportation. This has been made worse by the failure of officials to collect disaggregated data on AAs in prison. It has furthermore worked to silence Asian Americans who do understand the impacts of criminal justice on AAs due to a culture of shame. This creates difficulties for Asian Americans in prison, who are seen as "troublemakers" who ended up in prison but are still expected to behave as passive model minorities in prison who won't make trouble or get involved in fights and riots.

Another overlooked and inhumane aspect of the criminal justice system's impacts on AAs is the mandatory detention and deportation of noncitizens after incarceration. This double punishment created the school-to-prison and deportation pipeline for immigrants and especially Southeast Asian refugees.[4] Because of US foreign policies and the nation's proxy wars with the Soviet Union in fighting against communism, Southeast Asia was made into their battleground. The devastating results of the intergenerational trauma of war, the separation of families, and refugee resettlement in violent and poverty-stricken US neighborhoods created the school-to-prison and deportation pipeline. People who are not citizens of the United States who have committed a crime of moral turpitude and aggravated felony are automatically detained and deported after serving their time in accordance with the 1996 Illegal Immigration Reform and Immigrant Responsibility Act, which applies the law retroactively.

The perception of AAs as the model minority in prison and the lack of understanding of their peculiar presence are important to challenge. We must recover the history of AA activism within the prison system so examples of resistance by incarcerated AAs are known. We didn't know of any movement as part of our history of AA activism within the prison system until the fight for Asian American studies and ethnic studies in San Quentin State Prison began.

ACTIVISM IN PRISON VIA EDUCATION

I was introduced to activism before I was even politically and socially conscious through advocating for my fellow AA prisoners. Advocating for each other was a necessary survival tool for AAs due to our small population behind bars. We had to stick together to avoid being bullied and exploited by other prisoners, and I learned the importance of supporting other prisoners, especially those new to the system, so they could avoid some of the pitfalls that might lead them into dangers inside. It's known inside the prison that if you mess with one AA, then you have to mess with all AAs.

Another part of my introduction to activism was through studying Asian American figures and activism in US history—people like Richard Aoki, Grace Lee Boggs, Yuri Kochiyama, Philip Vera Cruz, and Helen Zia. This knowledge instilled in me an understanding of different kinds of activism, which planted the seeds for my eventual activism inside the prison system and beyond.

None of my activism would have been possible if I hadn't learned how to read, write, and think critically. When I was first incarcerated, I did not know how to read and write much English because I was a recent immigrant. Like many of the people of color in the prison industrial complex, I was impacted by the school-to-prison and deportation pipeline. Therefore, being able to read and write became part of my survival strategy. The motivation to survive enabled me to find my value and increased my self-esteem through becoming well-read. I was able to gain access to alternative literatures, which empowered me and fed my curiosity to learn and become a critical thinker.

As I was figuring out how to navigate the space of incarceration and learning about Asian American activists, I was also trying to figure out how to continue to empower myself and other people. Part of this path to empowerment and starting an activist movement in prison happened because I was already on the path to discovering my own political consciousness during my time in San Quentin State Prison.

When the federal Pell Grant was taken away from all California prisoners in 1992, it denied them access to higher education within the prison system. Even though it had been shown that access to higher education reduces recidivism, the targeting of crime and punishment trumped public safety.[5] But in San Quentin State Prison, located in the progressive Bay Area, volunteer professors led by Naomi Janowitz from the Religious Studies department at the University of California, Davis, started a free college program in 1996. This volunteer-run program started out by offering only evening courses to gauge interest from the prisoners, but it eventually became an accredited associate of arts degree program due to its popularity and success. As a participating student since its inception, I was extremely active in all aspects of the program. I was able to find my value and voice throughout this learning process and became one of the three students who graduated with an associate's degree in 1999.

Knowledge is power. That is a phase that I frequently heard as I was growing up. I experienced that power first hand as I gained more confidence and social consciousness with increased exposure to higher education. San Quentin State Prison's free college program became a popular place to which volunteer students and professors flocked to cultivate the minds of society's outcasts. But given that the existence of the program was dictated by the prison administration, there were many restrictions as to who could go in to teach and what could be taught. By about 2000 a new program coordinator was chosen by the administration. The idea that it was enough to give prisoners opportunities to learn how to read and write now became the basis for keeping the program. As more prisoners and volunteers became involved in the associate's degree program, reaching the goal of earning the sixty units needed to graduate was a huge accomplishment. However, for someone like me, who had been exposed to the power of learning and critical thinking, I was not satisfied. I wanted to have more access to alternative classes and literature, especially related to Asian American culture and history. After 9/11 I also saw white supremacist prisoners and prison guards scapegoating prisoners from the Middle East. It further motivated me to want to have more access to the histories and literatures of other cultures so we could humanize each other.

In early 2002 I reached out to the coordinator and expressed my thoughts about getting the college program to provide Asian American history and literature classes as a part of the curriculum. The initial response from the volunteer coordinator was positive, and I was advised to find professors who would be willing to come in to teach Asian American literature or other ethnic studies courses. The irony of this is that the coordinator was a free person and studied at UC Berkeley, while I was locked up, and yet I was expected to find professors to teach. So I reached out to other volunteers to help me find professors who might teach courses in San Quentin. Despite my success in identifying potential professors for the coordinator to reach out to, there was no follow-up even after multiple reminders. I was instead asked to write up a proposal of what I wanted, what I wanted for Asian American studies, and what I wanted to learn.

In March 2002 I submitted two proposals to the volunteer coordinator in the San Quentin College program that were signed by Viet Mike Ngo, Romerico Riemedio, Stephen Liebb, and me. In these proposals we advocated for ethnic studies and prisoners' rights. What began as a verbal request for Asian American literature classes quickly became a historical movement of activism inside San Quentin that would eventually extend outside into the free world. This form of activism was aligned with the struggle for ethnic studies and global studies that began at San Francisco State University with the Third World Liberation Front in 1968 and continued with the 1999 student strike at UC Berkeley.[6] I was able to publish my writing in the UC Berkeley student-led magazine *Hardboiled* because I met Momo Chang, Jeanne Loh, Alicia Yang, and Hua Xu. They were the first group of Chinese American student volunteers who came to the college program.

The original sentiment behind the first proposal was to offer elective classes that would allow people to learn about each other's cultures and histories of struggle against repression and occupation. In highlighting these struggles and allowing people to see where they had similar experiences and common histories of resistance, these classes would encourage cross-cultural understanding and challenge racial and cultural stereotypes. So we wrote the proposal, which presented the elective courses and topics we wanted to study and which also explained that we as a student body wanted to be involved in the decision making that was being made on behalf of us without our involvement.

The second statement we wrote focused on the need for transparency in the coordinator's decision to change the college program structure. There was talk about turning the all-volunteer program into a nonprofit organization with 501(c)(3) status, which allows it to seek funding from individual donors, philanthropic foundations, government grants, and corporate backing. We were not included or consulted in making these decisions, even though the shift to nonprofit status came with potential funding from corporations whose business practices exploited prisoners and profited off the prison industrial complex. As prisoners who participated in the college program, we were not made aware of those discussions. In our second statement we condemned the fact that programmatic decisions that would directly impact us were being made without involving us or engaging us for our input.

Our proposals were interpreted as a personal attack on the program coordinator instead of being understood within the bigger picture: people who had been historically disenfranchised were being excluded from the educational system and should have been given the opportunity not only to learn how to read and write but also to think critically about their conditions and how they got there.

One of the rare things that happened after we submitted our proposal was that we were able to bring people together, from prisoners who were participating in the college program to volunteers and professors who came in to support it. We were able to have honest, sometimes heated dialogues with each other about what was happening in a town hall–style environment. What came about during these discussions was very interesting. There were many conversations, disagreements, and conflicts between volunteers and professors that came out during this meeting and that we heard about for the first time. Some professors stated that they felt excluded from coming into the prison to teach because there was no transparency around hiring and curricular decisions. The prison administration had given the volunteer coordinator discretionary power to decide what to teach, who could teach, and what literature was taught, and she became a gatekeeper for the program. Another issue that emerged in the discussion was a conflict between one group of professors who wanted to maintain the associate of arts degree program through Patten College in Oakland, California, and a different group of professors who wanted to expand and create a bachelor of arts program through St. Mary's College.[7] Because we were excluded from access to this information and the decision-making processes and because the institution had total control over the function of the college program, we did not realize the extent of these conflicts and how they affected us until they came out in the meetings.

It is important to understand how all of these conflicts affected the prisoners and to situate this in the historical context of people of color who have been impacted by mass incarceration and who historically have been disenfranchised and excluded from the education process. According to Literacy Statistics, over 70 percent of inmates in America's prisons cannot read above a fourth grade level.[8] Therefore, when they are totally locked up in the institution, many are hungry for education when given the opportunity. Once they are exposed to education and understand their own ability to learn how to read and write, they are very enthusiastic, very involved, and eager to learn. This is why this college program was so important: it gave people an opportunity to find value and to learn how to read and write and think. However, it also created unexpected conflicts that began to turn the prisoners against each other.

There were two responses toward the people who signed the proposal. One was the administration's perspective: "You guys are making trouble. You're lucky that you have a college program. You shouldn't advocate or try to demand anything from us." They threatened to cancel the college program altogether. This threat was worrisome to some of the prisoners, who were concerned that they would lose their chance to earn their associate's degrees if the administration shut down the college program. The threat led prisoners to say, "We don't want the program to be shut down—we want it to continue," which in turn generated unanticipated disagreements, tension, and conflict between those who had already earned their associate's degrees and those who were still working toward their associate's degrees. Friends whom I broke bread together with and who had the same political sense said: "Eddy, we got love for you and totally understand where you're coming from, but we want our program. We want to keep the college program." I had to explain to them that I didn't want the program to be shut down—that I wanted to increase the resources of the program. I explained that we wrote the proposal because we wanted to get people to learn more, to grow more in this process, not to shut down the program. And they agreed with this. But the administration's threats and the conditioning pressured them to respond to the situation with this logic: "If you do this, then they're going to punish us and we're going to lose the associate's degree program. In order to not lose this program, you have to conform." Because much of the information about the college program, the decision-making around the college program, and the plans for corporate sponsorship had not been shared with us and were not transparent, there was a lot of conflict in the discussions that took place during and after the town halls. Sometimes it was heated, but a lot of truths came out from many people during these conversations.

THE ADMINISTRATION RESPONDS

Officers who witnessed these gatherings and heated conversations about the proposals wondered what we were discussing. After a few of these gatherings took place, the administration got a hold of the proposals and reviewed them. They called the coordinator in to discuss the situation and then put all the people who had signed the proposal under investigation. They took all of our paperwork, pieces we had written, photos, letters, articles, and books from all three of us Asian Americans—Mike, Rico, and me. We were questioned about all of the books, articles, and writings that they had confiscated from our property. They let the college program and the teaching continue but banned us from going into the educational buildings to participate in classes and programming. They shut down the town halls and meetings. We had to file a grievance demanding to know why the administration had banned us from going into the educational department. Then, one by one, the administration accused each of us of rule violations, thus creating reasons to put us into solitary confinement. The first person who was taken into solitary confinement was Rico. After that they took Mike. I knew I was next, so I was ready. At the time Rico, who was a life-term prisoner, already had a parole date. But as a result of signing the proposal, Rico's freedom eventually was taken away from him. He was put in solitary confinement, found guilty of his violation, and transferred to another prison. Mike was put in solitary confinement, put on bus therapy (he was transferred to different prisons), and then was found guilty of his violation. I was locked in solitary confinement for eleven months and found guilty of my violations. As we were put into solitary confinement one by one, the message was very consistent from the administration: "You're prisoners. You don't demand anything from us. You're lucky that we gave you this program." They used us as a way to demonstrate to the rest of the mainland population what would happen to them if they wanted to protest or advocate for themselves.

Once this got into the news, the community was in shock, from the volunteers to the people in the communities. There were a couple of reasons this made the news. One is because we were put in solitary confinement just because we signed a proposal. The second is because everybody had access to the proposal—the people on the outside and the people on the inside. The third is that, in the process, Mike filed a lawsuit against the prison for racially segregating inmates inside the prison industrial complex, a violation of the U.S. Constitution's Fourteenth Amendment.[9]

One of the very challenging pieces for me being in solitary confinement was that my mom and my family didn't understand why I would jeopardize my freedom to fight for this. My mom wrote to me and said: "Why do you have to advocate for other people? You've been in prison for this long, we're waiting for you to come home. We're getting old, our health is not that good. Why can't you just lay low and just come home?" It was very tough for me. I didn't know that I would end up in solitary confinement because I was exercising my knowledge and was trying to get people to learn more. I thought it was the right thing to do because I was advocating for everybody. I was not just advocating for myself but really advocating for improving the program and helping everyone to grow. I was trying to get us access to more critical thinking education, more literature, more classes that were inclusive of other cultures and other people so we could learn from each other and find better ways to treat each other.

ACTIVISM INSIDE IGNITES A SOCIAL JUSTICE MOVEMENT IN THE AA COMMUNITY

Once we were in solitary confinement, we had to go through the process of defending ourselves. This is when many people in the community began to come together. Because of my engagement with college students and community members, I was introduced to Yuri Kochiyama by Monica Wayie Ly and Anmol Chaddha. Yuri made it a point to write to me, to visit me in solitary confinement, and to continue to encourage me and reassure me that the community was supportive of all of us who were in solitary confinement. The students were organizing, and with Yuri as a mentor and as someone who was actively fighting this, they were able to create multiple ways to make sure the administration knew we had support on the outside, that we were not alone in solitary confinement. They called us the "San Quentin 3," a name that referenced the historical San Quentin 6.[10] Yuri, Anmol Chaddha, Sharon Luk, Wayie Ly, and others then created the Asian Prisoner Support Committee (APSC) as part of this grassroots effort. That was the beautiful and unanticipated thing that came out of it: people started having meetings and building up activism from the outside. Community activists, people in the colleges, and others all came together to start talking and brainstorming about what they could do to get the administration to let us out of solitary confinement. Slowly, they built a social justice movement.

One of APSC's big actions was to put on a community event in 2003 at Locus Arts San Francisco to educate people about what had happened. People like Ishle Yi Park, a Korean American poet; 18 Mighty Mountain Warriors, an Asian American comedy group; Shailja Patel, an Indian American poet; Bao Phi, a Vietnamese poet; Jason Mateo, a Filipino poet; and others came together to perform and raise awareness about our signing a proposal advocating for Asian American and ethnic studies programs. Activist lawyer Charles Carbone was on hand to provide updates on our situation. My family and Mike's family were there to speak and thank people for coming together. It was a packed house. They got people to sign postcards to advocate for our release from solitary confinement and sent a big batch of these postcards to the administration. Every week subsequently, they continued to send postcards and had the media regularly call the prison to ask about what was happening with us and what they were doing with us. This was the birth of the Asian Prisoner Support Committee.

While this activism was happening outside, I was still trying to do what I could inside to help the people who were voiceless inside. While in solitary confinement, I was able to utilize some of the basic knowledge that I had dealing with law in order to fight. I filed grievances about the violation of our rights inside and filed grievances for other prisoners whose rights were being routinely violated but who did not know the law and who did not know their rights or how to exercise them. I was able to help multiple people, including a monolingual Chinese speaker with mental health issues whom I helped to get a translator and an African American person at a halfway house who had been falsely arrested, brought back into prison, and was getting ready to be sent to Pelican Bay State Prison to do a one-year SHU (Security Housing Unit) term. I was able to teach him how to advocate for himself and exercise his rights, and eventually he was released.

We were able to create impacts in several ways. First, our activism inside, which highlighted the need to fight for our rights, for prisoners' rights, and for the incorporation of Asian American studies and ethnic studies programs into the prison college program all gave us the platform to uplift the challenges of AA prisoners' needs and invisibility. Second, our activism showed the importance of having ethnic studies in the college program. It raised the important question: how do we empower people? Third, the support from the Asian American community continued to uplift the issue of AA incarceration and its impacts, but it also exposed the need to become more involved and to support people who were experiencing injustice. This allowed an opportunity and space for many of the progressive students who were willing to step up, be involved, dedicate their time to creating this social justice movement, and see it through. This ties into how activists are born: because they were exposed to certain injustices or certain movements, once they get involved, then they know what it takes to win and what it means to be involved. There were two young students in particular who spent years of their time even after I got out of solitary confinement continuing to advocate for my release from state and immigration prisons—Anmol Chaddha and Ben Wang. Yuri was the glue and the mentor in the movement who continued to help empower these students and others to do that.

As a result of that activism, we were able to prove a couple of things. When we were in solitary confinement, the main population of the prisoners counted us out. Because many of them were all life-term prisoners, their sentiment was that we were not going to get out of prison and that if we were to get out, it would be years later. People just went back to their normal business because they were conditioned to think, "Make no waves, because if you do, look at what happens." But we all got out and way before those people who counted us out. The other outcome is even more important. Subsequent to our release, we never gave up on continuing to pursue the creation of ethnic studies or an Asian American studies program to help support the historically marginalized Asian American and Pacific Islander (AAPI) community in prison because in the prison system—aside from religious programs, which are a constitutional right—there was no culturally competent program that specifically supported AAPIs. We were able to create the ROOTS (Restoring Our Original True Selves) program, which is modeled after Asian American studies and ethnic studies curriculum to empower individuals inside as a way to heal intergenerational trauma. It has proven to be extremely successful with all the participants in the program, which include all volunteers, because the teaching and healing are from both sides.

The creation of this Asian American activist movement brought together all different professions of people, including the faith-based community, the grassroots community, educators, students, politicians, and especially members of the legal community. Mike, Rico, and I all filed a lawsuit against the prison administration for violation of our First Amendment rights. We each filed a section 1983 civil rights lawsuit against them and sued them for two million dollars for their violation. We had Bay Area lawyers from Asian Pacific Islander Legal Outreach (APILO), led by Victor Hwang, two lawyers from the Asian Law Caucus, and Peter Kang from Sidley Austin Brown & Wood LLP, who were all involved in representing us pro bono. With their assistance we were eventually able to settle our cases and remove the negative files on our records that could jeopardize our freedom. While this was only a partial justice, settling my case allowed for the later revitalization of APSC and the grassroots social justice movement that formed as a result.

THE CHANGING FORM AND REVITALIZATION OF APSC

In May 2003, after I had been in solitary confinement for eleven months, I was transferred to Solano State Prison because of the overwhelming pressure from the public and APSC's efforts to hold the administration accountable. Once I was transferred to Solano, some of the students who had been exposed to the movement initiated contact and started to visit me. One was Ben Wang, an undergrad student from UC Davis whom I had gotten to know through writing letters and who eventually came to visit me and to talk about how to support the AA prisoners in Solano. Ben encouraged some of his fellow students to come in with him, including Mike Cheng, Claudia Pacheco, and Josh Savala, and other people who had become familiar with our case, like Sun-Hyung Lee, Serena Huang, Joy Liu, and Monica Wayie Ly, also came as part of the visiting group. As we engaged with the students and as they were learning about the impacts of mass incarceration on the AAPI population, we began thinking about how we could start political education discussions that would educate the AAPI prisoners. We organically started the visiting program because there were many AAs who hadn't received visits from their family members or friends in years. One of our goals with the visiting program was to take up space in the visiting room and begin talking about politics so others would hear us and understand what we were doing.

The other goal came about because I was reading literature about impacted African American and Latino populations but noticed that there was no literature from AAPIs who were impacted by mass incarceration. I wanted to start an anthology with AA prisoners' voices that we could use to educate the public. I started reaching out to different prisoners in Solano prison, asking them to submit poetry, vignettes, and writing, and asked those people who couldn't write if they would be willing to contribute their artwork or be interviewed so they could be a part of the anthology. I believed we could sell the anthology, use it as a curriculum in schools and colleges, and educate the public about what was happening to AAPIs in prison. Initially, there wasn't a lot of enthusiasm among prisoners because many of them did not know how to write and they did not believe this project could happen. So I worked with Ben to expand the cause and the mission of the project to other prisons. We wanted to center women in prison, so we reached out to the Dublin women's prison and Chowchilla and invited them to submit material. Unfortunately, we were only able to highlight one woman, an ICE (Immigration and Customs Enforcement) detainee and a transgender woman. In New York we reached out to prisoner Hyung-Rae, a Korean American prisoner who was an artist, and asked him to contribute. Slowly, we were able to gather submissions, worked on the editing and design, and put the anthology together. Ben was instrumental in reaching out to other prisoners as well as editing and revising submissions through correspondence. In 2007 I was finally released from prison and ICE after being incarcerated for twenty-one years, and at my homecoming party on March 31, 2007, we released *Other: An Asian & Pacific Islander Prisoners' Anthology*, with funding support from the Agape Foundation.

APSC had turned a new chapter after we left San Quentin. Although they still focused on supporting my freedom, there was a shift in the kind of organizing done. In 2005 Ben, Sun-Hyung, Mike, Serena, and Kasi Chakravartula picked up the work that Yuri, Anmol Chaddha, Monica Wayie Ly, and Sharon Luk had begun while I was in solitary confinement, and organically we began organizing, first through the visiting program and then with the anthology. After I got out, in 2007, we started meeting at different people's apartments and houses because we wanted to continue to find ways as a part of APSC to support the people currently incarcerated. We were grateful to continue to be mentored by Yuri and Richard Aoki, who also joined our meetings, until they became our ancestors. We didn't have a budget. Our budget came from doing book readings of the anthology and selling it. Most of the money earned from selling the anthology went to supporting political prisoners, contributing to disaster relief, donating to nonprofits, and helping people who were less fortunate, which the people inside and anthology contributors had wanted. We were truly a grassroots group where people came together for a common purpose—to support AAPIs who are impacted by mass incarceration and deportation. Slowly, we gathered interest from people who were willing to volunteer to write to prisoners and wrote and sent annual holiday greetings with stamps to show them that they were not forgotten.

At the same time, I was still trying to figure out how we could bring in a culturally competent support program to the prisoners. Because of my complicated history with San Quentin, we tried to start a culturally competent program in the Solano prison; however, it was tough because self-help programs were seen as a privilege, not a right. When we couldn't get the program in Solano after a couple of attempts, we turned our focus back to San Quentin, where we were able to go in with an existing program called T.R.U.S.T. (Teaching Responsibility Utilizing Sociological Training), a program designed to transform incarcerated men from social liabilities into assets. We went there as participants and volunteers. For over a year and a half, we proposed and spoke with AAPI prisoners on starting a culturally competent self-help program, asking for their input and about their needs and asking what they wanted to see in this program. Finally, in 2013, with the advocacy from many of the AAPI prisoners who were serving life sentences, we were able to convince the administration to start a nine-month program called ROOTS—Restoring Our Original True Selves. The prisoners came up with the acronym and title of the program. The inside cofounders of ROOTS were Borey Ai, Nghiep Lam, Phoeun You, Stephen Liebb, and Sujat Shakur. Each Monday afternoon volunteer professors led by Roger Chung and Nathaniel Tan, devoted members Kasi Chakravartula and Tracy Nguyen, hip-hop artists, lawyers, health care workers, activists, and organizers would go in to work with people for two or three hours and talk with them about the history and culture of AAPIs as a way to heal intergenerational trauma. It seemed like a dream come true because ten years after I left solitary confinement for fighting for ethnic studies, we were able to create the only culturally competent program that centered on the empowerment and healing of AAPIs in US prisons. Ironically, I was banned from going into San Quentin on the inaugural day of the program with no explanation. However, at the first graduation of the first ROOTS cohort, I was finally allowed to go in to deliver the keynote speech and see the fruition of the program.[11]

The graduation of the first ROOTS cohort generated a lot of excitement. Once people finished their first year in the ROOTS program, they started thinking about what they would do in the second year. We were able to invite people inside who had gone through the program to become co-facilitators of the program and to help build the curriculum. We did this for the different cohorts each year, and it became very successful. We could see the transformation of individuals who had never had the opportunity to learn about their culture and history and who didn't understand why their parents, who came from war-torn countries, acted differently. They had not been able to make the connection between the trauma that they had experienced as a result of coming from a war-torn country and as a result of growing up in violent and poverty-stricken areas. But through this curriculum, which was modeled after ethnic studies, they were able to start engaging and learning from their history and experiences and used it to heal intergenerational trauma. The curriculum opened spaces in which individuals could have transformational conversations with each other and with their family members about some of those forbidden topics and intergenerational traumas. Although we faced some initial challenges in terms of figuring out how to train volunteers who were not familiar with the dynamics of the prison system, the program was equally transformational for the people on the outside who went in to co-facilitate the classes. They saw how people absorbed this type of information and used it as a tool to heal and teach other people.

During this time APSC was still a grassroots group with no budget that met in different houses and apartments as we expanded our membership. It was a volunteer-based group: everybody had full-time day jobs, but we came together on our own time to participate with APSC because we believed in supporting the people who were inside. It was amazing to witness the love and dedication and how people contributed because we cared about these issues. As more people learned about us through word of mouth and joined us, we needed to have an organizational structure. Ben and I were voted to be cochairs. Because at the time there weren't that many formerly incarcerated people getting out, especially life-term prisoners, I was responsible for informing the group about how people inside were impacted, what their needs were, and helping to guide the group about possible directions we could go. We were able to get a five thousand–dollar discretionary grant from the California Wellness Foundation thanks to the recommendation of an outgoing board member, which, aside from the money we made from selling the anthology, was the first five thousand dollars we had ever gotten from anyone. In 2015 I applied and received the Soros Justice Fellowship from Open Society Foundations to focus on raising awareness about the detrimental impact of mass incarceration on the AAPI community.[12] APSC was my host organization for the fellowship, and APSC became part of the Asian Americans for Civil Rights and Equality (AACRE) network under the advocacy organization Chinese for Affirmative Action (CAA). CAA became our fiscal sponsor. This meant that, as a grassroots organization, we were able to get the group's support with the financials and bookkeeping as well as with training and gaining access to meeting space. Though we operate like a nonprofit, we don't have 501(c)(3) status. Through my fellowship I was able to engage and connect other organizations, including the Asian Prisoner Support Committee, Southeast Asian Resource Action Center, Asian Pacific American Labor Alliance (APALA), National Education Association, and Asian Americans Advancing Justice Asian Law Caucus (AAAJ-ALC), Los Angeles, to start talking about how we could create a coalition in order to support each other and leverage resources to focus on incarceration and deportation. This was how we started the AAPIs Beyond Bars Coalition.

As part of this coalition, in 2015 we organized the historical AAPI Behind Bars convening of stakeholders at San Quentin State Prison, where direct service providers, health care providers, politicians, formerly incarcerated people, and funders from across the country visited our ROOTS program, interacted with people inside, and learned about both the transformational impacts of ROOTS and the impacts of mass incarceration and deportation on the AAPI community. Participants were blown away by this experience. After the convening at San Quentin, the Alameda Labor Council hosted a discussion among participants about their experiences, which led us to collectively write a report with the AAPIs Beyond Bars Coalition called *Asian Americans*

& *Pacific Islanders Behind Bars: Exposing the School to Prison to Deportation Pipeline.* In this report we examined the impacts of mass incarceration and deportation on the AAPI community and offered recommendations. With our partners in DC and the sponsorship of US Representatives Judy Chu, Barbara Lee, and Bobby Scott, we were able to hold a historic congressional briefing on this report inside the Capitol. The following year we went to Seattle with support from an AA group called FIGHT (Formerly Incarcerated Group Healing Together) and hosted a convening with AA grassroots and direct service communities from across the country where we met with AAs in prison and discussed the importance of having culturally competent resources and programs to empower the individuals inside. These experiences of movement building and working with AA communities across the country were very valuable and eye-opening but not without challenges. Although I had worked in nonprofits, I had not been in these spaces on the national level and was unaware of the ongoing tensions that had been generated from the unequal distribution of resources and representation among organizations. I had to become a mediator to bring people together, refocus them on a common cause, and not only validate their feelings but also remind them of their larger purpose and work as a community.

Through these convenings and forms of engagement, I was able to meet funders and eventually secured significant funding for APSC. In January 2017 we were able to hire four staff members—Ben Wang, Harrison Seuga, Nghiep Ke Lam, and me; besides Ben, all were formerly incarcerated juvenile life-term prisoners who had each been incarcerated for over twenty years but who could now work full-time to give back. We embodied a grassroots organization that is led by formerly incarcerated individuals and created a prison-to-leadership pipeline. As more people were being released due to statewide policy and political climate changes, we realized there were few resources and culturally competent programs available to support AAs. As an extension of the ROOTS program, we were also able to create the ROOTS 2 Reentry (R2R), a program designed to offer culturally competent peer reentry support, care management, and community immersion opportunities to people coming out of the prison. In July 2017 we partnered with Asian Health Services in Oakland, California, to create the Chinatown Ambassadors pilot program to hire formerly incarcerated individuals to beautify Oakland Chinatown and to engage with merchants as a way to change people's mindsets about formerly incarcerated individuals. It's also a stepping-stone to support people to find other employment opportunities. As more people, especially those who were serving life sentences, began to get out of prison and were granted parole through reform efforts in California to engage the life-term prisoner population, these three programs supported these individuals and created a prison–to–reentry to the workforce and leadership pipeline. From San Quentin many of the former participants of the ROOTS program became R2R participants, and from there we could start hiring more people to work because attitudes had shifted within the larger AA community about formerly and currently incarcerated people through the success of the Chinatown Ambassadors pilot program.

FIGHTING CAMBODIAN DEPORTATIONS: KEEPING FAMILIES TOGETHER

At the same time that the ROOTS 2 Reentry program was expanding, APSC was fighting against the immigration policies under the Obama administration that targeted Vietnamese and Cambodian refugees for deportation because of the repatriation agreements the Vietnamese and Cambodian governments had with the United States. APSC had a high population of Southeast Asians in our programs and thus supported refugees at risk of deportation throughout the state. As one of only a handful of organizations in the country that actually offered direct services for currently and formerly incarcerated AAs, we also fought for several people out of state as well. Despite the pressure to deport Vietnamese refugees, the repatriation agreement was renegotiated in 2008 so that any Vietnamese refugee who had come to the United States prior to 1995 would not be deported even if they had had brushes with the law or were incarcerated. For the Cambodian refugee community, however, the government did not negotiate the repatriation agreement, so many Cambodian refugees were actually deported due to political pressure from the US government. The community came together and started fighting. With the momentum generated from Asian American and Southeast Asian organizations and community members coming together to fight the deportations, they were able to push back and advocate changing the repatriation agreement between Cambodia and the United States so that it mirrored the one the United States had negotiated with the Vietnamese government.

But as the momentum grew and the organizations made progress, the 2016 presidential election changed everything. Once Trump was elected president, all the negotiations stopped. When Trump took office in January 2017, he was able to pressure and coerce the Cambodian government to take back refugees. At that point we saw hundreds of refugees being rounded up with orders for deportation and then actively deported and separated from their families. At the time Black and brown communities had begun to build momentum and efforts around starting criminal justice reform movements; however, AAs were not always included at the table or in these conversations, and the specific challenges our community faced around the possibility of being deported after serving our time because we were not US citizens were not always acknowledged or validated. The AA and Cambodian community had to become active in response to these policies in order to keep families together. APSC focused on building relationships across the state and the country within the AA and Cambodian community so we could collectively build a movement around the anti-deportation effort. Unfortunately, there aren't many pro bono immigration lawyers who are familiar with the intersection of criminal and immigration laws to support impacted people. We were able to find lawyers such as Anoop Prasad and Tin Nguyen from our community network who were committed to representing people who had deportation orders and to fight to get them relief. As family members who had historically kept to themselves and who had not previously faced the trauma of coming from war-torn countries saw lawyers, activists, and community members who were willing to fight for their loved ones, they also stepped up to fight for their own people. As they became more active and learned more, they started becoming active in other people's fights against incarceration and deportation. They began talking to local politicians, advocated for policy changes, and exercised their rights to engage in this political process.

As part of the anti-deportation effort in California, APSC partnered with AAAJ-ALC San Francisco, Survived and Punished, the Center for Empowering Refugees and Immigrants, the Interfaith Movement, and other community organizations, and we were able to win many of the fights against deportation of Cambodian and other Southeast Asian refugees and immigrants. This was possible not only because the progressive policies had been changing in California but also because of the collective advocacy of the people. The slogan "Hope is contagious" came out of these organizing efforts from activist Nate Tan and APSC's partnerships with different organizations across the country. "Hope is contagious" uplifts many of the successful campaigns to keep individuals in this country with their families. "Hope is contagious" reflects the anti-deportation campaigns led by the people to keep families together, the lessons learned from those campaigns, and the history of how those campaigns were activated.

In November 2019 the New Breath Foundation sponsored and funded the Cambodian Deportees' Listening Tour in which members of APSC, AAAJ-ALC San Francisco, and Southeast Asian Freedom Network went to Cambodia to do a listening tour and met with over one hundred deportees and family members in order to learn about the challenges and impacts that they had experienced after being deported and separated from their families.[13] Anoop Prasad held a legal clinic with everyone about their cases. He found that because of changes in the law, 20 percent of those individuals would be allowed to return to the United States, including a single father who we discovered was actually a US citizen. Two months later he returned to the United States and reunited with his family after being wrongfully deported for almost five years.

Though it started in the most unlikely place as a grassroots movement, APSC has eventually been able to expand into a nationally recognized organization. Even though it is still under-resourced and has room for improvement, we are able to do our work with the active support of volunteers, interns, directly impacted people, family members, allies, and funders. With more people being released from incarceration, there are more people needing support, both those coming out of state and immigration prisons, especially many juvenile life-termers, as well as those who are still incarcerated. Both within and outside of California, we receive many letters and requests for services, including questions about jobs, housing, lawyers, how to get relief from potential immigration detention and deportation, and how to demonstrate that those in prison have a place to stay and a support system when they are released. There is a huge demand for resources due to the scarcity of organizations providing similar direct services. APSC does our best to respond. We have also done frequent teach-ins, presentations in universities, conferences, and worked with community organizations to educate people on the impacts of mass incarceration and deportation on AAs and to encourage people to get involved. APSC and all it has accomplished over the years is an example of how once a social justice movement comes together, it can create lasting effects and will continue to fight for the impacted individuals, families, and communities.

The issues of ending mass incarceration and comprehensive immigration reform that connects to institutional racism have generated unprecedented momentum nationally. We have witnessed Black and brown communities stepping up in organizing and utilizing political education to shift the dominant narrative and policies. But in the mainstream the detrimental impact of mass incarceration and deportation on Southeast Asian refugees and AA communities is still mostly ignored. That is why the AA movement that fought for ethnic studies in San Quentin State Prison and created the Asian Prisoner Support Committee has become an integral part of the longer tradition of Asian American social justice activism that has existed for more than fifty years.

What this type of activism through learning and education allows for is the creation of history and lineage. When I was able to cultivate and maximize an environment of learning, I found my value and purpose. I utilized what I had learned through reading literature such as African American history, American writings, poetry, and songs and by listening to and singing those songs. These forms of critical thinking education gave me opportunities to participate in cross-cultural engagement and to navigate those spaces so I could build and deepen relationships with impacted individuals. This work essentially helped me to solidify my values and shaped who I had become as I exited the system. I used the same knowledge that I had learned when I was inside to engage different cultures, to engage different communities, and to build racial solidarity when I was outside. Because I had the ability to learn and understand where I came from, how I got here, where I was going, and how healing and liberation are tied to each other, I was able to understand the possibilities and necessity of using culturally competent political education to heal and deepen relationships as a practice. When engaging with educators, I always say that it doesn't matter if you're a janitor or doctor: how you are informed and what informs you and what you learn translate to how you engage with the people utilizing your services. It makes a huge difference if you're informed based on a multicultural narrative compared to an ethnocentric narrative. It changes the world.

The Asian American social justice movement has always been happening, but we need to continue to build that pipeline for the next generations as previous generations have done for us so that the momentum we have built will not die. In my own case much of the momentum of the movement that began in response to AA political activism in San Quentin stopped after I was freed. People thought that now that I was out, they could go back to their own lives and focus on other issues. There was nobody to hold the space to keep the movement activated until young people like Ben, Sun-Hyung, Mike, Kasi, and Serena picked it up, reactivated it, and built it again. But they did not necessarily recognize at the time that what they were doing was reviving and rebuilding a movement. This has unfortunately happened historically in the Asian American activism movements, in which there has been no intentional organizing designed to maintain these movements or networks over time. Instead of proactively engaging people so we can continue the fight against the ongoing injustices in our community and communities of color, we become reactive to injustices, starting to organize again only when injustices come up instead of having an infrastructure in place that we can always activate. The ability of future generations to carry on this work and to be informed is not just a matter of them stepping up and saying, "This is why we need to advocate for ourselves and advocate for other people." It is a matter of whether they have a lineage or movements that they can point to and say, "This is what they did for the past fifty years in order for me to have what I have right now and in order for us to do what we are able to do right now." What is important is the next generation's ability to understand how they can do the work we are doing now differently and on their own terms while also understanding the work we are doing now from our perspective. Understanding, preserving, being grateful, building off our history of Asian American activism, and continuing to maintain and build these existing infrastructures and networks are essential parts of sustained movement building. Because when we stay ready, we don't have to get ready.

I remember reading a quotation by Ho Chi Minh, "When the prison doors are opened, the real dragon will fly out." This quotation resonates with me because when someone is politicized inside of the prison system and survives, it's inevitable that this person is going to become a change maker in the free world. The same applies to people who are often trapped in their mental prisons. Once we become socially and politically conscious and understand the impacts we can create, we can't stay back. The unintentional consequences of our fight for ethnic studies in San Quentin created an unanticipated grassroots social justice movement that has had a historical impact in the AA community over the past two decades. People inside the prison system and individuals, families, communities, and organizations on the outside engaged in political activism and created the space in which people could contribute and come together. In doing so, they brought a movement to life. As Yuri Kochiyama eloquently stated, "The movement is contagious, and the people in it are the ones who pass on the spirit." We have a rich lineage of fifty years (and more) of Asian American activism, and I believe political education through ethnic studies and global studies will play an important role in driving the next fifty years of Asian American activism. We can't be complacent or simply reactive to the current administration and policies. We must be proactive in making systemic changes. We need to understand that once an intergenerational impact and unanticipated movement has been created, it can't be stopped or controlled. As we continue to fight for what we believe in, the outcomes are unpredictable, but we need to be fearless when fighting for freedom and liberation for all people.

NOTES

1   While terms such as *Asian American and Pacific Islanders* (*AAPI*) and *Asian Pacific Islanders* (*API*) are widely used, we chose to use the abbreviation *AAs* to accurately reflect the individuals and groups involved in the struggles discussed here. We recognize that Native Hawaiians and other Pacific Islanders are disproportionately impacted by mass incarceration and frequently overlooked (see Umemoto's contribution to this volume, "Ho'opono Mamo and Restorative Practices").

2   Korean American Chol Soo Lee was wrongfully convicted for a murder he did not commit and then later given more time when he defended himself against another prisoner. His case led to widespread pan-Asian activism for his release. Chinese immigrant David Wong was sent to prison for trying to recover back wages from his boss and later framed for a killing while he was in prison. Yuri Kochiyama and others in the AA community of New York started the David Wong Support Committee and eventually won the case. Because Wong was not a US citizen,

he was deported to Hong Kong after his release from the prison system. Japanese national Yu Kikumura was a US-held political prisoner of Asian descent. Yuri Kochiyama and others started the Yu Kikumura Defense Committee, and Rev. Michael Yasutake provided visits and supported Kikumura's many lawsuits, including to have access to materials in his native language. On Lee, see Chol Soo Lee, *Freedom without Justice: The Prison Memoirs of Chol Soo Lee*, ed. Richard S. Kim (Honolulu: University of Hawai'i Press, 2017). On Wong and Kikumura, see Diane C. Fujino, *Heartbeat of Struggle: The Revolutionary Life of Yuri Kochiyama* (Minneapolis: University of Minnesota Press, 2005); Diane C. Fujino, *Nisei Radicals: The Feminist Poetics and Transformative Ministry of Mitsuye Yamada and Michael Yasutake* (Seattle: University of Washington Press, 2020). On the draft resisters, see Eric L. Muller, *Free to Die for Their Country: The Story of the Japanese American Draft Resisters in World War II* (Chicago: University of Chicago Press, 2001).

3 AAs are officially categorized as "others" throughout much of the prison system, a fitting description for a population that is often overlooked. In 2013 there were 118,100 others in the state and federal prison system, comprising 9 percent of the state and federal prison system. Women categorized as others constitute 11 percent of the female state and federal prison system (E. A. Carson, *Prisoners in 2013* [Washington, DC: US Department of Justice Bureau of Justice Statistics, 2014], www.bjs.gov/content/pub/pdf/p13.pdf).

4 Deportations have increased for AAPIs overall and Southeast Asian Americans in particular. Since 1998 at least fifteen thousand Southeast Asian Americans from Cambodia, Laos, and Vietnam have received final orders of deportation, despite many having arrived in the United States with refugee status and having obtained a green card. Further-more, more than twelve thousand of the final orders of deportation were based on old criminal records rather than current offenses. Due to stringent immigration policies enacted in 1996, Southeast Asian American communities are three to four times more likely to be deported for old convictions, compared to other immigrant communities (Transactional Records Access Clearinghouse [online]. Syracuse, NY: Syracuse University, 2015, trac.syr.edu/phptools/immigration/court _backlog/deport_outcome_charge.php).

5 Jerry Holloway and Paul Moke, *Post-Secondary Correctional Education: An Evaluation of Parolee Performance*, research/technical report, 1986), search-proquest-com.proxy.library.ucsb.edu:9443/docview/63319582 ?accountid=14522.

6 Eddy Zheng, "Break These Chains: Ethnic Studies in Prison," *Hard-boiled* 5, no. 4 (April 2002).

7 Because the college program was accredited by Patten College in Oakland, California, the prison administration wanted to stick with

Patten College. But because Patten College does not offer accredited bachelor's degrees, the proposal for a bachelor's program came from a professor from St. Mary's College.

8 "The Relationship between Incarceration and Low Literacy," Literacy Mid-South, March 16, 2016, www.literacymidsouth.org/news/the -relationship-between-incarceration-and-low-literacy/#:~:text =According%20to%20the%20National%20Adult,are%20the%20 most%20prone%20to.

9 On Mike Ngo's lawsuit, see "Inmates Protest De Facto Segregation at San Quentin," *Jewish News of Northern California*, July 19, 2002, https://www.jweekly.com/2002/07/19/inmates-protest-de-facto -segregation-at-san-quentin.

10 For more information about the San Quentin Six, see Fania Davis Jordan, "The San Quentin Six: A Case of Vengeance," *Black Scholar* 5 (1974): 44–50; Karen Wald, "The San Quentin Six Case: Perspective and Analysis," *Social Justice* 40, nos. 1–2 (2014): 231–51.

11 For more information about the ROOTS program, see Saemmool Lee, "Refugee Advocate with Criminal Past Changes Life, Helps Others," *Oakland North*, December 12, 2017, https://oaklandnorth.net/2017/12 /12/refugee-with-criminal-past-changes-life-helps-others; Lydia Lum, "Group Addresses Incarceration among Asian Americans, Pacific Islanders," *Diverse Issues in Higher Education*, May 1, 2018, https:// diverseeducation.com/article/115575; Kimberly Yam, "Asian-American Prison Program Teaches About, Honors Inmates' Cultural Struggles," *Huffington Post*, May 3, 2018, https://www.huffpost.com/entry/asian -american-studies-program-california-prison_n_5ade42e8e4b0b2e811 32737b.

12 I initially had the very ambitious goal of using my fellowship to change the 1996 Illegal Immigration Reform and Immigrant Responsibility Act federal law; however, changing a federal law and starting a movement around it in only eighteen months was seen as too ambitious, and I was asked to modify my focus.

13 For more information about the New Breath Foundation, founded by Eddy Zheng, and its work, see https://www.new-breath.org.

CHAPTER 2

HOʻOPONO MAMO AND RESTORATIVE PRACTICES

Reflections on Scholar Activism in Juvenile
Justice Systems Change

KAREN UMEMOTO

WHAT IS AN "ACTIVIST-SCHOLAR"?

ASIAN AMERICAN SCHOLARS AND PUBLIC INTELLECTUALS have pioneered progressive change throughout history. Honored elders of earlier generations, including Yuri Kochiyama, Dr. Kekuni Blaisdell, Grace Lee Boggs, Puanani Burgess, and Philip Vera Cruz, pushed us to embrace a shared humanity to welcome a better world. Pioneering thinkers in ethnic studies and Asian American studies challenged Eurocentric paradigms to reposition ourselves as producers of knowledge and makers of history. Creative writers such as Carlos Bulosan, Viet Nguyen, Albert Wendt, and Maxine Hong Kingston connected generations and geographies to awaken a more empathetic society. And essayists such as Jeff Chang and Helen Zia embolden the voices submerged from within. What lies in common across these thinkers is the application of their pointed pens to touch our souls and enliven democratic discourse to improve life conditions for everyday people. Along with many others, they do the work of public intellectuals for the sake of creating a more compassionate, sustainable, and just society.

It is in this long tradition of idea shapers and change activators that we situate the activist-scholar. With the growing number of Asian Americans in university research and teaching posts, a new generation of authors and educators are navigating social justice work from their positions in academia. I use the term *activist-scholar* to describe public intellectuals who engage in social change within and beyond the traditional duties of an academic professional, using their privileged training, resources, and standing to participate in movements for social change. They come from different disciplines to play meaningful roles in a wide range of progressive campaigns. Some do their work in the trenches of grassroots organizing, while others lead national and international organizations, strategize issue campaigns, or join in legal cases. Talented orators crisscross the world, sharing ideas that have profoundly transformed the public imagination. This is all to say that activist-scholars can wear many hats, work in many corners of the world, and engage in a wide assortment of activities. There is no one role or one clear path, just as there are countless approaches to working for change.

I consider my work as an activist-scholar somewhat improvisational. I have taken advantage of opportunities that have opened up to me as a university professor and connected with community organizations, advocates, and state actors interested in systems change, albeit in light of more ambitious aspirations. For the first twenty-odd years of my career, I held a faculty position at a public university with scarce resources, continuously fitting together research, teaching, and service opportunities within my job duties to effect as much positive change as possible. I taught at the University of Hawai'i (UH) and had the privilege of working in and with many Native Hawaiian communities and community-based organizations. Through my ten-year involvement with the Asian Pacific Islander Youth Violence Prevention Center at the UH School of Medicine, I focused on youth issues and worked with schools, government agencies, and youth and youth-serving organizations. Like a quilt maker, I tried to piece together funded and unfunded research with public engagement, community mobilizing, classroom teaching, and student mentoring to support progressive tides of change within my orbit of work. I wish to reflect in this chapter on one such project that deployed Native Hawaiian knowledge and collaborated across many communities, including those of Native Hawaiians, and various agencies to create change on the ground.

The position of an activist-scholar is a relatively privileged one, however fraught with constant tensions and dilemmas. I explore some of the tensions here to deepen our discussions on the role and efficacy of activist scholarship and scholar activism and to draw insights about the project of social change more generally. I preface this with some personal background that helps to situate my ideas and concerns. I illustrate these tensions and dilemmas through a case of juvenile justice reform in Hawaiʻi that I, along with a committed group of colleagues, was involved in for seven years from 2010 to 2017, after which I relocated to California and maintained more limited involvement. I describe my participation alongside close colleagues over various phases of the project and interweave the main challenges and insights in each. I conclude with what I believe are some of the main implications of these reflections for the times we find ourselves in today.

FINDING MY WAY AS AN ACTIVIST-SCHOLAR

How we see ourselves as part of transformational movements for change is heavily shaped by our personal life experiences. As a third-generation Japanese American woman whose parents were incarcerated during World War II for the sole reason of their ancestry, a concern over racial justice and the harms of incarceration is part of who I am. And as a granddaughter of a devout female minister of a Japanese faith tradition called Konkokyo who dedicated her life to the well-being of others, I inherited a deep reverence for service steeped in humanistic values. In my freshman year of college at UCLA in the mid-1970s, I took my first Asian American studies class and worked as a tenant organizer, using my limited Japanese language skills learned from my grandmother to work with Little Tokyo residents and activists in the face of pending evictions.

This began a journey of activism and an exposure to radical critiques of the human condition. We grappled with the contradictions between democratic governance for the "public good" and the gross inequalities of an unfettered free market system. We schooled ourselves in geopolitical histories of conquest and military interventions that undermined movements for democracy globally. We thought deeply about how the problems we were trying to address in the organizing work—from evictions locally to nuclear threats internationally—grew from prioritizing profit seeking and individual wealth accumulation over ecological and collective human development to the detriment of untold generations. Scrawled on picket signs of those times were slogans such as "People before Profits" and "Books Not Bombs."

A persistent dilemma of the revolutionary 1960s was how to fix immediate, pressing problems while building critical consciousness and solidarities to address more systemic and existential ones. As a professor specializing in community planning and social policy, I was invited by the State of Hawai'i's Office of Youth Services to conduct a study of racial disparities in the state's juvenile justice system, a problem deeply embedded in a settler colonial context. I saw an opportunity to conduct rigorous research that might prompt interventions to reduce the harms of the juvenile justice system while building a foundation to address the underlying, historically rooted structures leading to youth entanglement and racial disparities in the first place. Researchers and advocates in the field had already come to some consensus on the devastations of the punitive policy swing, the latest stemming from the 1980s "tough on crime" movement and legislation. As a scholar and practitioner in the field of planning, I saw this work as an opportunity to facilitate change on both the long- and short-term horizons—with short-term reforms that could lead to more systemic change.

In the juvenile justice systems change work, a growing team pushed the idea to "huli" the system. *Huli* in the Hawaiian language means to "turn over." We proposed the idea of flipping a system of surveillance and punishment to one embedded in the ethics of healing, restoration, and community. As scholar practitioners, youth and youth-serving professionals, and cultural practitioners, our team asked participants to imagine what a juvenile justice system would look like if the powers of the state were shifted to give increased resources to community organizations, local agencies, volunteer groups, and families who can better support their youth. We asked what it would mean if each child in the justice system were to be treated as if they were one's own. This *huli*—or turning of the role of government from a punisher of bodies to enabler of restorative practices in agencies, schools, communities, and families—is in many ways a revolutionary idea, though it should not be. In fact, many of the concepts were born of Indigenous origins and long propagated in some of the more innovative youth and family programs throughout the state. Although many professionals in the juvenile justice system were already practicing from an ethic of care, a punitive model had become dominant for various reasons, including lack of both political will and resources to uproot a system of social control born of colonial domination.[1]

While my personal history buttressed my resolve to fight racial injustice, it also complicated and colored my work in Hawaiʻi as an Asian settler from the continent who is identified with an ethnic group that is politically dominant in Hawaiʻi. Because I had cut my teeth in West Coast activism focused on issues in communities within which I was embedded, such as redress and reparations for Japanese Americans, I had been used to advocating in the first person. Working primarily in and with Hawaiian communities as a settler on native land placed me in the position of an ally working in solidarity with Kanaka Maoli, with humility and a commitment to justice and decolonization. I had the advantage of having worked with "outside" supporters before moving to Hawaiʻi, some of whom "crossed the line" by imposing ideas that were not fitting or appropriate to the community to which we belonged. Back then we worked hard to find roles for supporters who respected the need for a type of self-determination within communities of color to find their voice and build their own capabilities for change. These lessons informed my changing role and what it meant to work in solidarity with Kanaka Maoli communities in Hawaiʻi, in the context of colonialism and their work to reclaim and restore sovereign spaces, to "live aloha" and "be Hawaiian."

ENGAGING JUVENILE JUSTICE REFORM TO "HULI THE SYSTEM"

In reflecting on insights gathered from the praxis of change, I find it helpful to see the juvenile justice systems change project within a larger analysis of social change processes. Change can transpire when there is a clear vision of the future that people can picture together, combined with the mobilization of political will to enact the change and see to its implementation. In this case the vision among a growing group of activists, professionals, and community practitioners was for a compassionate system of care rooted in Hawaiian or Indigenous ways of knowing. Current efforts at the time of this writing also include ending youth incarceration altogether.[2] Native Hawaiians were subject to the greatest entanglement in the juvenile justice system, from the point of arrest to sentencing and incarceration. In fact, Native Hawaiian youths were arrested at nearly double the rate of Caucasian youths.[3] We saw better ways to address problems that led to harmful behavior through *healing and getting to the roots of the problems they experienced.* This was a change from a nationally dominant system set to easily default to apprehension, punishment, and discipline. Harmful behavior among youths cannot be separated from deeper problems such as poverty, past individual and intergenerational trauma, and wrongs or harms that continue to be reproduced as part of a settler colonial reality.

Many of us believed that there was untapped promise for youths in various cultural practices of healing and community building. The state-defined problem of "overrepresentation" of Native Hawaiian and other Pacific Islanders in the Hawai'i justice system was embedded in a legacy that included massive death by disease, land dispossession, and cultural suppression. Healing practices of old to restore one's gene-alogical connection to an honorable past and laying the foundation for a *pono*, or "righteous" future, remained very much present in families as well as community life.[4] Some practices had been tried pro-grammatically in the justice system with successful outcomes, such as Alu Like's Kupuna Program, which served those arrested for sub-stance abuse offenses during the 1990s.[5] *Ho'oponopono*, in particular, was a long-established traditional practice of restoring balance and reconnection to all of one's relations in the living and spiritual realms. Wayde Hoapili Lee, executive director of Wahi Kana'aho (aka Kahua Ola Hou), along with other cultural practitioners, provided critical guidance. Lee with support from his wife, Adele Lee, had developed a program recognized for successful results in healing youths through *ho'oponopono*, originally designed for young people challenged by sub-stance use and addiction. To "huli the system" meant building these and other culturally rooted pathways to physical, mental, and spiri-tual health and wholeness.

In fact, this change effort was taking place in a growing sea of activities among Native Hawaiian communities seeking greater self-determination and control over their lands, education, and daily life. These activities were wide-ranging, including ocean and land stewardship, cultural immersion education, language revitalization, reclamation of sacred lands, restoration of fishponds, and the promo-tion of traditional cultural and livelihood practices such as hula, wood-working, canoe making, star navigation, martial arts, use of medicinal plants, and various healing arts. Native Hawaiian scholar Davianna McGregor used the metaphor of the kipuka—outcroppings of ancient growth bypassed by the flow of lava—to describe the significance of spaces where full expressions of culture are preserved and from whence they can propagate. The work to reform the juvenile justice system in Hawai‘i was approached with similar aspirations of creating spaces for Hawaiian knowledge and practices to take form, at least by those of us who followed the lead of our Hawaiian colleagues in this journey to foreground a Hawaiian epistemology to analyze and transform a Western logic that "*treated* the *problem* of youth delinquency" as an individual problem devoid of history.

Our efforts were buoyed by parallel initiatives to transform the juvenile justice system. While justice reform in Hawai‘i had been slow and, for the most part, under the public radar, there was a growing number of individuals and institutions, especially institutions like the State Office of Hawaiian Affairs, Kamehameha Schools, and the Lili‘uokalani Trust, with leading figures such as Kamana‘opono Crabbe and Mark Kawika Patterson, committed to ending mass incarceration and the school-to-prison pipeline. Grassroots groups like the Community Alliance on Prisons, led by Kat Brady, had long advocated for prison reform. A nationwide shift in public opinion had turned to the negative tolls of incarceration, both human and financial. Many philanthropic foundations had made it their mission to address the problems in the justice system, ranging from racial profiling at the front end to unfair sentencing on the back end. The Annie E. Casey Foundation's Juvenile Detention Alternatives Initiative invested in reform through the Hawai‘i Judiciary, with Carol Matsuoka coordinating this work. They had quickly begun to lower the number of arrested juveniles held in the detention facility. The Pew Foundation gave technical assistance to change state statutes to reduce youth incarceration. State agency leaders such as David Hipp, then executive director of the Office of Youth Services, and Judge Mark Browning of the Family Court had been taking active steps to reduce sentencing of youth to the correctional facility for low-level offenses and probation violations. These and other efforts dramatically lowered average daily incarceration rates from well over one hundred incarcerated at any given time to around a dozen or two as alternatives to incarceration were sought.

My work alongside then graduate student and now assistant professor Tai-An Miao, Native Hawaiian cultural practitioner Wayde Hoapili Lee, and many others represented a piece of these interrelated efforts. I agreed to take on a research project for the State of Hawai'i Office of Youth Services to study racial disparities and the experiences of youth in the juvenile justice system and to engage the public in problem-solving. I saw potential in this work to lower arrest and incarceration rates for youths and support communities to address the root causes leading to arrests. There was a growing alignment of people across agencies, organizations, and the public working to bring about systems change to shift the punitive paradigm that reproduced patterns of colonial subjugation. We saw the potential for incremental improvements in the treatment of young people entangled in the system and meaningful benefits for them and their families, even as this project, like other tangible reforms, may fall short of resolving deeper systemic problems. The work of juvenile justice systems change also complemented capacity-building work that we had been doing earlier with community-based organizations. The research and planning we had done led to the launch of Ho'opono Mamo, a juvenile justice diversion initiative.

There were many justice reform campaigns taking place across the country, but what was unique about Ho'opono Mamo was the lens through which our team of designers and proponents pursued this effort. This program to divert youth away from entering the court system was conceived through community consultation and represented the insertion of Hawaiian epistemology into the justice system. The inclusion of cultural values, philosophies, and meanings as *core* to the diversion system would not simply change the flow away from the court system to community-based organizations but could provide promising approaches and interventions that were rooted in Indigenous ways of knowing. Even more fundamentally, we believed that a program rooted in Hawaiian epistemology could strengthen an ethic of care embodied in everyday interactions among all those who interacted with youth along a journey of healing, reconciliation, and coming of age.

One way to illustrate the assertion of Hawaiian epistemology is by comparing the two representations of the program as illustrated in the implementation and evaluation plan created by University of Hawai'i planning students and submitted to the Office of Youth Services (figures 2.1 and 2.2).[6] The image in figure 2.1 represents the diversion model from the lens of a Hawaiian knowledge system as drawn by Kanaka Maoli student and now planning practitioner Lillie

Ho'opono Mamo
Flowchart Metaphor

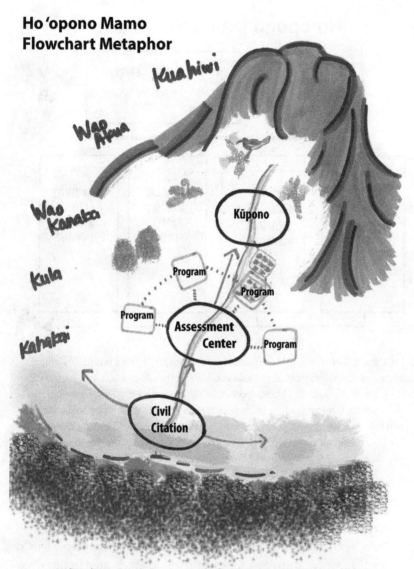

Kūlia i ka nu'u - strive to reach the summit; try to do your best

FIGURE 2.1. Ho'opono Mamo Flowchart Metaphor. This metaphorical depiction of Ho'opono Mamo, a diversion process to steer youth away from the court system to a "village" of supportive people and programs. It situates the process of healing in an *ahupua'a,* a traditional land division where youth connected to their community's progress upward toward the *kuahiwi,* or summit, where one's view is wide and clear and where one is closer to the heavens, captured by the phrase *Kūlia i ka nu'u* (Strive to reach the summit; try to do your best). The *kuahiwi* are symbolic of excellence to be sought after.

Ho'opono Mamo Flowchart

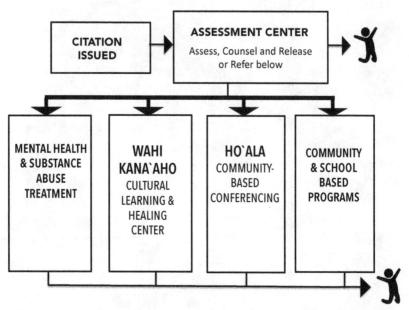

FIGURE 2.2. Ho'opono Mamo Standard Flowchart. The standard flowchart maps the formal steps that eligible youth can proceed through upon arrest if they are eligible for the Ho'opono Mamo and receive a civil citation. Rather than productively engaging in their community and striving for a summit, the outcome is to be free of connection to the court system and independent of program involvement. Any long-term reconnection to restorative and life-giving people and places is diminished from view.

Makaila under the guidance of participating Kanaka Maoli elders Bruce Keaulani and Kehaulani Lum.

Ho'opono Mamo seeks to support youths in finding their *pono*, or righteous, path and striving for excellence. As illustrated in this drawing, this approach foregrounds a Hawaiian epistemology by seeing juvenile justice system change and this diversion program as inhabiting spaces of Hawaiian knowledge and practices for healing and restoration. The land is seen as an *ahupua'a*, not only a watershed but an interconnected community whose well-being is tied to the health of the *'āina*, the living land. It is from this standpoint that healing oneself, healing the land, and restoring one's relationship to land, people, and a spiritual realm are simultaneous processes. The word *ho'opono* refers to a process of bringing into balance and harmony one's physical, mental, and spiritual dimensions of being. The metaphor of the mamo bird, now extinct, nods to Hawaiian history and puts into perspective the precious life of Hawaiian youths today and the precarity they face. That we treat each youth as precious as the mamo bird signifies the aspirational essence many hoped would imbue Hoʻopono Mamo as an Indigenous space of healing, reconnection, and growth. Addressing the challenges and needs of all youth is inseparable from the well-being of the larger community in a non-compartmentalized world.

In contrast, figure 2.2 represents the diversion system using a conventional flowchart, emphasizing the movement of bodies through institutional processes. The boxes represent the various stages of processing through various types of youth programs. Most diversion programs are seen as "second chance" programs for minor first-time offenses in order to address the "problem of youth delinquency." The underlying policy logic is to catch misbehavior early and provide both incentives and punishments to modify harmful or "antisocial" behavior. Completion of such programs leads to the expungement of the arrest record, at least in theory.

While the logistical steps in the process according to both images may appear similar (arrest to assessment to services to program exit), the deeper analyses of the fundamental nature of the problem as well as the cultural foundation of the intervention to address it are worlds apart. The metaphorical drawing is explicit about striving for excellence, charting a *pono* path, and seeing the world with clarity and perspective from the highest pinnacle.

One of the most difficult tasks was to translate the rich philosophical and programmatic perspective embedded in a Native epistemology to those who were accustomed to seeing boxes. Maintaining ways to build upon and expand a collective understanding of the meaning of the model in the fullness of its cultural meanings was perhaps one of the biggest challenges.

While our efforts did not accomplish what we would have liked in the way of a full paradigmatic and cultural shift, as of this writing many tangible reforms were initiated. Hoʻopono Mamo was implemented, which successfully channeled many youths away from the court system and directly to youth service organizations upon arrest. Youth who were stopped by police for first-time misdemeanors and status offenses in the pilot district received a citation and, in the ideal case, were connected to a youth service organization for immediate services. Youths received referrals for counseling, family therapy, mental health services, mentoring, sports activities, tutoring, cultural learning programs, and other supports. The evaluation of the first eighteen months of the pilot program showed a statistically significant decrease in rearrest rates. This success, however, was not seen for Native Hawaiians or other Pacific Island groups. A major setback came with the retraction and lack of funding of the two core cultural components, the Wahi Kana'aho residential program and Ho'ala Community Conferencing (a culturally adapted family conferencing program), because of an unintentional administrative error. This was a major setback that we believe likely led to its limited success for Native Hawaiian and Pacific Islander youth, though this correlation cannot be proved with existing data. Adjustments were made, and a second phase of the pilot was implemented, though again without those core cultural components.

ENVISIONING INSTITUTIONAL CHANGE

This particular juvenile justice systems change project grew out of an Obama administration effort to reduce racial disparities in the justice system. The Office of Juvenile Justice and Delinquency Prevention (OJJDP), which is the youth division of the Department of Justice (DOJ), required states receiving DOJ funds to address what they termed "disproportionate minority contact" in the juvenile justice system. The State of Hawai'i Office of Youth Services received OJJDP funds and oversaw this process for the state. African Americans and Latinos were deemed "overrepresented" in many US jurisdictions. But in Hawai'i, Native Hawaiian and Pacific Islander youths were the ones subject to disparate treatment at most decision points in the juvenile justice system.

The OJJDP requirement was designed to catalyze a cycle of change—from research, programmatic design, and implementation to the evaluation and refinement of programs and systems. This process was designed to facilitate incremental change within certain bounds. But it also had the potential to shift thinking and practices within a whole subsystem of state and local institutions. This was the timeline of activities that ensued:

2010–12: Research resulting in "Disproportionate Minority Contact in the Hawaiʻi Juvenile Justice System" report

2012–13: Dissemination of findings and public engagement on recommendations

2013–14: Development of Hoʻopono Mamo implementation and evaluation plan

2014–16: Implementation of Hoʻopono Mamo and developmental evaluation

2016–17: Outcomes evaluation

Many hands were involved in each of the phases. The research phase involved Professor James Spencer and doctoral students Tai-An Miao and Saiful Momen. Tai-An Miao continued as the lead coordinator for the four remaining phases. Hawaiian cultural practitioner Wayde Hoʻopili Lee played a leading role in the development of Hoʻopono Mamo. Founder of Kahua Ola Hou and developer of the Wahi Kanaʻaho, one of the culture-based programs for the initiative, "Uncle Wayde" was also member of the Hawaiʻi Juvenile Justice State Advisory Council. Other contributors included Matt Hom and Trina Jones Artis, graduate students in the University of Hawaiʻi Urban and Regional Planning Department, and scores of others too many to name here but whose participation is recorded in our planning process report.[7]

Trying to change institutional systems, such as the juvenile justice system, is challenging because it requires a change on three fronts. Each front requires different types of work and strategic thinking to effect desired changes.

1. Changing the policy paradigm and institutional logics that run a system *entailed shifting belief systems through collaborative learning.*

2. Changing policies, rules, and procedures *entailed altering policies and administrative procedures by garnering political will.*

3. Changing professional roles and behaviors among those who work in that system *entailed the introduction of new professional practices through education and training.*

These ambitious aims were beyond the scope of the formal contracts we had entered into with the state. And these aspirations did not necessarily reflect official priorities, though many state workers in the field were committed to change. Such was the tension that lay at the nexus of state-funded reform and the imperatives of deeper paradigmatic systems change. Under any contract one is beholden to its scope and must fulfill the deliverables. At the same time, many of us saw there was more that could be done to achieve the social justice aims related to the problems of the juvenile justice system. Activist-scholars across the disciplines can find themselves confronted with a twofold agenda: honoring contractual agreements while also expanding the boundaries of possibilities to reshape the social and institutional imaginary.

PLANNING FOR INSTITUTIONAL CHANGE

Trying to effect some change in all three facets of institutional systems requires us to play many different roles. They involve utilizing scholarly abilities and one's position as an engaged scholar and teacher in creative ways. It is difficult to explain them all, since many things we did were as intangible as they were immeasurable. But I briefly outline them here in relation to the five phases of work we engaged in.

Policy-oriented research for social change. As a research team of colleagues and students, we completed a study, entitled *Disproportionate Minority Contact in the Hawai'i Juvenile Justice System.* It was a mixed methods research project that examined racial differences in rates of penetration into the juvenile justice system, from the decision point of arrest and court referral to sentencing and incarceration. We also interviewed those who worked with court-involved youth to better understand how decisions were deliberated. We extended the project to examine the records of court-involved youth to delve deeper into their experiences from reading probation officer notes, letters of apology, mental health assessments, school records, and other documents. In a nutshell we found disproportionally higher rates of penetration for Native Hawaiian youth at all decision points in the system but most markedly at the point arrest. Other Pacific Islander youths followed a similar pattern. Court-involved youth suffered from a combination of challenges, including depression (32 percent), psychological or physical abuse (30 percent), low school achievement (77 percent), substance abuse (72 percent), and lack of positive relationships with maternal

(35 percent) and paternal (62 percent) guardians.[8] The more traumatic and dire the conditions, the more one could see the need for greater understanding and support.

Dissemination of findings and public engagement on recommendations. The next step was to disseminate our findings, which the Hawai‘i Office of Youth Services contracted us to do statewide. We had fourteen pages of recommendations that were actionable by different agencies, including law enforcement, probation, court officials, prosecutors, and youth service organizations. These ranged from replacing punitive practices with more restorative approaches, allocating resources to critical needs areas such as mental health, using civil citations as an alternative to arrest, and strengthening cultural, community-based and gender-appropriate programs.

In considering ways to share the recommendations, we consulted with the director of the Office of Youth Services, David Hipp, and decided to package the most important recommendations into a recognizable juvenile diversion model to gain policy traction. In order to divert youth away from the court system, police would issue a citation and transport a youth directly to a community-based agency for an assessment and services, rather than making an arrest and transporting this individual to the police station. We called this model Ho‘opono Mamo, a name given by a revered elder.

Another major consideration was the means of communication and order of presentations to capture the imagination of stakeholders and decision makers. Tai-An Miao, Wayde Lee, and I tag-teamed, starting with the presentation of statistics, then qualitative data, followed by stories. We realized later that this sequence communicated to the head, heart, and *na‘au*, or "gut"—different "receptors" of knowledge—and that may be why the presentations elicited such positive engagement. We were only contracted to make eight public presentations but ended up making over one hundred presentations across the state, including on neighbor islands. In an eighteen-month stretch we presented the findings and recommendations to the major youth-serving state and nonprofit agencies, grassroots organizations, and key agency heads. As for the order of presentations, we began with a presentation to the police chiefs of all four counties of Hawai‘i at their quarterly summit. Their enthusiastic endorsement of the recommendations gave it the life of possibility. Other agencies then took the recommendations much more seriously, with buoyed hopes for their implementation.

New paradigms are often difficult to comprehend if not experienced in a personal way. So, in addition to the presentations, we also organized a series of a dozen two-day or three-day trainings in the Wahi Kanaʻaho, a land-based, culture-based youth residential program model designed by Wayde Lee, who credits his many Hawaiian elders for their foundational knowledge and guidance. Participants from key agencies, including police and probation officers, received training in the cultural knowledge and practice of hoʻoponopono, including self-reflection, appreciation, apology, forgiveness, and reconciliation. The "homework assignment" after the first day was to call someone you love but with whom your relationship is strained and tell them you love them. The goal was to train youth to heal themselves and to become healers. A condensed curriculum based on the three-week residential program model provided a taste of what youth can gain from a diversion program deeply rooted in Hawaiian culture. The experiential nature of this training was profoundly transformative for many of the participants. Agency personnel and organizational representatives who took part became some of the strongest advocates of the new diversion model after seeing what it could do for their own lives.

Intervention and evaluation design. We invited those who attended the presentations and trainings to join a Hoʻopono Mamo Task Force to help with program design and possible implementation. The task force included the key potential partners for implementation, from the prosecutor's office to youth outreach workers. This would be the "village" that could support youth referred into the diversion program. But this was one phase for which the Office of Youth Services did *not* have funding resources. To fill that need and to provide students a real-life opportunity to learn through planning practice, I created a service learning practicum course for graduate students in our Urban and Regional Planning program for those interested in program design and evaluation. They worked with the task force and developed an implementation and evaluation plan.[9] This would later serve as a guide for the operationalization of the diversion program and its evaluation. It was a win-win collaboration; students gained valuable planning experience through a client project, and the Office of Youth Services had an operational roadmap.

Implementation and obstacles. Implementation took a difficult turn. Because of funding restrictions and procedural constraints, funds for the program were given to an agency with a strong history in serving youth but that had not participated in the task force and had a more traditional diversion model in mind. They implemented a caseworker model rather than an assessment center relying primarily on referrals to a village of agencies and organizations. Rather than flipping the system to mobilize community-wide support and resources, the caseworker model has a more limited range of resources available to youth participants, and caseworkers had less time than needed to work with the most vulnerable youths. As the diversion program launched, the Office of Youth Services also urged us to disband the Ho'opono Mamo Task Force, which we did. This left little in the way of an advocacy base to affect the course of implementation. In addition, the main culture-based program component, the Wahi Kana'aho, was shut down unexpectedly after only four months of operation due to the unforeseen shortage of state funds that had been earmarked for the program. This was a big blow since it was the cultural cornerstone for systems change. The effort also felt the unfortunate passing of Office of Youth Services' Juvenile Justice Program officer Ed Chargualaf, who was a major proponent of the initiative, with prior experience in his home country of Guam.

Evaluation. After the first year of implementation of the pilot program, we began the evaluation process. A *process* evaluation looked at the degree to which the program was implemented as designed. And an *outcomes* evaluation measured any changes in rearrest rates for those who had gone through the program compared to those outside the pilot program district. Dr. Earl Hishinuma, a well-respected faculty member in the Department of Psychiatry at the University of Hawai'i at Manoa, took the lead on the outcomes evaluation, while Tai-An Miao and I focused on the process evaluation. In short, the findings showed the program was successful for certain subsections of the population and not others. While the results were overall positive, the impacts were not as strong as we had hoped for. More specifically, the program did not see significant improvements for Native Hawaiians, the most overrepresented group in the system. The lack of fidelity to the model and the absence of the two key programs in the model—the Wahi Kana'aho and the Ho'ala Community Conferencing programs—aimed specifically for Native Hawaiian and Pacific Islander youth were major shortcomings. This made it difficult to determine the efficacy of a diversion model as originally conceived.

CHALLENGES AND DISCOVERIES

As an activist-scholar, there are certain limitations to what one can do, what influence one has, and what exactly one can change in the absence of greater collective action on an issue. This is particularly true when one is working in a settler colonial context in which individuals and organizations concerned about the issue are to varying extents politically hamstrung in their maneuverability. For example, many organizations that supported systems change were also funded by state and private foundations that made it difficult to take bolder actions. Other limitations arise when one is contracted with a government agency, no matter how committed its leadership and staff may be to a shared vision of change. Government workers are themselves restricted by their mandates, job descriptions, and the scaffold of bureaucratic regulations they are bound by. Here I share my reflections in an effort to learn from the successes as well as the shortcomings. I welcome dialogue, including differing views, as part of a collaborative learning community.

To be sure, the Hoʻopono Mamo Civil Citation Initiative itself was a major step forward. It continued to divert hundreds of youths arrested for status offenses and first-time misdemeanors away from the court system to supportive services. There was a marked decrease in detention and incarceration. This was part of gradual shift away from the punitive model and toward a more community-based approach emphasizing healing and growth. It opened possibilities for transforming key institutions of the carceral state in Hawaiʻi. Putting the spotlight on the high arrest rate of Native Hawaiian and other Pacific Islander youth (twice that of white youth) also led to a marked reduction in those disparities.

Despite the cautiously optimistic gains of the Hoʻopono Mamo launch, there were three major limitations—implementation of a traditional caseworker model rather than the original village model, the disbanding of the Hoʻopono Mamo Task Force, and the unexpected loss of funds for the Wahi Kanaʻaho—that impacted its fuller success. And with the lack of funding for the core cultural components of Hoʻopono Mamo to serve as a cultural anchor, the guiding values and principles of the program based on Native Hawaiian epistemology faded into the background.

One ever-present reality was the task of navigating our work within view of the larger ecosystem of politics, institutions, and movements. On one hand, there were many parallel efforts moving in a similar direction as juvenile justice systems change within existing institutions, as mentioned earlier with the Office of Hawaiian Affairs, Annie E. Casey Foundation, Pew Foundation, and advocacy by administrators at the Office of Youth Services and Family Court. There was also a growing movement among Native Hawaiian organizations for self-determination and justice reform more broadly and to create sovereign spaces to "be Hawaiian." Our efforts were aided, for example, by the on-the-ground success of the Annie E. Casey Foundation in reducing the number of youths in detention facilities as well as long-time calls by Hawaiian activists and advocates for radical transformation of colonial structures that have imprisoned Kanaka Maoli bodies. Our work both facilitated and were facilitated by these connected streams of discourse and advocacy. In retrospect, more could have likely been accomplished if there was more deliberate coordination and strategizing between these efforts than took place.

On an interpersonal level we enjoyed supportive relationships and healthy lines of communication with others involved and informally tried to make sure our efforts were in sync with one another. More formally, both Miao and Lee participated actively in the Juvenile Justice State Advisory Committee (JJSAC), convened quarterly by the Hawaiʻi Office of Youth Services, as well as other ad hoc bodies that facilitated formal communication and coordination. And there were many relationships that moved these initiatives forward. Collaborative relationships were built upon a shared vision that kept the well-being and future of youths at top of mind. They were maintained by honest and open communications, mutual support, cooperation, and a sense of camaraderie. We strove to live the Hawaiian values of *aloha* (including love, compassion, and mercy), *laulima* (as in many hands working together), *haʻahaʻa* (humility), and *lōkahi* (unity, expressed with harmony), among others. In short, the quality of relationships enabled a cross-fertilization of efforts and helped to sustain a working network of those willing to champion change. Without these relationships, the overall progress that was made would not have been possible.

This brings to light what it means to challenge dominant policy paradigms and what those paradigms consist of. The dominant "tough on crime" policies in effect in the United States since the mid-1990s were ensconced in a web of policies and procedures as well as philosophical belief systems. While the reform movement both in Hawai'i and nationally represent a shift in thinking, the policies and procedures are still embedded in decades of history as well as in the positivistic traditions of youth-serving professions that are not easily moved. What the Ho'opono Mamo diversion model represented was an attempt to bring Indigenous practices and ways of knowing into the juvenile justice system and make room for deeper emotional, spiritual, and relational healing practices in the face of intergenerational trauma. I believe that had there been a greater presence of those with a fuller understanding and appreciation for Native Hawaiian knowledge systems and practices, further progress would have been made. The limited number and political influence of Native Hawaiian professionals and advocates among the stakeholder groups involved at that time was symptomatic of the larger racial hierarchy that continues to plague Hawai'i. And to the extent that Native Hawaiian and other community organizations were dependent on public funding, their leeway to advocate in such situations was similarly constrained.

Of course, the story is unfinished as the program continues in its second iteration and related initiatives are flourishing. The evaluation of this second phase of the pilot is still in process as of this writing, and we hope more lessons and improvements will follow. At the same time, funding for the original two culture-based components remains elusive. It is our hope, however, that other culture-based activities, sensibilities, and ways of working have begun to permeate the program. Meanwhile, progress is being made on other fronts in which I try my best to remain involved even if from a geographic distance.

CLOSING REFLECTIONS

Like a rubber band, institutions have muscle memory so that one or two interventions over one or two years of operation are not enough to transform them in more permanent ways. It takes many people, from different angles, relying on a variety of tools over a long duration of time to move them toward a new way of functioning. These tools include education, legislation, public discourse, retraining, and changing policies and administrative procedures. It also means building social learning processes into institutions so they can be more responsive and malleable. Achieving change takes many champions, particularly when it involves a shift in philosophical outlooks or epistemic knowledge systems. And change requires sustained collective efforts and movements to resist the weight of inertia.

One important lesson is that the battle over hearts and minds is just as important, if not more important, as changing a law or making a rule. If there is no embrace of a policy move in a highly interpersonal field such as juvenile justice, change will be merely procedural and superficial rather than heartfelt and transformative. Not to belittle changes in procedures, but the devil is in the details, as they say. A fundamental transformation of a system like the justice system requires a change in understanding, a change in the way we see things, and a change of heart so that we can come to treat every child as if they were our own. If we do that, we might see a more lasting and impactful difference with results that can lessen the need for such systems in the first place. This points to a more emancipatory agenda, for which incremental social reforms can be a meaning part but only if seen within that longer horizon.

In fact, we may have found better ways to link the Wahi Kanaʻaho experiential trainings to the creation of a more organized and sustained learning community that could help facilitate transformative work across parallel initiatives, even with the dissolution of the Hoʻopono Mamo Task Force. As a teacher, I am naturally mindful of nurturing a healthy learning community that feeds the mind and soul through (re)discovery, exchange of thought, and (re)imaginings. In retrospect I wonder how we may have watered the seeds of knowledge creation and program innovation by leveraging the energy that had been generated through the trainings to cohere a body of fellow change agents that could sustain reflective action into the future, beyond the scope of any state-supported process.

My involvement with Native Hawaiian organizations and advocacy groups has been consistent throughout my career. Still, had we taken greater time to involve more Hawaiian advocates and grassroots organizations in the Hoʻopono Mamo Task Force, I wonder if we could have gathered sufficient people and resources to have generated meaningful paradigm shifts. In retrospect, if we had involved more grassroots organizations and relied less on funded agencies, I believe this would have impacted the outcome of the project and the creation of abolitionist futures, rooted in Native Hawaiian pedagogies. This is critical, as future success in any systems change in Hawai'i has its greatest potential in the larger movement for Native Hawaiian self-determination.

I, along with many others, was personally transformed through this process of learning and growing together. I am grateful to have had the privilege of helping with over a dozen of the Pono Lōkahi trainings led by Uncle Wayde. Each time I sat as a student to deepen my understanding and practice of *ho'opono* and *ho'oponopono*, to "make things right" within myself as well as in all my relations. It is not a skill but a philosophy and way of life. I continue to learn how to be in balance and harmony within myself and in all my relations—past, present, and future—in the material and spiritual realms. I feel blessed to have had this opportunity to learn. And I am still learning. As they say, the more you know, the more you see what you do not yet know. The personal transformations that many of us experienced have given us insight, strength, and humility that we bring to future endeavors.

Finally, I close by acknowledging that I have not discussed the challenges that this type of work poses for one's academic career and have instead focused more heavily on the concerns of the "activist" in scholar activism. Changing the reward system for faculty in higher education, heavily tilted currently toward peer-reviewed academic publications, is an even more intractable problem. Suffice it to say, activist-scholars at research institutions tend to do double duty. We invest a great deal of time engaging with real-life problems in intimate ways while balancing time for scholarly research and publications along with teaching, advising, and university service. Evidence of good praxis carries little weight in evaluations of faculty performance. That said, the life of an activist-scholar is fulfilling in ways that go far beyond the rewards of academia. Sometimes the journey feels like "two steps forward, one step back." But this is the nature of change, isn't it? For scholars as well as activists working in the space of conflicting paradigms, contested practices, and disparate interests, successful change requires a great deal of tenacity as well as continual learning. It is my hope that these reflections on practice are useful and that this story of one collective effort can inspire and inform further engagement in movements for social change.

NOTES

The author would like to thank Tai-An Miao and Krisna Suryanata for their valuable insights and Tai-An and Wayde Lee for their wisdom, thoughtfulness, and camaraderie in juvenile justice work. There are many others to thank, too numerous to name here but to whom I owe a lifetime of gratitude.

1 Katherine Irwin and Karen Umemoto, *Jacked Up and Unjust: Pacific Islander Teens Confront Violent Legacies* (Berkeley: University of California Press, 2016).

2 The Kawailoa Youth and Family Wellness Center was incorporated into the Hawaiʻi Revised Statutes (§352D-7.5) to provide an alternative to incarceration that allows for "mental health services and programs, substance abuse treatment programs, crisis shelters for homeless youth, crisis shelters for victims of human and sex trafficking, vocational training, group homes, day treatment programs, aftercare, independent and family counseling services, educational services, and other services and programs that may be required to meet the needs of youth or young adults." See also Karen Umemoto and Britta Johnson, *Kawailoa Youth and Family Wellness Center: Programmatic Plan*, State of Hawaiʻi, Office of Youth Services, 2018.

3 Karen Umemoto, James Spencer, Tai-An Miao, and Saiful Momen, "Disproportionate Minority Contact in the Hawaiʻi Juvenile Justice System, 2000–2010," report prepared for the Juvenile Justice State Advisory Council and the State of Hawaiʻi, Office of Youth Services, June 2012.

4 The Hawaiian word *pono* has different meanings depending on the context in which it is used, including righteousness, uprightness, and excellence. In the context of juvenile justice reform, the term was often used to refer to the state of being in harmony and balance in all relations—past, present, and future. In regards to youth, the term was also used in reference to walking a righteous path or doing right by oneself, by others, and by the physical and spiritual world.

5 Noreen Mokuʻau, "Culturally Based Interventions for Substance Use and Child Abuse among Native Hawaiians," *Association of Schools of Public Health* 117 (2002): S82–S87; Abbie Napeahi, Terry Kelly, Paula-Ann Burgess, David Kamiyama, and Noreen Mokuʻau, "Culture as a Protective Factor in Two Prevention Programs for Hawaiians," in *Responding to Pacific Islanders: Culturally Competent Perspectives for Substance Abuse Prevention*, ed N. Mokuʻau (Washington, DC: US Department of Health and Human Services, Center for Substance Abuse Prevention, 1998), 97–116.

6 University of Hawaiʻi Department of Urban and Regional Planning Practicum Students, *Hoʻopono Mamo: The Hawaiʻi Youth Diversion System Program Implementation and Evaluation Plan*, report prepared for the Hoʻopono Mamo Civil Citation Task Force, fall 2013.

7 Karen Umemoto, Wayde Lee, and Tai-An Miao, *Hoʻopono Mamo / Civil Citation Initiative: Planning Project Report,* prepared for the State of Hawaiʻi, Office of Youth Services, 2014.

8 Quantitative data included youths arrested in Hawaiʻi during 2000–2010 from the Hawaiʻi Juvenile Justice Information System, and qualitative data included a 20 percent sample of court-involved youths arrested in 2009. See Umemoto, Spencer, Miao, and Momen, "Disproportionate Minority Contact in the Hawaiʻi Juvenile Justice System."

9 University of Hawaiʻi Department of Urban and Regional Planning Practicum Students, "Hoʻopono Mamo: The Hawaiʻi Youth Diversion System," report, 2013.

CHAPTER 3

THE STREETS OF SOMA

Building Community amid Displacement in San Francisco

ANGELICA CABANDE, WITH KATHERINE NASOL

THE SOUTH OF MARKET (SOMA) NEIGHBORHOOD IS RACIALLY diverse, home to a sizable Filipino immigrant community, in addition to having pronounced poverty alongside marked wealth. In many ways it is a microcosm of the growing disparity between the rich and the poor in the city of San Francisco. Adjacent to San Francisco's Downtown and Financial Districts, in the local popular imagination it has not typically been thought of as a residential neighborhood. It has been seen as a place where tourists and seasonal workers come and go. Despite this perception of SoMa, it has been home to many of San Francisco's low-income residents, people of color, immigrant workers, and their families since the late 1840s. As Filipino immigrants and other tenants became displaced from Chinatown and the Fillmore neighborhood, these residents were forced to move and began calling SoMa their home.

This chapter tells the story of the SoMa neighborhood and the community's fight against housing displacement and gentrification, with a specific focus on the work of the South of Market Community Action Network (SOMCAN). SOMCAN was formed in 2000 after a major struggle in the late 1990s against the "dot-com" boom, in which internet companies flooded the neighborhood. During this time community leaders, including youth, seniors, and veterans, many of whom were Filipinos, realized the need for an organization addressing gentrification in the SoMa. We share how SOMCAN in many ways draws from the legacy of past tenant rights movements that organized to defend tenants' homes from greedy developers, like the struggle to save the International Hotel in the 1960s and 1970s. It has also taken the movement in new directions by empowering tenants to proactively come up with and fight for their own visions of equitable development as well as to advocate for city planning policies that prioritize the needs of low-income and immigrant families.

FROM THE "WALL STREET OF THE WEST" TO THE "DOT-COM" BOOMS: DRIVERS OF DISPLACEMENT IN SAN FRANCISCO

After World War II American city governments enacted "urban renewal," which prioritized demolishing and replacing large swaths of economically depressed older neighborhoods with new development that would purportedly result in lower crime, economic growth, and a higher standard of living. San Francisco was no different. At the same time, San Francisco's business community aspired to be the "Wall Street of the West" and made plans to attract more corporate headquarters into the area and expand the downtown business sector, particularly the area around the Financial District (Rosen and Sullivan 2014). San Francisco corporate and real estate leaders joined forces with the San Francisco Redevelopment Agency, or SFRA, to support the urban renewal movement. They targeted the Fillmore, Chinatown, Manilatown, and SoMa since these neighborhoods had become rundown and had a reputation for crime and violence. SFRA led the way in declaring these areas "blighted," paving the way for the government to begin land acquisition and evictions of neighborhood residents (Gans 1992).

By the mid-1970s Financial District expansion combined with the building of the Bay Area Rapid Transit (BART) system across the San Francisco Bay Area made it easier for white-collar workers to commute from the outlying areas into downtown to work in the major banks, trading companies, and other corporate entities that moved into the growing Financial District. It was this focus on economic growth and corporate interests, without addressing affordable housing needs and equitable development, that destroyed what was once Manilatown.

Manilatown had been the largest urban Filipino neighborhood in the country, with as many as twenty thousand residents at times

(Robles 2002). The ten blocks of Manilatown—in close proximity to what became the Financial District—running down Kearny Street to Market Street had residential hotels, including the International Hotel (I-Hotel), the Victory Hotel, and the Bell Hotel; restaurants like Mabuhay; barbershops such as Tino's; pool halls like the Lucky M; and dance halls like Club Mandalay. By the late 1970s the I-Hotel was almost all that was left of Manilatown (Habal 2007). After the I-Hotel was demolished, many of the residents of the former Manilatown moved to join large Filipino communities in the Tenderloin, Excelsior, and SoMa districts.

In the 1990s the first dot-com boom hit SoMa. The boom garnered massive wealth for new internet companies causing existing homes to be converted to live/work lofts for tech workers, thus leading to rising rents and the disappearance of many nonprofits and small businesses.[1] San Francisco city officials passed more development in the SoMa than any other neighborhood during this time.[2] By the 2010s a second dot-com boom would hit the neighborhood. It was during this time that the infamous Central Market Street and Tenderloin Area Payroll Expense Tax Exclusion, also known as the "Twitter Tax Break," was introduced, in 2011.[3] The tax break was believed to be a source of economic growth for the city similar to claims made about urban renewal initiatives decades earlier.

SOMCAN sees the housing crisis, gentrification, and displacement as rooted in four main drivers: real estate companies, the landlord, the developers, and the city government. Ultimately, we in SOMCAN see these drivers as all being pushed primarily by capitalism. Housing is perceived as a commodity, not a right. Just like how our environment is extracted for corporate gains, housing has become a money-driven business without consideration of its human impact, such as the people evicted from their home or displaced from their community.

Real estate companies and other businesses have deepened the housing crisis in SoMa through purchasing rent-controlled buildings and evicting existing tenants. For instance, the Academy of Arts purchased rent-controlled housing and single-room occupancy (SRO) buildings and turned them into private student housing units, thus removing affordable housing options for low-income people.[4] Landlords, meanwhile, threaten existing tenants through evictions, especially when there is the possibility of a buyout. They can also resort to harassment or making housing units uninhabitable (such as not addressing mold in units or fixing things in a timely manner) so tenants are forced to leave. There have been instances when real estate brokers even teach landlords how to get rid of tenants so they can sell their buildings for higher sale prices to prospective developers.

Developers exacerbate the crisis through the types of housing being built. Developers have been able to get zoning policies passed for more luxury housing, hotels, and tech offices in SoMa. Indeed, the private sector is strengthened by its own corporate lobbyists, such as Ron Conway. Conway is a lobbyist for over 350 tech companies, from start-ups like Square to existing big companies like Google and Twitter. Corporate lobbyists like Conway and the private sector interests they serve keep the power over land use and city planning in their control, ensuring that immigrant and low-income residents are kept out.

Thus, municipal government plays an important role in contributing to the crisis because of the tax breaks they provide to the private sector (like the Twitter Tax Break) and the type of jobs they prioritize for the city's economy. Facilitated by the Mayor's Office of Economic & Workforce Development (OEWD), the city prioritizes work in the tech and biotech sector, leaving out the working-class San Franciscan and instead bringing in new people from other parts of the state to fill those professional skills. The housing crisis is worsened when the mayor or other supervisors vote against legislation that will protect tenants and when city departments like the Planning Commission approve zoning changes without looking at the neighborhood holistically. Ultimately, municipal governmental agencies are neoliberal institutions that prioritize free market solutions to address the affordable housing crisis. They operate from the logic that supporting the wealthy somehow trickles down to everyone else. In reality wealth does not trickle down. Instead, economic and racial inequality in San Francisco is exacerbated.

The combination of different private interests together with the local government all drive displacement and intensifies the housing crisis in this second dot-com boom. As a result, SOMCAN aims not only to use the existing tools, knowledge, and experience we inherited from past tenant rights movements but also to look into different strategies to address these different drivers of gentrification. Before discussing our current organizing strategies, we will briefly discuss how SOMCAN came to be.

FORMING THE SOUTH OF MARKET COMMUNITY
ACTION NETWORK

In 1990, 30 percent of SoMa residents were Filipino, and over the course of the decade, Filipino American businesses, organizations, and other cultural institutions were established. For example, the Yerba Buena Center for the Arts would be the site for the yearly Filipino American Arts Exposition, now generally known as "Pistahan," drawing thousands of Filipinos from across the city and the Bay Area to enjoy cultural performances and goods from Filipino vendors. The very first exposition took place in the early 1990s. While many of the performances take place in the park, the exposition is preceded by a parade along San Francisco's Market Street.[5] By the late 1990s the Bayanihan Community Center would open its doors and play host to numerous community events, and the Bayanihan House, where the center was located, would offer low-cost housing to Filipino American World War II veterans.[6] Just across the street from the Bayanihan Center is the Mint Mall, home to many low-income Filipino immigrants as well as small businesses serving the Filipino community. Not far from the Bayanihan Center is Bindlestiff Studio, the very first and only permanent, community-based performing arts venue in the nation dedicated to showcasing emerging Filipino American and Pilipino artists.[7]

SoMa residents, many of whom had previously been displaced from Manilatown, would face the threat of displacement as the dot-com boom crept into the SoMa and the neighboring Mission neighborhood in the 1990s. In 1999 occupants of the Mint Mall, home to Filipino-owned businesses and organizations and low-income Filipino immigrant families, were given eviction notices to make way for the dot-com boom. More than twenty years after San Francisco's Filipino Americans fought for the I-Hotel, they came together in a fight to save the Mint Mall.[8] Filipino businesses, organizations, and community leaders came together to form the Mint Mall Organizing Committee (MMOC). The MMOC combined organizing, mobilizing, and advocacy and brought the Mint Mall issue to City Hall. Through their tactics Filipino businesses and nonprofits were able to stay in the Mint Mall, and it continues to be a cultural hub. The Mint Mall fight was ultimately what led to the formation of SOMCAN in 2000.

SOMCAN's mission is to nurture youth, family, and individual wellness and cultivate collective power among low-income and immigrant communities to create a more just society. We work on a wide range of issues, from housing, land use, and gentrification to language access and employment. SOMCAN provides culturally competent direct services ranging from tenant rights outreach and language access to workforce development and workers' rights. It is important to emphasize that unlike many other nonprofits, SOMCAN places a priority on organizing for change. Though we address people's immediate day-to-day needs through our direct services, it is though our organizing that we truly empower people. We help tenants understand that their individual, personal issues are not isolated but part of a larger systemic problem that requires collective power to address and change. Fostering critical thinking through political education is therefore important. Through our work SOMCAN has been able to engage low-income, immigrant families and youth in addressing issues affecting them collectively and to support them in mobilizing their peers and the broader community to fight for their basic human rights. I have worked for SOMCAN for nearly twenty years. I started first as a volunteer, supporting SOMCAN's organizing as a translator since I am a native Tagalog speaker. Later I was hired to be an organizer, and eventually I was hired to serve as the executive director.

INTERGENERATIONAL RELATIONSHIPS

SOMCAN's strategies and tactics did not form overnight. It was through past organizers such as the late Bill Sorro and Al Robles that we were able to learn about the I-Hotel struggle and what they did not only to keep the land where the I-Hotel once stood but to fight its numerous landowners from building luxury developments on that vacant land. Though the I-Hotel was destroyed, organizers like Sorro, Robles, and many others were able to ensure that the empty lot that was the original site of the I-Hotel would house new generations of low-income elders, and by 2005 a new I-Hotel was erected.[9]

In 2003 SOMCAN was approached by tenants from Trinity Plaza (on Eighth and Market Streets) who had received a demolition notice from their building management. The building was home to majority low-income residents, many of them Filipino. We organized with the tenants and helped them form the Trinity Plaza Tenants Association (TPTA). For over three years we met weekly to connect them to legal support from tenant lawyers; strategize tactics; provide peer-to-peer support; connect them to their city representative; and put pressure on the building owner, Angelo Sangiacomo.[10] SOMCAN and TPTA would door knock and phone bank tenants in the building to invite them to attend meetings, hearings, and actions. We also provided Filipino language support to the Filipino tenants to ensure that they were fully understood and were well-versed in the strategies and tactics. Finally, in 2006 Sangiacomo negotiated a community benefit agreement with TPTA that preserved the 366 rent-controlled units that were slated for demolition and negotiated an additional 135 affordable housing units, including a lifetime lease to tenants who had been living in their units since 2004. Tenants were also able to add their family members onto the lease.

I first became involved in SOMCAN as a volunteer during the Trinity Plaza struggle, in large part due to my relationship with Manong Al (Robles). I started spending time in SoMa as I began to develop my work as a spoken word artist. I wasn't a housing activist at the time. I was actually working as a customer service representative for a small business. While researching online about where to buy books by Filipino authors, I discovered Arkipelago books, located in the Bayanihan Building, and later learned that the entire SoMa neighborhood was actually a hub for Filipino culture. I had no idea that there was a Filipino community in SoMa though I worked only a few blocks from the area. Once I learned more about SoMa, I would hang out in the neighborhood during my lunch breaks and after work, spending time at Arkipelago Books, attending events at Bindlestiff, and eventually meeting Manong Al and other artists. I was close to Manong Al, but mainly we connected through his poetry. Manong Al, however, would often talk-story about Manilatown and the activism to save it. He would share stories about what would take place behind the scenes in the I-Hotel, describing how he would spend time with the elderly *manongs* there, having coffee or tea and listening to their migration stories, even as he and other activists fought alongside the *manongs* against eviction. Manong Al taught me about the importance of relationship building as essential to organizing. I would eventually meet the executive director of SOMCAN at the time, Jeanne Battalones, while hanging out in the neighborhood. At some point she told me that SOMCAN needed support in working with the Trinity Plaza residents because there were not enough Filipino speakers on staff and asked if I was interested in volunteering. I decided to pursue the opportunity.

The Trinity Plaza campaign was really my first time organizing on the ground. Though I didn't have experience, I applied the lessons I learned from Manong Al as I helped SOMCAN in door knocking and tenant visits. I would bring food and just listen as tenants shared their migration stories and discussed their kids and their experiences growing up in the neighborhood. Tenants would share details about their lives in the Philippines, what province they were from, and what their families did there. Of course, I, and other organizers, would also discuss the actual campaign to save their building, but we also made time to listen to their personal issues. As the fight continued—it was a long and drawn-out fight that lasted more than three years—we would listen to the tenants' insecurities about their leadership and helped to train them in skills such as public speaking, often organizing mock sessions to prepare them for speaking out at public hearings. We listened to tenant leaders as they vented about the prolonged nature of the fight and questioned whether it was even worth it to continue leading the struggle when it seemed that nobody cared. We strived to encourage and empower them to persist while also helping them understand the long-haul nature of the campaign. Our efforts proved successful as the tenants were able to get the building owner to negotiate terms that allowed them to stay in their homes.

DEVELOPING INNOVATIVE WAYS TO RESIST, ORGANIZE, AND SHAPE PLACE

From our organizer-elders we learned the importance of mixing direct organizing and advocacy, land use policy change, equitable community planning, tenant protections, and ongoing engagement of youth and families in the SoMa and other parts of San Francisco. It is through them and other housing and tenant movements from the Mission neighborhood that we learned that when it comes to city planning and land use decisions, the participants have primarily been land developers, lenders, businesses, and the rich, both through access to elected officials and by creating markets for certain types of development. As SOMCAN, we wanted to change that.

Alongside our work in the Trinity Plaza, SOMCAN led the SoMa Community Coalition in winning a historic piece of legislation from the San Francisco city government in 2005 that established a SoMa Community Stabilization Impact Fee, which would generate thirty million dollars for the SoMa Community Stabilization Fund. Mayor Gavin Newson had championed the so-called Rincon Hill Area Plan, which tenant rights and housing activists feared would trigger even further gentrification in the SoMa. The SoMa Community Stabilization Fund helps to offset the gentrifying impacts of the Rincon Hill Area Plan by charging developers twenty-five dollars for each square foot they wish to purchase in the area, with the funds going toward various community programs as well as supporting affordable housing and economic development.[11] The fund is overseen by the Mayor's Office of Housing & Community Development and the SoMa Community Stabilization Fund Community Advisory Committee.[12]

STATE OF THE SOMA: PLANNING FOR THE PEOPLE

After the Rincon Hill Area Plan was pushed through by the city, SOMCAN made a strategic decision to organize a "State of the SoMa," a community-led visioning process through which the needs and wants of SoMa residents themselves are reflected in planning in contrast to the planning visions articulated by those in power. State of the SOMA included a series of town halls organized by SOMCAN that were facilitated by resident leaders (both youths and adults) that combined demographic census maps with photographic storyboards as a way to engage neighborhood residents in discussing the issues of the streets, housing, jobs, youth, seniors, stores, and services.

We conducted numerous community meetings focused on sectors with resident-led facilitation to find out what people love about the SoMa, what people dislike about the SoMa, and what a healthy community would look like for community members. The meetings were held with seniors, people with disabilities, families, workers, and transitional-age youths. We provided language support in Spanish and Filipino.

As a result, of the State of the SoMa process, the "Healthy SoMa Community," a social and economic justice agenda committed to working toward fairness and opportunity for the existing low-income, people of color, immigrant, and working-class residents of SoMa, was formed. By defining an equitable and comprehensive community development strategy on their own terms, existing SoMa residents were able to have a voice in their social, economic, physical, and political environments so that they can live, work, and thrive in the South of Market, and San Francisco generally, regardless of race, income, or language spoken.

The State of the SoMa process was timely because the neighborhood was being butchered by the city's Planning Department into different area plans.[13] Figure 3.1 illustrates the simultaneous area plan that the Planning Department was facilitating in the SoMa neighborhood. This made it hard to organize and mobilize because each area plan held its own planning process and hearing. It was evident that the SoMa community, especially the Filipino community, did not have the time and resources to challenge each one.

LAND USE POLICIES

With this limitation in mind, SOMCAN decided to be proactive in land use policies. Looking at our Healthy SoMa Community agenda, what was echoed across sectors of residents was the feeling that "my neighborhood is not seen as a neighborhood—it is seen as a gateway to downtown. But there is an existing community here of children growing up, of families settling here and calling this area home, of seniors and people, the Filipino community being here since the 1920s." This prompted us to advocate for a SoMa Youth and Families Special Use District (SYF SUD) in 2007. The creation of the SUD would ensure that the city recognize and acknowledge the concentration of youths and families in SoMa.[14] Advocacy for the SUD mobilized youths, parents, and families to speak at City Hall. Fortunately, the SUD was passed and was established in 2009 by the city to protect and enhance the environment and health of youths and families in the neighborhood. It restricts certain types of development so youths, families, and seniors can continue to live, work, and thrive in the SoMa. The SUD's boundaries include Natoma to Harrison, spanning the area between Fourth Street and Seventh Street, and establish a vision for how the area will grow over the next fifteen to thirty years. The SUD aims to ensure the provision of affordable housing and to protect and enhance the health and environment of youths and families by encouraging open space, community-based organizations, schools, and pedestrian safety as well as uses that support youths' and families' livelihoods, such as employment opportunities, workforce development, and more small businesses. Because of the political climate at the time and rezoning of the neighborhood, we were only able to establish twelve blocks for the SUD, but it was always our intention to expand it to include the majority of the SoMa.

It is important to emphasize while we engage in processes and struggles to shape city policy, we continue to do relationship building on the ground with community members, just as we learned from our elders. At SOMCAN we always try to celebrate wins, big or small, whether they are organizational or even personal. For us, when we say we're building community, it means more than just fighting together; it's also having fun together, whether it's celebrating a birthday, hosting a karaoke session, going on group outings, or just chitchatting. We want to foster a genuine sense of community and not just bring people together over an issue.

There are risks, however, to our commitment to genuinely empowering SoMa's community members. SOMCAN often has doors closed to us because we are seen as too radical. For example, because we fought the Rincon Hill Plan championed by former mayor Gavin Newsom, he fought against SOMCAN getting city resources, saying that groups that are "too political" should not be funded by the city. Yet the city does fund organizations that support "civic engagement." It became clear to us that civic engagement is encouraged but only within limits.

Since the SUD's adoption in 2009, within its boundaries and throughout the entire South of Market neighborhood, in contrast to the child-friendly, family-friendly development visions and goals established by the SUD, more commercial and luxury development has taken place. This can be largely attributed to the second dot-com boom that began phasing into San Francisco and the Bay Area shortly after the SUD's adoption. Arguably worse than the first dot-com boom of the late 1990s, the city's response to the resurgence of the high-tech industry has ushered in rampant speculation, the privatization of public services, hyper-gentrification, mass displacement, and heightened spatial and class polarization (Goldman 2013).

The surge in high-tech companies moving northward from the Silicon Valley surpasses the original dot-com boom that created a new submarket called the "South Financial District." Not everyone benefited from this economic activity. For instance, there were no local hiring requirements that came along with the Twitter Tax Break.[15] SoMa's low-income residents were not being trained for the thousands of jobs that these tech firms were offering. Additional gains from the Twitter Tax Break included the city investing in a new bus line to cater to the Twitter employees so they could travel more easily between Tenth and Market to the Caltrain station. In the meantime the South Eastside, which is home to poor and middle-income immigrants and people of color, has been advocating for years to have better transportation in the area but has continued to be neglected by the city. The city also invested city tax dollars in adding more police patrols around Tenth and Market, where Twitter headquarters is located.

Right after passage of the 2011 Twitter Tax Break, evictions went up by 115 percent. In 2013 the San Francisco rent board had 716 people reported as being displaced; however, eviction groups estimate the number was closer to 3,580 citywide.[16] The citywide minimum rent for all types of apartment units grew to $3,414, an 8.2 percent increase from 2012.[17] After eight years since the Twitter Tax Break, new District 6 supervisor Matt Haney requested a hearing to analyze what was gained by the city from the tax break. Newspapers showed the lack of benefits to the Mid-Market neighborhood with headlines reporting: "SF City Hall Fed Up with Twitter Tax Break! Shame and Disgrace."[18]

BALLOT MEASURES

In the current era SOMCAN has resisted through new and old tactics in our neighborhood. Since 2008 SOMCAN has engaged in electoral organizing with San Francisco Rising, a coalition of base-building organizations located in San Francisco's various working-class communities. We especially focus on educating and mobilizing thousands of San Francisco Filipino voters on ballot measures that protect tenants, provide legal representation, hold the rich accountable to pay their fair share, and ensure equitable funding for schools. Participating in electoral organizing gives us an opportunity to understand and discuss local issues that impact Filipino voters. We focus on Filipino voters because of our cultural and linguistic capacity.

One ballot measure SOMCAN worked on is Proposition F, or the Tenant Right to Counsel.[19] Proposition F guarantees any tenant the right to counsel in an eviction matter. Although there is a law that protects tenants against wrongful evictions, those who are unable to afford an attorney struggle to protect themselves in a system that favors landlords who can pay for legal representation. Studies have shown that having an attorney in an eviction case increases a family's chance of avoiding homelessness by over 70 percent.[20] The universal right to counsel in eviction cases is a proven and cost-effective way of keeping people housed. This measure, which we successfully passed, ensures that all San Francisco renters facing eviction have access to an attorney, regardless of age, income, or the amount of time they have lived in San Francisco. In addition, we successfully mobilized over the citywide ordinance Eviction Protection 2.0, which reforms the city's existing rent control law to address the city's eviction crisis.[21] The ordinance's aim is to reduce evictions by fixing loopholes in the law that are being exploited by speculators and landlord lawyers.

PROPERTY FOR THE PEOPLE

As SoMa becomes an "up and coming" neighborhood where speculators purchase rent-controlled buildings and resell them for higher profit, we resist by partnering with the San Francisco Community Land Trust (SFCLT) to purchase rent-controlled buildings that are up for sale and take them off the speculative market, thereby saving tenants living in the buildings from eviction. In 2012 tenants living at 534–536 Natoma Street, fearing eviction, approached SOMCAN for support when their building went up for sale by their landlord. This building was home to immigrant Filipino tenants, seniors, people with disabilities, and families that had called the building home for over twenty-five years. SOMCAN organized the tenants and in 2012 went to the SoMa Stabilization Fund to help purchase the building, with the SFCLT land trust serving as the new landlord. SOMCAN and the SFCLT were able to take other rent-controlled buildings out of speculators' hands, such as 568–570 Natoma Street and 1353–1357 Folsom Street.[22] To further ensure we are able to protect rent-controlled buildings, in 2019 we organized the long-awaited Community Opportunity to Purchase Act (COPA) legislation.[23] COPA provides us a step up in competing with speculators by informing us about buildings for sale and giving us a chance to purchase them; fortunately, it was approved.

THE CULTURAL DISTRICT

In 2015 SOMCAN organized against the 5M Project, a large-scale development, and questioned the city's intentions of replacing neighborhoods like SoMa for billion-dollar developers, even though the project put residents at risk of displacement.[24] SOMCAN mobilized residents, seniors, youths, workers, artists, and concerned San Franciscans from the Filipino community to share over two and a half hours of public comments on the impact of displacement at the September 2015 San Francisco Planning Commission hearing. We questioned city officials with the question "Who are you building for?" and demanded an anti-displacement and stabilization plan. Since we knew the city would be bowing down to corporate interests and would ultimately approve the 5M Project, we strategized ways we could counter the impact. Our first solution was to file a lawsuit against the city of San Francisco. The other was to demand that the city approve the SOMA Pilipinas-Filipino Cultural Heritage District.

The cultural district was first proposed in 2008 as part of the Western SoMa Plan. The Planning Department published *Recognizing,*

FIGURE 3.1. Community planning session with SOMA residents identifying areas they would like to be part of the public realm to reflect Filipino culture, heritage, and history for SOMA Pilipinas-Filipino Cultural Heritage District, 2008. Photo courtesy of SOMCAN.

Protecting, and Memorializing SoMa Filipino: Social Heritage Neighborhood Resources, which presented a discussion of the Filipino community in San Francisco from the 1920s through the 1980s, identifying buildings or sites in the SoMa neighborhood that are viewed as cultural assets by the Filipino community. However, the efforts in making the plan a reality were put on the back burner by the city until it was brought back to light by SOMCAN and the Filipino community in the 2015 fight against the 5M Project. In 2016 SoMa finally became designated as "SoMa Pilipinas, a Filipino Cultural Heritage District" by the San Francisco Board of Supervisors. The board's designation represented a shift away from private development to the needs of the community living in the SoMa district, a shift pushed and activated by the community itself. Juvy Barbonio, a Filipino resident, said: "Passing SoMa Pilipinas is an opportunity to make sure that our organizations, our businesses, and residents like me can continue to be rooted in the city. It's an opportunity to make sure everyone can see SoMa how I see it—a neighborhood of beautiful cultures, a rich heritage, and full of loving, friendly, and talented people that we need to recognize, invest in, and protect."

To ensure SOMA Pilipinas's status, SOMCAN, along with the Filipino American Development Foundation, made sure that funding was allocated from the city's general fund to staff the cultural district as the regional center of Filipino culture, further recognizing the historical and present contributions of the community and stabilizing Filipino residents, businesses, and community-serving institutions. Because of SOMCAN's lawsuit against the city on the 5M Project, which it had simultaneously led, we decided it was best that SOMCAN not lead the cultural district work. The city's bureaucracy and politicking have often delayed the city from addressing community members' concerns. We did not want to give the city any reason to put our community's efforts on the back burner yet again, so instead we are creating a more proactive platform for community control over housing and neighborhood development. SOMCAN still heavily participates in the work of the cultural district, sharing our community planning, art, and community organizing experience. We continue to help facilitate meetings and created a progress report on the cultural district that encouraged youths, families, seniors, and artists to be a part of the process of shaping it.[25]

In recent years the Twitter Tax Break epitomized the relentless onslaught of tech companies into San Francisco. Though the Twitter Tax Break is no longer in effect, the gentrifying impact it had in San Francisco still continues. Indeed, gentrification in the San Francisco Bay Area more broadly shows no signs of slowing. In fact, it's accelerating. As housing prices rise and tech jobs continue to flood the region, more people in San Francisco and neighboring cities are at risk of displacement. According to UC Berkeley's Urban Displacement Project, an interactive map that shows regional demographic data and case studies, researchers found that neighborhoods that have easy access to rail transit are experiencing rising housing prices and are especially at risk of losing low-income households (Chapple and Zuk 2015).[26] It is also not just low-income communities that are at risk. Higher-income areas with low-income households in the mix are rapidly losing population. Between 1990 and 2013 census tracts undergoing or at risk of displacement lost approximately twenty-five thousand low-income households. More than half of the neighborhoods lost low-income Black households, far more than any other demographic.

In spite of these challenges, SOMCAN offers an important model of resistance to gentrification. Building on the lessons of earlier tenant movements, most notably the struggle to save the International Hotel, we continue to value listening and learning from those most affected by gentrification. We continue to strive to have tenants lead and speak for themselves (and not the staff leading or speaking for them). We continue to do the hard work of base building and truly empowering tenants to advocate for themselves individually and collectively. We strive to celebrate every win no matter how small because those little things help to build people's spirits, especially when many of the struggles we engage in can be very protracted.

At the same time, we have also taken the tenant rights movement in a new direction. Like many of the tenants we organize, I did not really know anything about community planning jargon. Unlike some of my counterparts, I did not have the college education or advanced training that might make it easier to understand. The fact is the jargon can feel really alienating for immigrants or for people who did not study planning in school. As an organization, we keep in mind that we are here for a higher purpose. Policy work can suck your energy and take a lot from you. It requires understanding and knowing how much you're willing to negotiate, but at SOMCAN we always try to stay true to the people we are representing.

NOTES

1 Marisa Lagos, "San Francisco Evictions Surge, Report Finds," *SFGate,* November 4, 2013, https://www.sfgate.com/bayarea/article/San -Francisco-evictions-surge-report-finds-4955020.php.

2 Richard Walker, "Boom and Bombshell: New Economy Bubble and the Bay Area: Historical Essay," in *The Changing Economic Geography of Globalization,* ed. Giovanna Vertova (Oxfordshire, England: Routledge, 2005), reprinted in *FoundSF,* www.foundsf.org/index.php?title=Boom _and_Bombshell:_New_Economy_Bubble_and_the_Bay_Area.

3 Marcus Wohlsen, "San Francisco Lawmakers Approve Twitter Tax Break," *PhysOrg,* April 6, 2011, https://phys.org/news/2011-04-san -francisco-lawmakers-twitter-tax.html.

4 A single-room occupancy (SRO) building is a form of permanent housing typically aimed at poor and working-class residents. The rooms usually have a bed, chair, and small desk, while residents share a kitchen, toilets, and bathrooms. In the past few decades SROs have been converted into condominiums as gentrification has increased.

5 James Sobredo, "Filipino Culture Thrives South of Market: Historical Essay," *FoundSF,* 1996, https://www.foundsf.org/index.php?title =Filipino_Culture_Thrives_South_of_Market.

6 SOMA Pilipinas, "Bayanihan Center," 2018, https://www.somapilipinas .org/cultural-assets-1/2018/7/25/bayanihan-center.

7 Bindlestiff Studio, "About Us," https://www.bindlestiffstudio.org/our -mission.

8 Ryan Kim, "Hub in Crisis / Evictions Dispersing Filipino American Businesses / Mint Mall on Mission St. Down to 5 Firms Rally Will Publicize Plight," *SF Gate,* December 14, 2000, updated August 6, 2012, https://www.sfgate.com/news/article/HUB-IN-CRISIS-Evictions -Dispersing-Filipino-3236232.php.

9 "Home," The I-Hotel—San Francisco, www.ihotel-sf.org, last modified in 2021.

10 Ken Werner, "The Sangiacomo Family's Pattern of Behavior," *Beyond Chron,* January 3, 2006, http://beyondchron.org/the-sangiacomo -familys-pattern-of-behavior.

11 Joshua Sabatini, "SoMA Fund to Add 10m to Buy Small Housing Sites in the Neighborhood," *San Francisco Examiner,* May 12, 2017, https:// www.sfexaminer.com/news/soma-fund-to-add-10m-to-buy-small -housing-sites-in-the-neighborhood; Ken Werner, "Rincon Hill: The Next Stage of Manhattanization," *Beyond Chron,* April 26, 2005, http://beyondchron.org/rincon-hill-the-next-stage-of -manhattanization.

12 Mayor's Office of Housing & Community Development, SoMa Community Stabilization Fund, https://sfmohcd.org/soma-community-stabilization-fund.

13 San Francisco Planning, "Eastern Neighborhood Plans: Area Plans," 2020, https://sfplanning.org/eastern-neighborhoods-plans-area-plans.

14 J. Laberinto, "Prioritizing Children, Youth, and Families in the Urban Context: Implications for an Equitable SoMa Youth & Family Special Use District" (August 2018).

15 Marissa Lang, "Companies Avoid $34M in City Taxes Thanks to 'Twitter Tax Break,'" *SF Gate*, October 19, 2015, https://www.sfgate.com/business/article/Companies-avoid-34M-in-city-taxes-thanks-to-6578396.php.

16 Anti-Eviction Mapping Project, "San Francisco's Housing Crisis in Numbers," *Causa Justa*, 2013, https://cjjc.org/mediapress/san-francisco-s-housing-crisis-in-numbers.

17 City and County of San Francisco Board of Supervisors, Budget and Legislative Analyst, *Analysis of Tenant Displacement in San Francisco*, October 30, 2013, https://sfbos.org/sites/default/files/FileCenter/Documents/47040-BLA%20Displacement%20103013.pdf.

18 Adam Brinklow, "SF City Hall Fed Up with Twitter Tax Break," *Curbed San Francisco*, June 7, 2019, https://sf.curbed.com/2019/6/7/18657092/twitter-tax-break-mid-market-hearing-haney.

19 Eviction Defense Collaborative, "Tenant Right to Counsel," http://evictiondefense.org/services/right-to-counsel.

20 Heidi Schultheis and Caitlin Rooney, *A Right to Counsel Is a Right to a Fighting Chance: The Importance of Legal Representation in Eviction Proceeding*, Center for American Progress, October 2, 2019, https://www.americanprogress.org/issues/poverty/reports/2019/10/02/475263/right-counsel-right-fighting-chance.

21 Jun Nucum, "Renters Triumph, San Francisco Toughens Tenant Protections," *Inquirer.Net*, October 20, 2015, https://globalnation.inquirer.net/129712/renters-triumph-san-francisco-toughens-tenant-protections.

22 Jessica Christian, "SoMa Stabilization Fund Helps Prevent Eviction of Low-Income Tenants," *San Francisco Examiner*, April 12, 2016, https://www.sfexaminer.com/photo-galleries/soma-stabilization-fund-helps-prevent-eviction-of-low-income-tenants/nggallery/image/sflandtrust_natoma_009; "San Francisco Tenants Beat Ellis Act Evictions," KTVU Fox 2, February 11, 2016, https://www.ktvu.com/news/san-francisco-tenants-beat-ellis-act-evictions.

23 Ida Mojadad, "Grants Non-Profits First Priority in Building Sales," *SF Weekly*, April 16, 2019, https://www.sfweekly.com/news/city-grants-nonprofits-first-priority-in-building-sales.

24 Dyan Ruiz, "SoMa '5M' Project Will Push Out Families," *San Francisco Examiner*, September 20, 2015, https://www.sfexaminer.com/opinion/soma-5m-project-will-push-out-families.

25 SF Planning Department and SoMA Pilipinas Working Group, *Progress Report: Filipino Cultural District Community Planning Process*, October 2016, https://static1.squarespace.com/static/5b2c30b58f51305e3d641e81/t/5b63f522352f53676d5d7cba/1533277482339/FINALSoMaPilipinasProgress+Report.pdf.

26 UC Berkeley's Urban Displacement Project and the California Housing Partnership, *Rising Housing Costs and Re-Segregation in San Francisco*, 2019, https://www.urbandisplacement.org/sites/default/files/images/sf_final.pdf.

WORKS CITED

Chapple, Karen, and Miriam Zuk. "Case Studies on Gentrification and Displacement in the San Francisco Bay Area." Center for Community Innovation, University of California, Berkeley, July 2015. https://www.urbandisplacement.org/sites/default/files/images/case_studies_on_gentrification_and_displacement-_full_report.pdf.

Gans, Herbert J. "Second-Generation Decline: Scenarios for the Economic and Ethnic Futures of the Post-1965 American Immigrants." *Ethnic and Racial Studies* 15, no. 2 (1992): 173–92.

Goldman, Alexandra. "The 'Google Shuttle Effect': Gentrification and San Francisco's Dot com Boom 2.0." PhD diss., University of California, Berkeley, 2013.

Habal, Estella. *San Francisco's International Hotel: Mobilizing the Filipino American Community in the Anti-Eviction Movement*. Philadelphia: Temple University Press, 2007.

Robles, Al. "Coming Home to Manilatown, International Hotel." *Amerasia Journal* 28, no. 3 (2002): 181–94.

Rosen, Marcia, and Wendy Sullivan. "From Urban Renewal and Displacement to Economic Inclusion: San Francisco Affordable Housing Policy, 1978–2014." *Stanford Law & Policy Review* 25, no. 1 (2014): 121. https://law.stanford.edu/publications/urban-renewal-displacement-economic-inclusion-san-francisco-affordable-housing-policy-1978-2014.

PART 2

INTERNATIONALISM AND LOCAL STRUGGLES

CHAPTER 4

DISMANTLING THE "UNDOCUMENTED KOREAN BOX"

Race, Education, and Undocumented Korean
Immigrant Activism for Liberation

GA YOUNG CHUNG

> There is an "undocumented Korean box." This box is
> transparent and invisible, so nobody knows you are caged.
> You'll never get targeted or profiled like the Latinx, because
> "you Koreans don't look like an undocumented." But there are
> internal struggles coming from [our] Koreanness—our Korean
> family and Korean values. . . . Sometimes you may try to
> challenge the box of glass, but whenever you reach out your
> hands to the things outside the box, you realize they are not
> allowed to you. They will say "No!" to you. Instead, you see
> your parents making sacrifices for you and your community
> saying to you, "You will be fine as long as you study hard."
> You get to learn that staying inside the box might be the best
> way to protect yourself. Because you can't completely be apart
> from your family, community, [who] are Korean.
>
> —JINHEE, UNDOCUMENTED KOREAN
> IMMIGRANT AND ACTIVIST

IT WAS ONE SUMMER AFTERNOON IN JUNE 2016 WHEN JINHEE
mentioned the "undocumented Korean box" to me at a café in Koreatown, Los Angeles. Recalling her adolescence as a time when she was

without any legal protection as an undocumented Korean immigrant youth, she related how different modes of racialization and expectations shaped her identity both as an Asian American and as an undocumented immigrant. The model minority image, combined with parental sacrifices and the ethnic community's dominant social norms, created apprehensions among undocumented Asian immigrants that both paralleled and differed from those of the undocumented Latinx community. She also remembered that the image forged the particular dynamics of being both Asian and undocumented that remained invisible for a long time to the broader undocumented immigration movement and to the Asian American community. However, despite the pressures of not being able to break out of the undocumented Korean box, Jinhee and others have been ceaselessly resisting the pressure to assimilate through organizing rallies, giving speeches at press conferences, conducting community reach-outs, and creating art, texts, and videos. By risking everything for what others take for granted, they have been attempting to dismantle the glass undocumented Korean box instead of fitting into the racialized deservingness frame. In doing so, undocumented Korean immigrant youths have formed a new political subjectivity to become one of the leading groups in the undocumented immigrant activism movement in the United States.

In this chapter I argue how education allowed the undocumented Korean activists to be uniquely positioned to challenge depictions of them as "deserving" or "disposable," two dominant narratives framing undocumented immigration. Their aspiration for education was shaped by the pressure to prove their citizen worthiness through conformity to the existing system, but education also became a way for them to fight for justice for everyone. Caught between the model minority logic—which relies on education, hard work, and political passivity as pathways to mobility—and near-complete neglect and invisibility, they have faced multilayered oppression. Ironically, however, their liminal and precarious living experiences, coupled with persistent racialization, motivated them to create radical spaces for racial dialogue through multiracial and intersectional solidarity with other minoritized groups. Focusing on their activism for liberation, I attend to such contradictions to demonstrate how young activists have been transforming US society into a more inclusive and democratic space for all. In doing so, I argue that ultimately young undocumented

Korean immigrants are helping to create a new vision of Asian American activism in an era of continued US imperialism and uneven globalization.

My study draws on several years of multisite and community-based participatory research in Chicago, Los Angeles, New York, and the Washington, DC, area, including 112 in-depth interviews. I center the narratives of those who were teenagers and in their early twenties before the Deferred Action for Childhood Arrivals (DACA) program was announced in 2012. Using critical race theory in education that inspires us to consider sociohistorical and transnational approaches in understanding the experiences of ethnic subpopulations, I pay attention to the ways in which transnational Korean ideologies of the ideal youth-citizen, in combination with the model minority myth, affected the young undocumented Korean immigrants' identity formation.[1] In the first part of this chapter, I describe how young activists clung to the promise of education as a route to a better future, an aspiration that was shaped by transnational circulations of Korean state ideology of schooling, the racialized myth of the model minority, and the US discourse of meritocracy. Although the imperatives came from different sources, they converged on the same goals: to make youths contribute with productivity and employability to their own and the global project of future making. In the second part I examine how education functions as a tool for critical action and liberation for the undocumented Korean activists. While these immigrants worked hard to pursue education with the hope that it would lead to less precarious lives and a stable legal status as indoctrinated by the multiple subjects, these proved unattainable. They felt betrayed by the promise of education. However, their political reworking of this betrayal into critiques of exclusive citizenship and racism led them to practice the liberatory notion of education through their activism. As Richard Shaull stated in the foreword to Paulo Freire's *Pedagogy of the Oppressed*, a neutral education process does not exist. Education either facilitates the integration of generations into the logic of the present system to instill conformity or it becomes the "practice of freedom," the means by which people deal critically with reality and discover how to participate in the transformation of their world.[2] The experiences of my research interlocutors precisely reflect these two aspects of education.

Currently, there are 1.7 million undocumented Asian immigrants in the United States, making up 16 percent of the nation's 11 million undocumented immigrants.[3] Among them 192,000 are undocumented Korean immigrants.[4] They are the eighth largest undocumented population in the United States, and one of every seven Korean immigrants is undocumented.[5] According to the data, the number of undocumented Asian immigrants increased more than three times, from nearly 500,000 in 2000 to more than 1.7 million in 2015, which has made them the most rapidly growing undocumented group in the United States.[6] In spite of this remarkable statistic, the undocumented Asian immigrants have not received much attention publicly. Instead, the media has largely invoked the model minority image to frame them as "hardworking immigrants poised for high socioeconomic success."[7] But much has been changing as Korean and Asian American undocumented youths make visible their conditions and their resistance.

Scholars have written about the ways that DACA, while offering important protections for undocumented youth, created other kinds of problems that kept DACA recipients, especially during the transition from adolescence to adulthood, structurally bound in the same kinds of low-wage jobs available to their undocumented parents.[8] This realization created a shift in the immigration movement away from fairly uncritical mobilizations for DACA to make visible the ways DACA divided "deserving" and "disposable" immigrants. Enacted as an executive order by President Barack Obama in 2012, DACA offered a renewable two-year period of deferred action to the undocumented minors who satisfied the program's requirements in terms of age, education or military service, and criminal record. It distinctly targeted these individuals but only for those who were considered innocent, moral (having no criminal record), and educated, in order to grant them temporary support. Many Korean American community groups pursued a comprehensive immigration reform for all the marginalized and organized the previously uninvolved undocumented Korean immigrant youths, moving them to political action while supporting them with DACA applications and related resources.[9] This also created a movement away from more patriotic and optimistic views of the nation open to and supportive of all immigrants toward stronger demands for structural change and immigration "justice" rather than immigration "rights."[10]

METHODOLOGY

This chapter draws on my multi-sited and community-based partici-patory research from 2013 to 2020. I conducted this research in Los Angeles, Chicago, New York, and Annandale, Virginia, where large Korean immigrant communities are located. In each area I worked closely with Korean American organizations, including the Korean Resource Center, the Korean American Resource and Cultural Center (now HANA Center), the MinKwon Center for Community Action, and the National Korean American Service & Education Consortium. By working, cooking, and living together with young undocumented Korean activists, I was able to gain a deeper understanding of their life experiences. As time went by, my responsibility and roles in their activism increased as well. I worked as a campaign assistant, summer youth program facilitator, and media contact and translator for Korean American and Korean media outlets. By contributing to their activ-ism with my ability as a native Korean speaker and my formal experi-ences organizing undocumented migrant workers back in Korea, I was able to participate in and contribute to the community I was research-ing. Although I was called a "doctoral student from Illinois" at the beginning of my fieldwork, at some point I became more often called a "Korean–Korean sister," a "supporter of undocumented Koreans," and later a "fellow activist." All the specific cases in my research are based on the ethnographic data that I gathered by working with and interviewing my research participants. With the consent and support of my research interlocutors, I conducted 122 interviews, including those with undocumented Korean youth activists, their parents, com-munity organizers, and non-Korean undocumented immigrant activ-ists. I also took field notes on the participant observation I conducted at rallies, campaigns, community reach-outs, family gatherings, work-places, and casual gatherings and analyzed my ethnographic data gathered from the field notes and interviews. The names of my research collaborators used here are pseudonyms, except for Ju Hong, who has been featured by multiple national media outlets and wanted to be identified by name.

It is noteworthy that all the data collection was possible because of the generous help I received from my research interlocutors, who did not hesitate to share their experiences and struggles with me. Our con-versations often were accented with tears, sighs, and silence due to the unending burden of their lives. In spite of all the emotional challenges of looking back on the painful moments and struggles they had experienced, they chose to join my research because they believed that the voices of undocumented Korean immigrants should be recorded and heard in public. This chapter was structured, analyzed, and written with the hope that their challenges and stories will become more visible.

EDUCATION AS THE KEY TO REDEMPTION AMONG THE UNDOCUMENTED KOREANS IN THE PRE-DACA PERIOD

The undocumented Korean youths who had their teen-hood long before DACA was announced in 2012 said they were encouraged to believe in the promise of education as the key to resolve their liminal status during the time they spent in their K–12 education. I found three commonalities in their narratives that shaped their educational aspirations: their desire to repay their parents' devotion and sacrifice through educational attainment; the transnational Korean state ideology of meritocracy in combination with the Korean American community's belief in the model minority trope; and the US policies and laws that sent the message that only educated and moral undocumented youths would be protected by the state. Overall, the youths were consistently expected to be well educated and moral, by not committing any criminal act, so that they could contribute to their own, their family's, and the state's future.

Jinhee's story, which opened this chapter, speaks to the pressures to maintain the behaviors of respectability aligned with Korean meritocracy and the US imposition of Asian American representations of success. Kyungeun, the other research interlocuter from Pasadena, California, also shared a story akin to Jinhee's. She was born in Inch'ŏn, South Korea, in 1990 and came to the United States after her family went bankrupt during the 1997 Asian financial crisis. This crisis, shaped by global capitalism, caused the collapse of the middle and middle-lower classes and led to an increase in family separations, suicides, and homelessness in South Korea. For some families, like Kyungeun's, leaving South Korea was an inevitable choice to survive. They headed to the United States, where Kyungeun's uncle lived in Koreatown, Los Angeles, chasing a new hope. While working under the table day and night at a restaurant, gas station, and liquor shop without days off, her parents hired a lawyer to obtain green cards for the family. It was only when the lawyer disappeared, seven years later, that her parents realized that they had been scammed. Kyungeun was in the ninth grade when her parents informed her that she was undocumented. While she was frustrated about what it meant, she pushed herself to study hard as a way to repay her parents' sacrifice and fix her family's legal status. The issue of education was deeply intertwined with how the undocumented Korean American youth thought about not only her own future but also her families' dream for tomorrow.

Meanwhile, the undocumented Korean youths' hope for education was also affected by the transnational Korean state's ideology of meritocracy shared by their parents and the ethnic community. Yoomee, an undocumented Korean youth from New Jersey, said: "Elderly Koreans in the Korean community often said, 'There will be a good day in the future as long as you believe *hamyŏn toenda* [you can do it] and work hard.' . . . Growing up in the Korean community, I knew how the folks in the community degraded 'the illegals,' comparing them to Korean Americans, 'the good immigrants.' I knew I was undocumented, so there was a certain pressure that I should do my best at school so that I could be free from the 'illegals, the lazy and irresponsible cheaters.' I tried my best to fit the Korean American phenotype."

As many scholars have noted, contemporary immigrants are not the uprooted.[11] Instead, the newcomers traverse the borders while sustaining their connection with their home country that includes its culture, history, and social norms (Levitt and Jaworsky 2007). After the Korean War in the 1950s, South Korea was in ruins. Over decades its rapid recovery from the war and economic growth rendered a sense of pride, confidence, and most important, belief in meritocracy—that anyone is able to acquire better economic status and power through education and hard work. Young people were encouraged to adopt the transnational Korean state's ideology of meritocracy and hardworking "good" immigrants, but this ideology was also reinforced by the tenets of the model minority myth. Understanding the narratives of the undocumented Korean youths in relation to their transnational connectivity with the sociohistorical background of South Korea is important as it helps us to challenge the monolithic discourse applied to Asian Americans' educational experience. By emphasizing this transnational connection, researchers can not only avoid reproducing the exaggerated perception of the dominant racial discourse, but they can also provide a more comprehensive explanation of the educational aspirations of Asian Americans.[12]

US law and immigration policy also sent the message that only the educated and those considered "moral" would be protected. For instance, the 1982 decision in *Plyler v. Doe*, which guaranteed K–12 education for undocumented children regardless of their legal status, aimed to educate children in consideration of their becoming possible future US citizens.[13] Judge William J. Brennan Jr. stated, for example: "Today, education is perhaps the most important function of state and local governments. . . . It is required in the performance of our most basic public responsibilities, even service in the armed forces. It is the very foundation of good citizenship. . . . By denying these children [of the undocumented aliens] a basic education, we deny them the ability to live within the structure of our civic institutions, and foreclose any realistic possibility that they will contribute in even the smallest way to the progress of our Nation."

The value of education for undocumented children and youths in the United States was defined in terms of its utility for the state. As shown in Brennan's statement, along with their right to be educated was the expectation that they would contribute to the United States if they became citizens in the future. Likewise, there was similar value placed on education in the DREAM Act, which was introduced in 2001 to provide permanent residency for certain categories of undocumented immigrant youth and later became the model for DACA. Senator Dick Durbin, cosponsor of the DREAM Act, stated before the Senate Judiciary Subcommittee on Immigration, Refugees, and Border Security in 2011: "Thousands of immigrant students in the United States were brought to the United States as children. It was not their decision to come to this country, but they grew up here pledging allegiance to our flag and singing our national anthem. They are Americans in their hearts. The DREAM Act would give these young people a chance to earn legal status if they have good moral character and go to college or serve in the military. The DREAM Act would make America a *stronger country* by giving these talented immigrants the chance to fulfill their potential."

While appealing to popular sentiment about the citizenship worthiness, Senator Durbin's speech also created a divide between undocumented youths who could become ideal youth-citizens and those who could not, and in doing so, it situated undocumented youths within normative political state ideology. In this regard the DREAM Act can be understood as a smart mechanism aimed at selectively including the undocumented immigrants as long as they are young, educated, and moral. It reflects that the value the DREAM Act embraces is aligned with neoliberal ideology that seeks to bolster "greater efficiency, productivity, and accountability in public education."[14] This characteristic of the DREAM Act was inherited by DACA and was institutionalized more exquisitely once the executive order was enacted.

In sum, although the educational aspirations of undocumented Korean youths came from different sources, they converged on the same goals: they were encouraged to believe education would guarantee a stable future with state inclusion. However, they started to see the limits of the redemptive value of education and their ability to access this promise of future state acceptance. As indicated earlier, my research interlocutors in this study had spent their adolescence in the United States and turned nineteen years old long before DACA was established in 2012. Without a social security number, work permit, and driver's license, they could not freely move, work, or plan for their postgraduate life. They recognized that they were not able to apply for in-state tuition fees, government scholarships, or loans in order to enter higher education. For the many who were already experiencing financial stress in their households, the difficulty in accessing the next step made them less motivated or even caused them to give up. They began to fully realize that their liminal legal status was not going to be solved by their educational pursuits.[15] Activism became a mode for some young people to channel their frustration.

THE EXPANSION OF ACTIVISM AND EDUCATION FOR LIBERATION

Through activism undocumented Korean youths found a different kind of value in education as a tool for critical action and liberation. They had formally aspired to embrace the neoliberal value of education, but once they became involved in activism, they engaged the progressive knowledge created and practiced by various activists from other marginalized groups. It brought them a sense of education as liberatory practice, one that Paulo Freire discusses as a humanizing practice for the oppressed that raises consciousness and transforms social structures.[16] The undocumented Korean youths also shared the critical knowledge and analysis they had learned through their activism with their fellow undocumented youths and Asian American communities. Their efforts to envision a new future for social and racial justice through their activism occurred in three distinct waves: before, during, and after DACA.

The first wave of Korean undocumented youth activism occurred in Los Angeles with the Korean American Students in Solidarity (KASS).[17] Consisting of undocumented Korean youths, the KASS worked to obtain in-state tuition and federal financial aid coverage for undocumented students. California Assembly Bill 540 was passed in 2001 to provide access to in-state tuition rates for undocumented students at California's public colleges and universities. Even up to the early 2010s, however, the administrative staff in higher education as well as teachers and counselors in secondary education were often unaware of this bill. They did not adequately communicate the assistance available to undocumented students or tell them about their ability to enroll in universities. As a result, some undocumented students abandoned their plans for attending college. Activists took up the challenge to raise awareness. Janghoon, from KASS, was one of them. He said: "Some undocumented Koreans were rejected by college and reached out to us. They were afraid of even talking to the college officer in person due to their legal status. There was no DACA yet, so it was not a delusion. We helped them out. We visited the administrative offices explaining about AB450, and then students finally got admissions. We felt achievement from helping the other undocumented students. The more we learned about their struggles and advocated that they shouldn't be discriminated against in higher education, the more we realized our activism mattered. We continued to fight against institutional restrictions, and it expanded our activism." KASS tirelessly continued to raise awareness about AB 540. According to one member, KASS made more than one hundred visits to educational institutions in Southern California over several years around 2010 and helped their peers gain access to higher education.

Some undocumented Korean college students also fought against tuition increases, broadening their advocacy for educational access. In the fall of 2009 the University of California system voted to increase student tuition by 32 percent, to a total of $10,000 per year per undergraduate student. This tuition hike created hardships for many and was especially difficult for undocumented students. Through the practice of petition drives, rallies, sit-ins, and civil disobedience, the youth activists asked the public universities to provide more inclusive accessibility and financial resources to undocumented students. They discussed fundamental questions about the broad value of education, such as: "Who is to be protected and cared for in higher education?" "Who belongs and who speaks in universities?" and "Whose university is it?" In doing so, they framed the conversation about the ideals of public higher education at a time when universities were rapidly becoming corporatized and privatized. They were articulating the values of public education by reminding the greater community of the importance of maintaining inclusive and democratic spaces for all students.

Along with KASS the DREAM Act played a huge role in expanding the undocumented Korean immigrants' activism. As discussed earlier, the DREAM Act was a limited type of immigration reform for undocumented persons because of its selective permission and approval guidelines. Despite its shortcomings, however, many activists considered it to be the most feasible goal to achieve legal status at the time. They hoped to move forward from it to address comprehensive immigration reform.

For undocumented Korean youths, organizing around the DREAM Act shifted them from pursuing individual educational goals to developing a social and political consciousness. Several key undocumented Korean youths became highly visible in calling attention to the racialized discourse that overgeneralized the undocumented immigrants as Latinx and made invisible the undocumented Asian immigrants. For instance, Ju Hong, who later became well-known for heckling President Barack Obama to stop the mass deportation in 2013, came out publicly to disclose his legal status through a YouTube video in 2009. In the video, titled "Korean Student Shares a Secret," he said: "Today I'm taking a risk because I'm going to tell you something I don't normally tell other people. I'm an undocumented immigrant. Many people don't think that there are any Korean undocumented people. Actually, there are about 230,000 undocumented Korean people living in the United States. We are the seventh largest group of undocumented immigrants. . . . Some of you may think that I should not talk about this issue. Maybe you think I should keep silent because I'm bringing shame to the Korean American community. But I can't be silent anymore. I need your help. I need your voices, your leadership, and your advocacy. So please, don't be ashamed to talk about this issue.[18]

For Ju Hong what critical race theorists Daniel Solórzano and Tara J. Yosso (2002) call "counter-stories" served as methodological and pedagogical tools to meaningfully challenge racism and discrimination. As he urged the Korean American community to support the DREAM Act, he recognized how his undocumented status put him at risk. It was before the DACA program was implemented; thus, making his full name, personal information, and face public through online video could bring trouble not only to himself but also to his mother and older sister, who were also undocumented. Despite this threat, Ju Hong continued his testimony, challenging the mono-vocal and master narratives that created and reproduced the criminalization and racialization of the undocumented immigrants. His testimony pushed against racism in his community and the exclusions of immigration policy, showing the power of such counter-narratives. In doing so, he demonstrated his solidarity with others affected by racism and other forms of oppression.

The undocumented Korean activists' attempts to dismantle the racialized and exclusionary immigration policy continued through various actions, ranging from educational events to speeches at press conferences, rallies, and protests outside of governmental buildings. In a 2010 press conference in New York City, undocumented Korean youth activists gave a speech representing the voices of undocumented Asian immigrants in solidarity with undocumented Latinx activists. Also, at a May Day rally in Chicago, undocumented Korean youths and their allies played Korean *poongmul* drums and urged the government to respect working-class immigrant rights. In this process they met with day laborers, domestic workers, senior Asian American activists, undocumented Latinx activists, and African American community organizers, which inspired undocumented Korean youths to develop a critical analysis of racism and forge multiracial alliances. These connections provided a different kind of education for the undocumented Korean youth activists, including Booyoung, from the Midwest, who participated in the activism in the early 2010s. She said: "It was an eye-opening experience. Through the activism I met with the activists from other generations with different backgrounds. It was like I was reading a new history textbook about the land I lived in. Nobody taught me things like that until I went to high school. It was only when I became an activist that I began to understand the critical issues from the structure and history of the US society. My shame and anxiety [as an undocumented youth] disappeared, and I felt unafraid. I wanted to help the others to be out of the shadows and feel the liberation too." Through mutual engagement with other activists, youth activists like Booyoung became aware they were not fully protected by their formal education. By learning about the civil rights, Black Power, and Asian American Movements, they gained critical perspectives on social systems—and found value in an education that enabled them to pursue a liberatory and progressive future.

In 2012 then president Barack Obama announced DACA as an executive order. DACA had similar components to the DREAM Act in that it also aimed to fulfill the state's needs to maintain productivity and efficiency, but DACA provided a renewable work permit, social security number, and exemption from deportation, which motivated more undocumented Korean youths to join the activism without fear of deportation. The Korean American organizations that had organized the community since the 1980s actively played a pivotal role in providing resources and a safe space for the undocumented Korean DACA applicants in which they were able to share their concerns and hopes and get involved in the activism.[19] Undocumented Korean youth activists from the pre-DACA period became more invigorated in their activism through the influence of these new members. These young people's practice of liberatory activism and its expansion were evident during what was called DREAM Riders Across America conducted in 2013 and 2015 and the Undocu Black-AAPI Action in 2017.

Inspired by the Freedom Riders of 1961, the undocumented Korean youth activists organized DREAM Riders Across America 2013. The purpose of the road trip campaign was to raise awareness about undocumented Asian immigrants in solidarity with Vietnamese and Filipino youths and to celebrate the first anniversary of DACA. I participated in this effort as a campaign assistant, translator, and media contact. We drove from the nation's capital to cities throughout Virginia, North Carolina, Georgia, Louisiana, and Texas. We held a presentation at the White House for Asian American summer interns, met with Arne Duncan, secretary of education, and had a workshop with Freedom University, an underground Georgia institution providing undocumented young people with tuition-free college courses.[20] We also reached out to various immigrant, labor, and faith communities and communities of color. Through this process the youth activists raised their voices to advocate for undocumented youth ineligible for DACA, calling attention to undocumented high school dropouts, undocumented people in their early thirties just over DACA's age limit, and the overall invisibility of undocumented Asian immigrants.

In 2015 undocumented Korean youth activists organized the second national road trip campaign—consisting of Vietnamese, Thai, Latinx, and Black youth in twelve different cities in nine states—to illustrate how racialized illegality had shaped similar yet unique struggles among different racial groups. They held community meetings with youth members of the Southeast Asian Coalition in Charlotte, North Carolina; they facilitated a workshop with Vietnamese youths in New Orleans about post-Katrina struggles; and they met with social justice activists in Selma, Alabama, to discuss the history of race and illegality. These efforts, seeking the practice and expansion of the liberatory value of activism, formed a multiracial and intersectional solidarity in connection with the contemporary injustice issues.

The third case of political and educational collaboration was called the "Undocu Black-AAPI Action," held in Washington, DC, in 2017. Undocumented Korean youth activists coordinated the workshop with Black youths from Southern Africa and Central America to create radical spaces for racial dialogue. Its purpose was to show the collective response to DACA's official cancellation and reduction of Temporary Protected Status (TPS) to ask Congress to pass a new act protecting undocumented immigrants. About 110 members gathered to discuss the significance of bringing non-Latinx undocumented groups' struggles into the public eye. They examined how Asians and Blacks have been manipulated to perpetuate racism, which confirmed their understanding of structural racism. They also discussed the interracial conflicts between Asians and Blacks during the 1992 Los Angeles uprising and the interracial solidarity in initiatives such as the Black Lives Matter movement. In doing so, they forged solidarity based on their minoritized identities, continuing the history of multiracial movements in this current political moment.

The examples I have introduced here reveal how undocumented Korean immigrant activists have continued and broadened their activism since the 2000s. Their activism, motivated by a sense of betrayal surrounding their education, energized their progressive voice. As

FIGURE 4.1. Asian American and Black activists rally to call for a clean Dream Act and a permanent solution for Temporary Protected Status holders in Washington, DC, on December 7, 2017. Photo by the National Korean American Service & Education Consortium.

critical education theorists Leigh Patel and Rocío Sánchez Ares have pointed out, youth resistance has progressive and liberatory aspects as a process of negotiating power, identity, and inclusion that moves social justice forward.[21] Through their relentless efforts and direct engagement with other marginalized groups fighting for racial, economic, and political justice, undocumented Korean youth activists gained knowledge and perspectives to interpret their liminal legal status and precarious living conditions within an oppressive social system. They found a sense of liberation in activism and dreamed of a new future with hope.

RETURN OF DANGER, THE PERILS OF FUTURELESSNESS

Herein I have shared examples of how undocumented Korean immigrants engaged in activism and found liberation in it. Even as they found purpose and joy in their struggles for justice, they also faced moments of despair. As time went by, they often felt a sense of fatigue as their lives were continuously destabilized over fluctuations in US immigration policy. In particular, the rise in explicit anti-immigration speeches during the 2016 presidential election campaign and the waning of DACA made them feel vulnerable about their futures once again. This fatigue and disappointment were found especially among the activists who had been involved in the movement for a long time, eight to ten years or longer. While they were still passionate to continue their social justice work for other community members, they encountered many complicated feelings, sometimes even a feeling of tragedy because the long fight seems never to fundamentally improve the situation. Sangha, from Southern California, shared his concerns: "My older sister was part of the DREAM Act activism in the late 2000s. She was quite passionate but then was disappointed because it [the DREAM Act] never came true. When DACA was initiated, we felt hopeful, thinking it would lead to better policies. I joined the activism with passion, and like you know, I've been very active in it for five years. But look, DACA could be canceled at any moment. . . . I'm sick of putting my life at the mercy of another. Once I believed I could still decide my fate but no more. I'm not even one of their favorable innocent 'children' anymore. I'm getting older."

As queer theorist Lee Edelman has noted, society is organized by the belief in the middle-class logic of reproductive temporality.[22] It defines the appropriate age one should be and the steps one should take to be "normal," such as when an individual is supposed to be educated, graduate, secure a job, start a family, give birth to their children, and so on. Undocumented youths who cannot follow these social conventions because of their restricted legal status often feel their lives are being denied in spite of their desire to observe traditional social norms. The gap becomes more visible as they grow older. While their peer group moves forward and follows the appropriate passage into adulthood and citizenship ruled by the heteronormative regime, young undocumented immigrants are still referred to as "innocent children" in the political discourse. They have aged out of the DACA-created category of "safety" but are required to stay young forever in exchange for the state's benevolent relief of their legal status.

Like Sangha, many of my research interlocutors, who had been dedicated to activism for a long time, sometimes felt trapped. Their sentiments echoed Jinhee's description, early in this chapter, of being stuck in the undocumented Korean box and her predicament of being caged.

FIGURE 4.2. Undocumented Korean immigrant youth activists and allies protest the Trump administration's cancellation of the Deferred Action for Childhood Arrivals (DACA) program in Washington, DC, on September 7, 2017. Photo by the National Korean American Service & Education Consortium.

The sense of futurelessness loomed large in their minds. They had believed in the liberatory value of activism, but given the unchanging immigration system, they felt their future was in danger once again. They continued to fight from where they were, though, in spite of this challenging situation. Sangha stressed: "I fight because I don't want the next generation to deal with this pain that I have gone through. I know the previous generations who fought for the abolition of slavery, women's rights, civil rights movement, and worker and queer rights probably were hurt and exhausted over and over by the cruel system. It can't be changed all at once. But they didn't give it up, and because of their efforts I now can live in a bit better world than the one they lived in. I won't stop here. I will keep on fighting. I keep organizing, echoing what they did for all the marginalized."

The problems that undocumented Korean activists have criticized are evident everywhere. We are witnessing some disturbing changes in education. Public higher education is being ever more rapidly privatized and neoliberalized, with noticeable budget cuts and restrictions.

Universities are praising diversity while being less involved in critical debates over structural race, class, and immigration status barriers to higher education. Hate speech targeting people of color and anti-immigration rhetoric are growing both on and off campuses. At this critical moment the voices of undocumented Korean activists remind us that we must reject the imposition of a system that pressures us to accept gains for the so-called deserving at the expense of the so-called disposable. The immigrant justice movement itself is in a moment of transformation, making greater demands for justice for all outside the objective of formal citizenship and creating new ways of living in community and collectively resisting inequalities. The ideas developing today build on the struggles and experiences articulated by pre-DACA youths, including those in my study, who came to realize that the provisions made by a policy that distinguished between the deserving and the disposable ended up having many costs, not only for those who fell outside of the moral categories of DACA but also for those who gained the "right" education and exhibited the "right" behavior, only to be timed out of their DACA-created benefits.

Moreover, DACA eligible or not, undocumented Korean youth activists today are confronted with the risk of deportation. When DACA was rescinded in 2017, they felt their futures were threatened once again. However, they have been continuing their activism. On September 12, 2019, they spoke at the Democratic Presidential Debate in Texas, requesting collective support for the upcoming Supreme Court's oral hearing on the legality of DACA termination. Wearing T-shirts that read, "Defend DACA, Abolish ICE, Citizenship for All," designed by a member of the DREAM Riders Across America 2015, they shouted out, asking the audience to fix the broken immigration system. In addition, in November 2019 they organized the "Home Is Here: March for DACA & TPS" campaign and marched 230 miles over eighteen days to the Supreme Court in solidarity with multiracial organizations of immigrants, laborer, students, and faith groups. And amid the global COVID-19 pandemic, they continue to fight against the white supremacist hegemony that racializes and pathologizes Asian immigrants while they support the people at risk through mutual aid fundraising. As reflected in the catchphrase "Citizenship for All" that has been promoted by the undocumented Korean activists since 2017, now their fight aims to bring human equality to all the marginalized people. They continue to urge people to pay attention to the uneven accessibility to education, health care, housing, and food security and to racism, which intersects with class, gender, sexuality, religion, dis/ability, and legal status.

Critical education theorist Henry Giroux noted that we can begin to rethink and reform an oppressive system by asking questions about the forms of resistance already employed by the young.[23] What should we do in solidarity after we learn about the struggles and hopes of the undocumented Korean immigrants? In the shadow of racism and uneven globalization, they remind scholars, students, and community members that the purpose of education is to advance justice.

As Paulo Freire pointed out in 1970, education cannot be divorced from politics. In particular, education has been a foundational theme in the field of Asian American studies. Ethnic studies was born fifty years ago by a protest movement in higher education that was part of a larger social movement to change US society's power structure and the racialized culture of its institutions and international relations. Through their political reworking of education, the young activists for ethnic studies were eager to achieve self-determination and to serve the people.[24] The struggles and activism of the undocumented Korean youths not only furthers the legacy of the value of education in Asian American studies but also helps us reimagine the world we want to live in and the type of education we should engage in.

To return to numbers I gave at the beginning of this chapter, there are 1.5 million undocumented Asian immigrants, including 192,000 undocumented Korean immigrants, in the United States. Undocumented Asian immigrants might be invisible to you, but they are everywhere. They might be your neighbors, your coworkers, your students, or your teachers. The future of undocumented immigrants is just one part of how our society reflects its history of settler colonialism and continues to practice the lesson learned from the birth of Asian American studies. I suggest that we can start the conversation for these changes in solidarity with the undocumented immigrant youth today.

NOTES

1 Tracy Lachica Buenavista, Uma M. Jayakumar, and Kimberly Misa-
   Escalante, "Contextualizing Asian American Education through Critical
   Race Theory: An Example of US Pilipino College Student Experiences,"
   New Directions for Institutional Research 142 (Summer 2009): 69–81.

2 Richard Shaull, foreword, in *Pedagogy of the Oppressed*, by Paulo Freire (New York: Continuum, 1970).

3 "State-Level Unauthorized Population and Eligible-to-Naturalize Estimates," Center for Migration Studies, http://data.cmsny.org, accessed March 1, 2019.

4 Marc R. Rosenblum and Ariel G. Ruiz Soto, "An Analysis of Unauthorized Immigrants in the United States by Country and Region of Birth," Migration Policy Institute, August 2015.

5 Rosenblum and Ruiz Soto, "Analysis of Unauthorized Immigrant in the United States."

6 Karthick Ramakrishnan and Sono Shah, "One Out of Every Seven Asian Immigrants Is Undocumented," AAPI Data, September 8, 2017, http://aapidata.com/blog/asian-undoc-1in7.

7 Soo Mee Kim and Aggie J. Yellow Horse, "Undocumented Asians, Left in the Shadows," *Contexts* 17, no. 4 (December 2018): 70–71.

8 Roberto G. Gonzales, *Lives in Limbo: Undocumented and Coming of Age in America* (Berkeley: University of California Press, 2016).

9 Ga Young Chung, "At the Crossroads of Change: Deferred Action for Childhood Arrivals, Undocumented Korean Americans' Political Participation, and Upcoming Challenges," *Asian American Policy Review* 27 (2016–17): 1–10.

10 Elizabeth Hanna Rubio, "We Need to Redefine What We Mean by Winning: NAKASEC's Immigrant Justice Activism and Thinking Citizenship Otherwise," *Amerasia Journal* 45, no. 2 (October 2019): 1–16.

11 Floya Anthias, "Transnational Mobilities, Migration Research and Intersectionality," *Nordic Journal of Migration Research* 2, no. 2 (2012): 102–10; Peggy Levitt, "Transnational Migration: Taking Stock and Future Directions," *Global Networks* 1, no. 3 (2001): 195–216; Nina Glick Schiller, Linda Basch, and Cristina Szanton Blanc, "From Immigrant to Transmigrant: Theorizing Transnational Migration," *Anthropological Quarterly* 68, no. 1 (1995): 48–63.

12 Buenavista, Jayakumar, and Misa-Escalante, "Contextualizing Asian American Education," 70.

13 Plyer v. Doe, 457 US 202 (1982).

14 Adalberto Aguirre and Jennifer K. Simmers, "The DREAM Act and Neoliberal Practice: Retrofitting Hispanic Immigrant Youth in US Society," *Social Justice* 38, no. 3 (2012): 3–16.

15 Gonzalez, *Lives in Limbo*.

16 Paulo Freire, *Pedagogy of the Oppressed* (New York: Continuum, 1970).

17 I use a pseudonym for the name of this group.

18 Ju Hong, "Korean Student Shares a Secret," YouTube video, November 10, 2009, https://www.youtube.com/watch?v=L5G5F5_CrZQ.

19 Chung, "At the Crossroads of Change," 1–10.

20 On Freedom University, see https://freedom-university.org.

21 Lisa Leigh Patel and Rocío Sánchez Ares, "The Politics of Coming Out Undocumented," in *Youth Resistance Research and Theories of Change*, ed. Eve Tuck and K. Wayne Yang, 151–64 (New York: Routledge, 2013).

22 Lee Edelman, *No Future: Queer Theory and the Death Drive* (Durham, NC: Duke University Press, 2004).

23 Henry Giroux, "Literacy and the Pedagogy of Voice and Political Empowerment," *Educational Theory* 38, no. 1 (1988): 61–75.

24 Karen Umemoto, "'On Strike!' San Francisco State College Strike, 1968–69: The Role of Asian American Students," *Amerasia Journal* 15, no. 1 (1989): 3–41.

CHAPTER 5

DRIVERS ON THE FRONT LINES

The New York Taxi Workers Alliance, Neoliberalism, and
Global Pandemic—An Interview with Javaid Tariq

DIANE C. FUJINO

THE NEW YORK TAXI WORKERS ALLIANCE (NYTWA) WAS
founded in January 1998 to struggle for taxi drivers, 60 percent of whom
were South Asian—primarily Indian, Pakistani, and Bangledishi—
and more than 90 percent were immigrants. The NYTWA emerged
from the Lease Drivers Coalition (LDC), established in 1992 as the
first workers project of the Committee Against Anti-Asian Violence
(CAAAV) to organize against the violence and threats of violence
faced daily by taxi drivers. CAAAV itself formed in response to the
most widely known case at that time of anti-Asian violence, the Vincent Chin case, and to the widespread police violence in New York City.
Together, the NYTWA and the LDC have done extraordinary organizing across their thirty-year history. In August 1997 cabdrivers and
the LDC organized the first massive motorcade of taxi drivers to protest the harsh and dangerous working conditions of taxi drivers. In
May 1998 the newly formed NYTWA organized a historic one-day
strike of twelve thousand taxi drivers in response to a Mayor Giuliani's
proposed seventeen-point plan to the Taxi and Limousine Commission that would dramatically increase fines for drivers, turn minor
violations into suspension of licenses, and in other ways push drivers
out of work. Bhairavi Desai noted that at the time India and Pakistan,
where the majority of drivers were from, were on the brink of nuclear
conflict. The NYTWA showed the possibilities of united work across

FIGURE 5.1. Javaid Tariq is a cofounder and senior staff member of New York Taxi Workers Alliance and treasurer of the National Taxi Workers Alliance. Over the years he has organized numerous successful strikes, campaigns, and actions to promote economic and social justice for taxi drivers, a workforce that is 94 percent immigrant and primarily people of color. Photo courtesy of Javaid Tariq.

significant differences. When Uber and Lyft drivers flooded the market, rather than treating them as competition, the NYTWA organized with them as well, gaining important victories such as a recognition of app-based drivers, not as independent contractors but as employees entitled to worker rights and benefits. Since the coronavirus pandemic in early 2020, the NYTWA organizers have been working tirelessly to supply information, get full unemployment benefits, and provide other crucial resources to drivers. As frontline workers, drivers are at particular risk. The NYTWA reported that in the first three months of the pandemic, sixty-two drivers died of COVID-19 and the organization received ten thousand calls or emails from member-drivers.[1]

Javaid Tariq, Bhairavi Desai, and Biju Mathew, along with others who have since left, are founding members of the New York Taxi Workers Alliance. Tariq, while a student activist in college in Pakistan, fled his country in 1978, following the military coup to overthrow Z. A. Bhutto. He traveled to Germany, where he studied Marxism and became a DJ influenced by the music of Bob Marley, and immigrated to the United States in 1990. With an interest in photojournalism and wanting to document the conditions of South Asian drivers, he became a taxi driver himself in 1994. By 1996 he was organizing cabdrivers with Desai and Mathew.[2]

DIANE FUJINO: The New York Taxi Workers Alliance was established in the 1998 to organize taxi drivers in a period of global restructuring and deindustrialization. In the recent period the huge influx of app-based, for-hire drivers has dramatically impacted the taxi industry. How has the rise of neoliberalism and the gig economy changed the taxi industry and also created other kinds of problems for Uber and Lyft drivers, including the rising and then falling prices of taxi medallions and the suicides of drivers?

JAVAID TARIQ: It is a hardship. The gig economy is neoliberalism on steroids. This economy is based on a business model that is unsustainable and entirely dependent upon destroying the life of drivers. It is based on the situation after 2008 of rising unemployment, a model of part-time work, and lowering income. The drivers end up with no

benefits and not enough money to put food on their table.
So workers are forced to work two or three jobs. This
model is not working.

We started out working with Yellow Cab drivers and
FHV (for-hire vehicle) drivers. When Uber and Lyft started,
they were making good money. But as more and more cars
entered the market, their income was reduced. Before,
there were only 13,600 Yellow Cabs around, and now
there are about 120,000 Uber and Lyft cars. So Uber
drivers and Yellow Cab drivers were becoming the enemy
of each of other. But in time Uber drivers were not making
much money either. We were trying to figure out how we
can stop this exploitation. You can only win that fight
when you unify the drivers. That's what we started doing
in 2008.

"Uber starves the Uber driver to starve the Yellow Cab
driver," our executive director Bhairavi Desai says. The
Uber business model is based fundamentally on the
part-time-ization of work, where the sub-minimum rates
that Uber pays its drivers makes consumers happy but
ensures that the only drivers who can sustain driving Uber
are those who do it for additional or part-time income. As
Uber drives the wages down for its drivers, it undercuts
the Yellow Taxi drivers' business. In this model nobody can
make a full-time living—neither the full-time Uber driver
nor the Yellow Taxi driver. The only way forward then is
that all drivers must be unified under one union that has a
vision for a just and sustainable system of urban transportation. NYTWA built a Unity Platform in 2017–18 that
brought Uber/Lyft and Yellow Taxi drivers together to
fight on both fronts. NYTWA is probably the only union in
the United States and possibly in the world to have united
the traditional taxi sector drivers with the Uber and Lyft
drivers.

DF: The gig economy has indeed created horrendous hard-
ships for workers and has also made labor organizing
really challenging. Yet in 2018 the NYTWA won at least
two major victories. One was that the New York unemployment appeals board specified that drivers are employees,

not independent contractors, so Uber could no longer
bypass overtime and minimum wage protections.[3]

JT: There is a misunderstanding about minimum wage and
overtime protection. In that struggle we won that they can
no longer control us calling drivers contractors. The
drivers are employees. But we, in others ways, still don't
have any kind of protection. We had to fight separately
for minimum wages and overtime. So last year we fought
the minimum wage issue through the city council, and
they passed a law that Uber and Lyft drivers would earn a
minimum wage of $17.33 per hour after all expenses. But
then, to avoid paying that, Uber started blocking the
drivers from working longer hours. That's the way they
were playing games with the drivers.

So before, there was about 13,000 Yellow Cabs, 20,000
FHV cars, and 7,000 plain cabs, which was more or less
working. But as they kept adding more cars, drivers were
making less money, but the company was making the same
profit. So we wanted to put a cap on the number of cars.
When the number reached to around 120,000 cars in 2014,
we went to the city and introduced a bill to protect the cab
drivers. We had enough votes on the city council to win
that. But two weeks before the city council vote, Uber's
lobbyists came to New York and put $15 million into
advertisements on TV. They showed African American
faces on TV saying they could now get a ride when they
had previously been discriminated against. So we lost
that vote.

But a couple years ago we got the vote of the majority
of council members, and the city agreed that they would
limit the number of FHV vehicle licenses for Uber and Lyft
drivers. So that was a big victory for us. Our main principle is to not pit drivers against one another.

We see all drivers as workers trying to put food on their
table. How can we unify them together? That's the only
way that we can win some campaigns. On one hand, we
are fighting for the Uber drivers for their minimum wages
and fighting the state Department of Labor for unemployment insurance. On the other hand, we are fighting for

Yellow Cab drivers, who are around six thousand individuals who put their life savings into buying those medallions. In 2014 no one seemed to know where this industry was going. They were advertising to become medallion owners, and a lot of drivers bought those medallions at $850,000. At the same time, when 120,000 Uber/Lyft drivers came into the market, the price of medallions started falling. Yellow Cab drivers used to pick up a million passengers a day but now had less and less work. The taxi drivers who bought medallions got into $500,000 or $600,000 debt. By 2015 some medallion owners were up to $1 million in debt for their vehicles, and the banks were still charging them for that price, though the value of the medallions had gone down drastically. They were under so much stress and the suicides started happening. Around nine drivers committed suicide. In the 2008 financial crisis the government bailed out the banks. So we started this movement to organize a campaign for loan forgiveness for the individual medallion owners.[4]

DF: What you're describing is the intensified greed and profit making made possible under capitalism [JT: yes!]. In the 1990s worker centers started forming to address the restructuring of the economy and the problems of the union movement. The NYTWA emerges out of CAAAV. By contrast to traditional unions, worker centers tend to promote the leadership of ordinary workers to collectively organize on their own behalf, to engage in popular education, and also to view labor struggles as part of broader movements for social and racial justice. I'd like to hear about the NYTWA's model of leadership, especially developing the leadership of the workers themselves? And I know you used to be a taxi driver.

JT: I started driving a taxi in 1994, end of 1994. The NYTWA model is totally different from worker centers and traditional unions. We started from CAAAV [Committee Against Anti-Asian Violence; now CAAAV Organizing Asian Communities] in New York City. CAAAV had different projects. One was domestic workers with Ai-jen Poo. One is for housing with Helena Wong. Another was the

LDC [Lease Drivers Coalition], which Bhairavi Desai, who
is our leader, headed when she joined CAAAV in 1996.[5]
They started the LDC because at that time there was so
much police brutality happening against taxi drivers. It's
not just the police but also the Taxi and Limousine Commission. They have their own police, which has so much
power that they can, with very little violation, beat or
handcuff or harass taxi drivers. When any driver had
problems, they could come to CAAAV to get help. When
Bhairavi Desai started, she had some other visions.
CAAAV's office was on Third Street, between Avenues A
and B and near Houston Street, which was a big space for
shift change. Most of the workers there were South Asian,
especially Indians. At 5:00 p.m. they were changing their
shifts. When Bhairavi Desai went out to pick up some
dinner, she started talking to the drivers hanging out
there. She had her notebook with her and kept writing
everything down. She was listening and analyzing what
they said.[6]

That's how I met Bhairavi Desai. I had started driving a
taxi to do my photographic project about cab drivers' lives.
I was studying to be a photojournalist at the New School
in New York. I was reading stories about drivers getting
killed on the job, and most of them were South Asians,
mostly Pakistani. The drivers were half a world away from
their home and were working very hard to send money
back home. When they die, what kind of benefits do
they have? Their family hasn't anything. I couldn't just
take my camera and go talk to drivers. So I became a
taxi driver, and I'd have my camera with me. When I met
Bhairavi Desai, she gave me a flyer, and I went to the
meeting. That was the first time I met Ai-jen Poo and we
started working together and seeing each other in CAAAV.
We talked about that, about taxi drivers' rights. Meanwhile, I was learning through my own experience about
how dangerous and exploitative the job is. You work
twelve hours a day, very hard work. You are always in
danger. The taxi driver is eighty times more likely to be
robbed on the job, sixty times more likely to be killed on

the job.[7] They have no protection. Nobody was talking about that. So Biju Mathew, Bhairavi Desai, and I reached out, one by one, and it was to three hundred drivers. All of them were South Asian. At that time 60 to 70 percent of cab drivers were South Asian; the majority were Indian (mainly Punjabi), Pakistani, and Bangladeshi.[8] Our drivers were sick of all this exploitation. They organized a motorcade against Mayor Giuliani. He was cracking down on taxi drivers, against street vendors, against many workers. We were the first South Asian movement to get a motorcade against Giuliani from Fourteenth Street to City Hall. We did enormous outreach by flyering and talking one by one to the drivers. We were broadcasting our message through CB [citizens' band] radio in different languages, primarily in Urdu, Hindi, Punjabi, and Bangladeshi. We were expecting a rally of three to four hundred. But on that day in August 1997, over two thousand Yellow Cabs showed up for the motorcade!

It was big, and it was not only South Asians. People of color from many communities came because they heard that taxi drivers were having this protest motorcade against labor exploitation and police brutality and the harsh rules and regulations. These were everybody's problems. We had a very successful motorcade in 1997.

Our members voted that we should be separate from CAAAV and have our own organization. We have a very great respect for CAAAV. We still talk to them. But there were some political differences because we believed in mass membership. In 1998 we incorporated as the New York Taxi Workers Alliance. We didn't have any office space. We didn't have any funds. Thanks to the Brecht Forum, which said come into our office. We started with one table and one chair and a phone. Luckily, the Chinese Staff and Workers' Association was at the office there too. So we learned a lot from the Chinese staff about these activities happening at the Brecht Forum, and we were learning about Marxism.

Worker centers usually work for the community. They are solving community problems. We are a new kind of

model in the middle of worker centers and traditional
unions. Traditional unions are declining because these big
bosses sit in their offices and don't interact with the
members. Because they are automatically getting their
monthly dues, they don't have to go to the workers to
convince them to join the union. We have to work hard to
reach out to our members. We are 85 percent running our
organization with membership dues. Our model gives
workers the power of accountability. It gives the organizers
the responsibility to fight for the workers, for our members, because they are paying their membership dues. In
the beginning we were thinking of becoming a union but
decided against that.

Then in 1998 we had a historic strike in New York City,
where 95 percent of Yellow Cab drivers were out of work.
This was the first time since last century when the
people of New York coalesced because the Yellow Cab is a
symbol of New York. The Yellow Cab drivers are ambassadors of sorts for New York City. At the airports people
come from all over the world, and after the immigration
officer, they meet the cab driver. Cab drivers know everything about New York City. In the '98 strike people of color
stood with us. We have members from over one hundred
countries. We started this organization as South Asians,
but we cannot win alone. We are open for everybody, any
ethnicity. We became global.[9]

DF: And you organize Dominicans, Haitians, and others?

JT: The majority of South Asians are Bangladeshi, Pakistani,
Indian, Nepalese, Tibetan, Burmese, and Malaysian, and
Chinese too. Our members are also West Africans from
Ivory Coast, Burkina Faso, and even Senegal.

DF: I'm wondering what challenges you face in organizing
across differences of language, race, culture, religion.
Also, what kind of strengths you find in this diversity?

JT: Bhairavi Desai and Biju Mathew are from India. I'm from
Pakistan. I'm Muslim; Biju Mathew is Hindu; Bhairavi is
Christian. So while we started as South Asians, the drivers
were not united. Indians were on one side, Pakistani on
the other, Haitian drivers elsewhere. Before the 1998

strike we had this strategy. Our OC [Organizing Commit-
tee] members are drivers in the field. They talk to other
drivers. The OC members speak different languages—
Urdu, Punjabi, Bangladeshi, Nepalese, Arabic, West
African languages, French, Spanish, and Chinese—and so
they could talk to the different workers. We are not each
other's enemy. We have similar problems as cab drivers.
We talked to workers one on one to bring awareness to
drivers. It took years and years of work. We went out day
and night, whether hot or cold, we'd go to the airport and
talk to drivers one by one, give them a flyer or our newspaper that we started, *Shift Change*. In the newspaper we
included diverse faces and problems, not just those of
South Asians. At the Brecht Forum, in our one chair and
one table, we talked to the drivers. The majority of our OC
members voted to have a strike. They were very enthusiastic. They gave money to make flyers and spread them all
over New York City. As they were driving around, they put
flyers under the windshield wipers of cars. We told our
members, if you're a Pakistani driver stopped at a red light
and see a Pakistani driver on your right and an African
American driver on your left, talk to the African American
driver about the strike. Will you join the strike? That
strategy worked well.

That historic strike of 1998 built our power base. Today
we have twenty-four thousand members—Uber and Lyft,
Yellow Cabs, green cabs, liveries. Our principle is to unify
them all. We are clear that if you get money from the
company, like Uber, you won't stand with the workers.
To break the power of workers, companies start their own
company union to divide the workers.

After 9/11, with the rise in Islamophobia, we stood
strong against this new kind of racism. We have a lot of
Muslim drivers. It was also affecting South Asians because
some Americans don't know the difference between
Muslims and Sikhs. They only see the turban and the
beard. Cars were vandalized. People got assaulted.

DF: Javaid, I get a sense of the kind of strategies that NYTWA
uses. It's an industrial union model, organizing across all

workers across all skills levels. It's also about connecting with issues happening in the community around race, religion, racism, and not just narrow labor issues.

JT: Ninety-nine percent of cab drivers are immigrants. In their families maybe his wife is a domestic worker, his son a construction worker. So we think broadly about the labor issues. We have good relations with different organizations. We always stand in solidarity with them against racism and Islamophobia. We stood against Trump's Muslim ban, and 60-70 percent of our members are Muslim from Pakistan, Bangladesh, Egypt, Morocco, Sudan, Ivory Coast, Burkina Faso, and Senegal. We went to the JFK Airport strike in solidarity with our members against the Muslim Ban.

DF: Your ability to organize strikes in this day is incredible. It reminds me of the post–World War II moment in union organizing. I want to ask about influences on the NYTWA. You talked about what I'm calling industrial unionism. I'm not sure if your thinking is along lines of the IWW [International Workers of the World]. You also mentioned Marxism. What are the influences on the NYTWA? Do you see yourself as part of the Asian American Movement?

JT: Our founder is South Asian. But the taxi industry is not easy to organize. Yellow Cab drivers used to be unionized. But when the immigrants from India and Pakistan started coming to the United States in the mid-1970s and driving cabs, they didn't want to give them the benefits of unions and changed the whole system. They started them as lease drivers. As lease drivers, they started with negative money. They had to pay the lease up front, though they didn't know how much they'll make. They were not employees but were working on a commission basis, called dependent workers. They also had to pay three dollars every day or ninety dollars a month. They said the three dollars was for union dues, but there was no union. But it was going into the pockets of the union. So the unions sold out the rank and file. When we started talking to the drivers about organizing, they didn't trust us because the unions had sold them out. We are between worker centers and

traditional unions, a new labor movement. When we
started, taxi workers started as contractors. We were not
under the NLRB [National Labor Relations Board] and
received no benefits from that. We started ourselves, now
twenty-two years of struggle. Because we received our
money from our membership, this provides necessary
checks and balances. It gives us the responsibility to work
tirelessly. It's not just about protesting. We are doing the
persistent and tedious work of organizing because we want
to create change, to get better wages.

In time the NYTWA became a national TWA [Taxi
Workers Alliance] affiliated with the AFL-CIO. Traditionally, almost all AFL-CIO affiliates represent workers who
are classified as employees and are therefore entitled to a
"union" that will represent the employees in the collective
bargaining process and for other matters. But this does not
mean that to be a union of workers you necessarily have to
be covered under the NLRB or be a collective bargaining
agent. If you fight for workers' rights, every so often the
AFL-CIO recognizes this. Because of NYTWA's organizing
successes and because of the growing presence of independent contractors and contingent workers in the American
economy, the AFL-CIO recognized the need to bring in
new affiliates that don't fit their traditional model. That's
how we became one of the few unions not under NLRB.
We have chapters in Philadelphia, Austin, Maryland, San
Francisco, and other cities too.

We also work with the International Transport Workers'
Federation (ITF). In 2014 I went to the ILO, the International Labor Organization, in Geneva, Switzerland. What
model is Uber bringing? Uberization means sweatshop on
wheels. I spoke there: "Be careful of Uberization. It will
kill workers." I had meetings with taxi unions to plan how
to force the government to crack down on Uber. We had a
plan to organize the hundreds of drivers who are loyal to
the drivers' union, to block every exit of the highways on
a single day. It became big news. The French government
stopped Uber from working there. So we're also part of
international transportation organizing. In terms of

strategy the main thing is to establish the trust of drivers and to unify them. Now Uber, Yellow Cab, Green Cab, look to each other not as enemies but as working together.

DF: I want to turn to the current moment of pandemic. New York was the epicenter of the coronavirus. Then we had the Black Lives Matter protests, on top of neoliberalism already driving workers to ground. I see from your website that the NYTWA has been doing intensive organizing to respond to this moment. Can you speak to work you're doing and what this moment has been like for workers and for organizers?

JT: America has the biggest airports, where planes come from all over the world. Cab drivers are always on the front line. In America they don't take any precautions for COVID-19. Travelers are free to come out of the airport without any checks. Early in the pandemic, one driver in New York picked up a passenger from the airport. That passenger was coughing. The pandemic was on everyone's mind. The driver worried he might have COVID and quarantined in his home. But after one week he was getting sicker. He went to the hospital, and two days later he died. His wife and kids were also admitted to the hospital, but thank God, they were saved. I got the message from a member who told us his cousin died. It was alarming for us. There was no protection for the drivers. Yellow Cabs have a partition between the driver and passengers, but Uber has no partition. We started to alert all the drivers. We did e-blasts, phone calls—you need protection, gloves, hand sanitizer, masks. You're on the front lines.

We had to shut down our office because COVID cases were rising in New York. All our staff began working from home. In the first two to three months we got over ten thousand calls from members. Every two to three days another driver died. We got information from our members and found that sixty-two drivers had died from COVID. We asked the city for the number of drivers who died of COVID in New York City. They couldn't tell us. We started our own survey and worked with ACLU [American

Civil Liberties Union] California on this project. Bhairavi Desai wrote a thirty-page information guide not just for drivers but for every person. Every immigrant, every undocumented person, every worker, could get that link for the information guide. The city didn't provide that broad information, but you can see the guide on our website.[10] We got lists and started calling drivers to find out how they're doing. The government was afraid because 95 percent of drivers stopped driving. The Taxi and Limousine Commission started to give jobs to drivers and paid them seventeen dollars per hour to pick up food and deliver it to people who were stuck in their home. Drivers are heroes. They are essential workers. They help people to not die of hunger during the pandemic. Delivery workers, cab drivers, nurses, doctors, are all essential workers. Looking at the value of essential workers under capitalism, the big bosses cannot treat them as they did five years ago.

Many of our workers don't speak English, don't have internet. Our drivers turn to us for help. We're there helping them fight to get unemployment for Uber drivers and Yellow Cab drivers too. The applications in English are hard to understand, so our lawyers started helping. We put information on Facebook, sent out e-blasts with our lawyers showing picture by picture how to fill out the forms. The drivers started getting unemployment. But Uber wouldn't provide the earnings data to the Department of Labor. Workers are supposed to get $504 in unemployment, but they were getting only $182. We filed a lawsuit in federal court against the state Department of Labor and Governor Cuomo, and in two months we were able to get unemployment for the Uber/Lyft drivers raised from $182 to $504.[11] They also got the $1,000 [stimulus that went to all working-class workers] that they don't have to pay back. The drivers needed this support because they were not able to make money, so how will they pay insurance on cars, mortgage on cars? They got SBL [small business loans] for thirty years with 3.75 percent interest. We're now working to help drivers with rent problems. Any working-class person can fill out the applications.

We started Zoom meetings on Tuesdays—we had one today at 2:00 p.m.—and every Friday we also have Zoom meetings where our lawyers talk to drivers to show how to get benefits from the city's rental programs.[12]

The first three to four months we were working 24/7. I'm upstairs calling from my cell phone. Drivers call at six o'clock at night, two o'clock in the morning, anytime. They need to know that people are there for us. There are tons of heartbreaking stories from drivers. We've been working for them for the last twenty-two years; we cannot run away from them. Maybe some think we're crazy. Bhairavi Desai spends all her time helping drivers though her health is not that good, but she keeps working. She wakes up at six o'clock in the morning, going through emails, giving interviews, writing letters to congresspeople. There is so much work to do. We're working round the clock. Unless we're in touch with our members, there's no way to build more trust.

DF: Congratulations as well. You won your lawsuit for unemployment just a week ago. Your work is extraordinary. You're providing direct services and mutual aid and also organizing in multifaceted ways. What would you say are the most crucial actions we can take to create a liberatory future?

JT: Just keep fighting the fight. Never give up. Unify the workers. This is the only way to liberate us. This is our strategy.

DF: Javaid, you've shared so many lessons, history, stories, and great organizing strategies. Is there anything else you'd like to add?

JT: Our way is not the way of the bosses. We have meetings day and night so drivers can attend. Hundreds of drivers are coming to the day meetings, and we're talking to them, trying to find out what their big issues are. We vote, and based on what the majority of workers want, we start that campaign. We pick up the most difficult problems of the workers, and we have to work on that.

DF: You are building deeply democratic ways of working, and it comes through listening to the workers.

JT: Correct, because our members are drivers, and they know the issues best from their own experiences and from talking with other drivers. When I was driving, I knew from talking to other drivers all the time. Traditional union bosses sit in their offices and make decisions on their own.

DF: Thank you so much for all of your tremendously important work over the decades.

JT: It's an honor for me. Thank you for thinking of us and spreading the message of the NYTWA. We're proud to be South Asian. We've been here twenty to thirty years as an organization and reached this level. We are gaining something for the workers.

NOTES

This is a slightly edited version of the interview conducted by phone on August 4, 2020, in the midst of the coronavirus pandemic and requiring several communications before and after the interview.

1 Monisha Das Gupta, *Unruly Immigrants: Rights Activism, and Transnational South Asian Politics in the United States* (Durham, NC: Duke University Press, 2006), 227–54; Helen Zia, *Asian American Dreams: The Emergence of an American People* (New York: Farrar, Straus and Giroux, 2000), 195–204; Biju Mathew, *Taxi: Cabs and Capitalism in New York City* (New York: New Press, 2005); Anuradha G. Advani, "Against the Tide: Reflections on Organizing New York's South Asian Taxicab Drivers," in *Making More Waves: New Writing by Asian American Women*, ed. Elaine H. Kim, Lilia V. Villanueva, and Asian Women United of California (Boston: Beacon Press), 215–22; Bhairavi Desai, founding member of the New York Taxi Workers Alliance, recorded by Deepa Ranganathan, 2005, Crossing East Oral Histories, Interviews, and Transcripts, www.crossingeast.org/crossingeastarchive/2017/05/02/bhairavi-desai-director-of-new-york-taxi-workers-alliance.

2 Sonny Singh, "The Free-Spirited Journey of a Taxi Union Organizer," *Margins*, June 2, 2016, https://aaww.org/the-free-spirited-journey-of-a-taxi-union-organizer; Javaid Tariq, cofounder of New York Taxi Workers Alliance, recorded by Deepa Ranganathan, 2005, Crossing East Oral Histories, Interviews, and Transcripts, www.crossingeast.org/crossingeastarchive/2017/05/02/javaid-tariq.

3 Another major victory won by the NYTWA in 2018 was legislation that made New York the first city to place a cap on app-based, for-hire vehicles and to require a minimum wage for Uber and Lyft drivers. Chris Brooks, "How New York Taxi Workers Took on Uber and Won,"

Labor Notes, August 23, 2018,https://www.labornotes.org/2018/08/how-new-york-taxi-workers-took-uber-and-won.

4 Bhairavi Desai, "NYC Taxi Driver Kills Himself at City Hall after Condemning Uber & Politicians for Financial Ruin," interview on *Democracy Now!*, February 7, 2018, https://www.democracynow.org/2018/2/7/nyc_taxi_driver_kills_himself_at.

5 The Lease Drivers Coalition (LDC), established in 1992, was CAAAV's first worker project; see Das Gupta, *Unruly Immigrants*, 227–29.

6 The NYTWA organizers would talk to the drivers, who were then working twelve-hour shifts, at their shift changes at 5:00 a.m. and 5:00 p.m. as well as hold meetings at all different times to accommodate the drivers, including "on top of a taxi cab . . . on the street at 3 a.m." (Desai, recording; J. Tariq, recording).

7 Zia, *Asian American Dreams*, 202.

8 Das Gupta, *Unruly Immigrants*, 231.

9 South Asian cabdrivers and the newly formed NYTWA organized the twenty-four-hour strike of the twelve thousand Yellow Cab drivers on May 13, 1998, creating a shocking day of "near-absence of taxis" in New York City and making headline news; see "Commuters Brace for a Cab-less Wednesday as Drivers Protest," *New York Times*, May 13, 1998; "Miles of Street with Nary a Yellow Taxicab," *New York Times*, May 14, 1998; "Renewed Call for Motorcade against Giuliani's Taxi Rules," *New York Times*, May 21, 1998.

10 The *NYTWA Resource Guide for Drivers and Families to Get Through COVID-19 Pandemic* is a thirty-two-page, detailed how-to guide explaining the resources, criteria for eligibility, and process to obtain services, including unemployment, stimulus check, small business loans, food, health care, tenants' rights, and more. See http://www.nytwa.org/home/2020/4/20/nytwa-resources-guide-for-drivers-and-families.

11 Noam Scheiber, "Uber and Lyft Drivers Sue for New York Unemployment Benefits," *New York Times*, May 26, 2020; Noam Scheiber, "Uber and Lyft Drivers Win Ruling on Unemployment Benefits," *New York Times*, July 28, 2020.

12 On the NYTWA's intensive organizing during the COVID-19 pandemic, see http://www.nytwa.org/resources.

CHAPTER 6

BAYAN USA

Filipino Transnational Radical Activism in the
United States in the Twenty-First Century

JESSICA ANTONIO

ECONOMIC DISTRESS IN THE PHILIPPINES PUSHES MORE THAN
sixty-five hundred Filipinos to escape the Philippines daily, resulting in
the various formations of Filipino communities in over 190 countries.
Philippine census figures indicate that Filipinos in the United States
constitute the largest overseas Filipino community. It is not only one
of the Philippines' largest diasporic communities but also the oldest,
as Filipinos were displaced from the Philippines beginning with the
US colonization and occupation of the country with the Philippine-
American War of 1898. Nominal independence granted by the United
States in 1946 and continued US imperialism to this day have ultimately contributed to the continued growth of the Filipino diaspora
in the United States.

The formation of Filipino transnational political organizational
structures in the United States have engaged Filipinos in the diaspora,
including many who were born and raised in the United States, to participate in Philippine politics. In this chapter I discuss the history and
structure of BAYAN USA, an alliance of organizations that engages
Filipinos in the United States to participate in movements working to
fundamentally transform Philippine society. Though there are a number of Filipino groups based in the United States oriented toward
homeland politics, the BAYAN USA alliance is among the most radical in analysis and practice and among the few that is directly linked

to radical movements in the Philippines. BAYAN USA is an overseas chapter of BAYAN Philippines, which is an alliance of people's organizations united by a program of advancing national democracy in the Philippines. Through BAYAN USA, Filipinos in the United States—many who are US born and/or US citizens—can become direct participants in the Philippine National Democratic movement, a movement for Philippine national liberation that strives to root out what we believe are the "three basic problems" of the Philippines: US imperialism; bureaucrat capitalism, or what most might think of as government corruption; and feudalism because the Philippines continues to be a peasant society dominated by a centuries-old landlord class. BAYAN USA is significant as a long-standing diasporic organization with multiple US chapters working in solidarity with the national liberation movement in the Philippines. We also seek to build relationships rooted in anti-imperialist solidarity with non-Filipino groups, though this area of work has not been as strongly developed.

To better understand why and how Filipinos in the United States get politicized to engage in transnational activism, I discuss the politicization process of BAYAN USA members. I analyze interviews of BAYAN USA members to pull key information, looking for ways in which identity formation, politics, history, and current connections to the Philippines have affected organizers and activists. I look in particular at the impact of what BAYAN USA calls "exposure," or "integration," programs that facilitate US-based Filipinos' travel to the Philippines. Through these programs Filipinos from the United States travel to the Philippines and integrate with—that is, live with, learn from, and work alongside—individuals from different sectors of Philippine society (including youths/students, peasants, workers, fisherfolk, and urban poor) as well as the BAYAN Philippines–affiliated people's organizations of which these sectors are part. Generally, exposure allows US Filipinos to directly witness the struggles of the most exploited, marginalized, and oppressed in the Philippines; they get to directly experience—however temporarily—the three basic problems of Philippine society. For many participants BAYAN USA exposure/ integration programs may well be their first time visiting the Philippines or a rare opportunity to connect to their Filipino roots independent of their families, who often introduce them to the Philippine culture and society through primarily familial connections and tourist activities. Those who come back from a trip to the Philippines from an

exposure/integration program often come back with a (re)invigo-
rated commitment to transforming Philippine society while living in
the United States and simultaneously shaping the political landscape
in the United States by sharing stories of inspiration and lessons
learned from organizers in the Philippine liberation struggle with
greater numbers of Filipino Americans and non-Filipino progressive
and radical allies.

What is striking about Philippine exposure/integration programs
is that they can be equally impactful for even those who do not necessarily identify as Filipino. BAYAN USA's Peace Missions, which are
similar to the exposure/integration programs that are geared toward
those who identify as Filipino, also have the effect of deepening the
resolve of those who participate in them to commit to sharing their
firsthand experiences of the impacts of US imperialism—along with
bureaucratic capitalism and feudalism—to a broader American public. Through our work in BAYAN USA we find that to grow our movement among non-Filipinos in the diaspora, as well as to strengthen
relationships with allies, it is vital for people to directly experience
and witness what plagues Philippine society as well as to feel hope
and inspiration from experiencing and witnessing the Philippine liberation struggle. Though we live in a world that might seem so transnationally connected through media and other communications
technologies, there is something that continues to be distinctively
important about the experiential and interpersonal relationships that
get formed through exposure/integration programs. This chapter
therefore builds on themes laid out in the introduction of this anthology that include the importance of relationship building; we illustrate
how relationship building is important not only in forming international solidarity but also in extending the diaspora's participation in
the Philippine liberation struggle transnationally.

FILIPINO TRANSNATIONALISM HISTORICALLY

Filipino radicals in the Philippines have an expansive understanding
of what it means to be Filipino and therefore who can and should legit-
imately engage in the struggle for Philippine liberation. Antonio
Tujan, a leftist intellectual of the Institute of Political Economy, Manila,
for example, stated in 2019: "By its definition (displaced collective
community), diaspora is an adjunct to the homeland, and shares

history, social and cultural characteristics. This means compatriots identify with and share the responsibility to focus on the lot of the homeland and intuitively identify with the struggle for freedom and democracy."[1]

Indeed, Filipino transnational radicalism in the United States has been similarly expansive and has a history that even predates the formation of BAYAN USA in the early 2000s. During the dictatorship of President Ferdinand Marcos from the 1970s to 1980s, anti–martial law activists in the Philippines actively engaged Filipinos in the diaspora, most notably in the United States, to support the struggle to depose Marcos. Some fled the Marcos dictatorship and immigrated to the United States to join relatives and would eventually form anti–martial law groups. The Katipunan ng mga Demokratikong Pilipino (Union of Democratic Filipinos, KDP), launched in July 1973 in Santa Cruz, California, was one such group. The KDP united on the basis of a "dual-line" program of supporting national democracy in the Philippine and simultaneously promoting socialism in the United States. The radical politicization of Filipino youth during the late 1960s and 1970s in the United States shifted the political landscape of Filipino communities in the diaspora. Not only did members of KDP become active in their local Filipino communities; they also began mobilizing around issues based in their ancestral homeland, most significantly the rising fascism of the Marcos regime. In investigating Filipino history through their conversations with the *Manong* generation of Filipino migrants, members learned about the *Manongs*' experiences of fighting against racism, including white supremacist vigilante violence and labor exploitation during the 1930s and about their current situation of eviction and housing rights issues at San Francisco's International Hotel. The KDP was able to unite Filipino immigrants and Filipino Americans on these varying issues.

At the same time, the KDP became engaged in vigorously opposing martial law in the Philippines. Though KDP provided Filipinos in the United States, many of whom were second-generation (or even later) Filipino Americans, an opportunity to engage in homeland politics, the KDP's framework with respect to Philippine politics remained limited to a notion of solidarity. In other words, though Filipinos in the diaspora based in the United States were engaging in the issues affecting their ancestral homeland, they still saw themselves as separated from and not direct participants in the National Democratic movement in the Philippines; that is, they were in solidarity with the Philippine movement but not necessarily part of it. This distinction has become more apparent in retrospect through reflections from former KDP members but was not always so clear at the time. For some the KDP's dual revolutionary program meant that they supported both the revolutionary movement in the Philippines as well as the socialist movement in the United States. This, among other organizational issues, caused stress and confusion for KDP members, and eventually the KDP fractioned into variant groups. Estella Habal, a former member of the KDP, notes in her book, *San Francisco's International Hotel: Mobilizing the Filipino American Community in the Anti-Eviction Movement*: "We also suffered because of conflicting priorities, along with limited people power. The dual program seemed accurate, correct for the time, but our practice often lagged far behind."[2] Eventually, the KDP dissolved, with many choosing to focus primarily on socialist transformation in the United States, and others who would eventually go on to organize a new generation of Filipino Americans to engage in Philippine radical politics transnationally.

FROM SOLIDARITY TO PARTICIPATION: A CLEARER ROLE FOR FILIPINOS IN THE DIASPORA

BAYAN USA, in many ways, emerged to fill the gap left with the dissolution of KDP. Those who would eventually lead in the formation of BAYAN USA, including some who were involved in the KDP and other anti–martial law formations, came to understand that there was a need for a political organization of Filipinos in the United States that was not just a solidarity organization but one that was directly involved in the National Democratic struggle alongside activists in the Philippines and primarily oriented toward Philippine politics. Moreover, there was the view that when issues of Filipinos in the United States are addressed, it is necessary to frame these issues as ultimately due to the fact that Filipinos have been massively displaced from their homeland as a consequence of the root problems persisting in the Philippines. Thus, from this perspective Filipino issues in the United States are best addressed by rooting out the problems that force Filipinos to migrate to the United States to begin with and thus ultimately through the genuine liberation of the Philippines. US-Filipino National Democratic activists, focus their energies primarily on the liberation of the Philippines, their ancestral homeland, to which they hope they or their descendants can return. Though the effort to dismantle the current structures of society in the United States, where they are currently residing, is also vital to them, it is of secondary importance. Drawing from these understandings of transnational activism, BAYAN USA was established as the first overseas chapter of BAYAN in the Philippines; other BAYAN alliances would later form in the Filipino diaspora in Australia, Canada, and Hong Kong, and other countries where Filipino migrants have settled. As an overseas chapter, BAYAN USA maintains direct communication with BAYAN Philippines. Moreover, BAYAN USA maintains organizational accountability to BAYAN Philippines. This represents a major shift from the Filipino transnational activism during the anti–martial law movement, when communication and accountability across the Pacific was loose at best.

Notably, BAYAN Philippines was actually formed during the anti–martial law movement but did not form chapters abroad at the time. According to the website for BAYAN's Bagong Alyansang Makabayan Philippines (BAYAN, New Patriotic Alliance of the Philippines), the group formed in 1985, operating as an umbrella alliance of thousands of organizations representing different class backgrounds and sectors of society committed to the people's struggle for national freedom and democracy across the seventy-one hundred islands.[3] BAYAN's analysis of Philippine society claims that the Philippines remains semifeudal and semicolonial, and only through uniting in the National Democratic movement's objectives for national industrialization and genuine agrarian reform can the Philippines be truly free from foreign domination and internal corruption.[4] In order to achieve these goals, BAYAN states that the power of the workers, peasants, youths, students, women, educators, and professionals—all sectors of society—is needed to engage in the long process of struggle to transform Philippine society as a whole and for the benefit of future generations of Filipinos. BAYAN Philippines believes that while the Philippines continues to be controlled by corrupt puppet governments that serve imperialist nations and the wealth of the country remains in the hands of the few, the people will continue to organize broadly and boldly. BAYAN Philippines is composed of numerous people's organizations, including the Kilusang Mayo Uno (KMU, or May First Movement), a militant trade union confederation; and the Kilusang Magbubukid ng Pilipinas (KMP, or Peasant Movement of the Philippines), an alliance of peasant organizations as well as organizations representing faculty (CONTEND), government workers (COURAGE), Indigenous peoples (Cordillera People's Alliance), and many, many more.[5] Since the ouster of Ferdinand Marcos, BAYAN Philippines has been the leading force mobilizing thousands upon thousands of Filipino people to push back against the antipeople policies that each successive regime has introduced to preserve the economic dominance of multinational corporations, traditional landlords, and corrupt politicians.

BAYAN USA: AN ESSENTIAL TRANSNATIONAL LINK

With the launch of BAYAN USA, BAYAN Philippines formed an essential transnational link in order to mobilize the largest number of Filipino compatriots living abroad. BAYAN USA formed in 2005 as the first international chapter of BAYAN Philippines and was created to "organize, mobilize, and raise the consciousness of Filipinos in the United States, linking their basic issues of rights and welfare to the National Democratic struggle against three roots problems: imperialism, feudalism, and bureaucrat capitalism." Thus, BAYAN USA's primary task is to raise the consciousness of Filipinos in the United States by mobilizing them around issues in the Philippines. The establishment of BAYAN USA as an international chapter of BAYAN underscored our political orientation on the National Democratic movement in the Philippines and as a campaign center for Filipinos in the United States.[6] Taking the lead from BAYAN Philippines, BAYAN USA is able to concentrate on advancing the progress of the Filipino people's movement for true democracy, genuine land reform, and national independence from US imperialism in the Philippines.

BAYAN USA modeled our bylaws and structure after BAYAN Philippines and primarily operates as an alliance of youth and students', women's, and migrant workers' organizations represented, respectively, by Anakbayan USA, GABRIELA USA, and Migrante USA. To clarify further, BAYAN USA is a multisector alliance, engaging groups representing different sectors of the Filipino diaspora in the United States—youth/students, women, and migrant workers at present, though conceivably other sectors in the future—composed of member organizations and not individuals. Most of our campaigns are driven by issues being taken up by BAYAN Philippines and its allied organizations. As of this writing, for example, our chapters have been exposing the rising fascism under the Duterte regime. We have launched major social media campaigns and educational programs aimed at raising awareness of the dire human rights situation in the Philippines. Together with other Filipino and non-Filipino progressive organizations, BAYAN USA is working to support passage of the Philippine Human Rights Act (PHRA). In the past we have worked to support boycotts of specific products consumed by Filipinos and others in the United States in response to calls from the KMU in the Philippines; rallied behind GABRIELA Philippines for justice for transgender woman, Jennifer Laude, who was murdered by an American marine stationed in the Philippines; and supported the Save Our Schools Campaign championed by the National Democratic organization Lumad, made up of Indigenous people in the Mindanao region of the southern Philippines (figure 6.1). Notably, Indigenous groups in

FIGURE 6.1. Over 250 Filipinos and allies from across the United States rallied in front of the Philippine embassy in Washington, DC, in April 2019, in a protest organized by BAYAN USA that brought together people from multiple generations, political views, and organizations calling for the ouster of President Duterte. Fourteen people staged a die-in at the gates of the embassy, to symbolize the fourteen peasants and farmers killed by the Philippine National Police and Armed Forces of the Philippines in a joint "anti-criminality" operation in Negros Island. Photo courtesy of BAYAN USA.

the United States hosted Lumad activists from the Philippines, which led to important new ties among movements.

Though our primary focus of BAYAN USA is the struggle for national democracy in the Philippines, we cannot ignore the issues pervading our backyards as Filipinos in the United States, and therefore we also engage in local community issues, especially those concerning Filipino migrants. What we do that is different, however, is that we offer a transnational perspective by linking these issues to the overall conditions of Filipinos in the Philippines. Participating in localized issues is a way to approach and understand the complex layers of the diasporic realities that Filipino communities face. However, we strive to continue to link diasporic Filipinos' issues back to the three basic problems in the Philippines in our political education programs. Though we support Filipino Americans' and US-based Filipinos' issues such as wage theft and housing displacement and we fight alongside them to get justice from their employers or landlords, we emphasize the fact that we would never have had to live in the United States to begin with if our ancestral homeland was genuinely free.

For example, members of Anakbayan chapters in California took up a legislative campaign supporting AB 123, which was signed into law by Governor Jerry Brown in 2013 and requires the state curriculum to include the contributions of Filipino Americans to the farm labor movement in California. We believed it was an important struggle to support. Our organizations pay particular attention to Filipino and Philippine history, especially in relation to the United States, and utilize the slogan "Know History, Know Self" as a way to deepen identity politics among Filipinos from past to present. We especially highlight the role of US colonialism in ultimately producing the Filipino diaspora in the United States, which is a history few Filipinos in America grow up knowing. To support AB 123, therefore, would mean that Filipinos in the United States could develop a more critical understanding of their historical presence in this country by better understanding the role of US colonialism, and now imperialism, in displacing our people. Moreover, with its focus on Filipinos' leadership and participation in the farmworkers' movements, which led to the formation of the United Farm Workers, they can have activist role models to aspire to, including the likes of Philip Vera Cruz, who was also very committed to Philippine liberation.

Through our transnational analytic framework, Filipinos participating in BAYAN USA are engaging in the transnational struggle for national democracy in the Philippines while situated in the United States and also incorporating struggles Filipinos face as Filipino Americans and Filipino migrants (figure 6.2). This is different from KDP's dual revolutionary program, in which they ultimately saw themselves as part of the socialist revolutionary movement in the United States and only in solidarity with the revolutionary movement in the Philippines. BAYAN USA's political framework focuses on addressing the issues in the Philippines with the analysis that the root cause of the forced migration of Filipinos globally is linked to the three basic problems in the Philippines. At the same time, BAYAN USA promotes a clear, anti-imperialist analysis that underscores the importance of building international solidarity with other oppressed people around

FIGURE 6.2. In this BAYAN USA Peace Mission 2017, the exposurists visited Lumad communities in Mindanao, where they learned about the fight for Lumad rights to ancestral lands, the Lumad schools that incorporate their Indigenous cultural practices, and the need for basic healthcare in their communities. This photo further shows the solidarity between the Lumad and the Standing Rock Indigenous rights to land and protection of natural resources. Photo courtesy of Jessica Antonio.

the world against the common enemy of US imperialism by participating in the International League of People's Struggles (ILPS),[7] International Migrants Alliance, National Alliance Against Racist and
Political Repression, and other alliances.

In summary, what makes BAYAN USA different from its predecessors is that it propagates the idea that Filipinos in the United States
can and should take an interest in the liberation of the Philippines,
their ancestral homeland. Filipinos in the United States can ultimately
claim a liberated Philippines as a place to which to return and genuinely belong. We believe that by participating directly in the national
liberation struggle of our ancestral homeland, we or our descendants
can return to an independent and self-reliant economy that can sustain Filipino families and end the economic need for forced migration
abroad. BAYAN USA thus leverages Filipinos' presence in the United
States to play a role in directly combatting one of the three basic problems—that of US imperialism—right in the belly of the beast. A liberated Philippines, moreover, can contribute to further breaking the
chains of US imperialism as it exploits the people and resources of
the entire planet.

PHILIPPINE EXPOSURE PROGRAMS: CULTIVATING A
TRANSNATIONAL CONSCIOUSNESS IN THE DIASPORA

BAYAN USA has been able to maintain its multi-sector alliance for over
ten years, with now more than thirty member organizations. Through
conducting interviews with BAYAN USA members, we found that there
is a significant importance for Filipino Americans—that is, Filipinos
who mostly grew up in the United States—to participate in integration and exposure programs. These exposure programs are coordinated between BAYAN Philippines and BAYAN USA and the sectoral
formations part of BAYAN and BAYAN USA, such as between Anakbayan and Anakbayan USA and GABRIELA and GABRIELA USA, in
which Filipino Americans travel to the Philippines, work alongside
National Democratic activists, integrate in communities by living with
peasants, workers, urban poor or squatter communities, and Indigenous people, among others, to experience the issues and struggles
faced by ordinary Filipino people in the Philippines. In addition, these
programs contribute to strengthening our member organizations and
our alliance.

The transnational relationship between BAYAN Philippines and BAYAN USA fosters the ability to have well-organized exposure programs that facilitate the important face-to-face interactions between Filipino activists in the United States and in the Philippines. These programs primarily facilitate a deeper understanding of the concrete conditions in Philippine society for the US "exposurist" who may or may not have any direct experience of living in the Philippines. In addition, these programs also help to maintain and strengthen relationships between BAYAN USA and BAYAN Philippines, especially when activists who are part of BAYAN USA integrate with BAYAN Philippines' main office in Quezon City. It is through these exposure programs that many Filipino activists based in the United States describe their experience as transformative.

Filipinos residing in the United States are physically, and at times mentally, separated from the Philippines. This is especially true for Filipino Americans born and raised in the United States who have no experience of what life is like growing up in the Philippines. This common feeling of disconnection is challenged through the process of connecting to the Philippines beyond concept and theory, beyond culture and identity politics, by physically going there and experiencing firsthand a sample of life through the organization's integration programs. Moreover, BAYAN USA activists are able to directly observe the three basic problems up close. BAYAN USA activists typically undergo a political education process that starts with the *Philippine Society and Revolution* (*PSR*), a book by Amado Guerrero, a pseudonym of Jose Maria Sison, published in 1970. The book fleshes out exactly how US imperialism, bureaucratic capitalism, and feudalism have shaped the Philippine economy, politics, and culture and lays out why a program of national democracy is therefore necessary to Philippine liberation.

Jill Mangaliman, BAYAN USA, explains how she was able to internalize educational materials such as the *PSR* through the exposure program:

> When I traveled on expo [the exposure program], I started to truly
> understand the conditions in the Philippines. I had taken the
> Philippine Revolution and Society educational series, but it wasn't
> until I saw what multinational corporations had done to the land,
> the large-scale logging and the clear-cut hills, and the massive

graves of townspeople were killed in the landslides following
Typhoon Pablo, that I finally internalized [the *PSR*]. I carry the
stories of people I met on the expo trips with me, not just to
remember that there are people counting on us to keep fighting
but also to give me courage while being in the belly of the beast.
We don't have the same conditions, so it's easy to become complacent
or numb here. ("Things are bad here but not so bad.") Also, the
larger society thinks that "the US is great and imperialism is
great," but we know the truth; we saw it. US imperialism is what
is killing our *kababayan* and our homeland.[8]

Not only does the exposure program bring the *PSR* to life for Mangaliman; the relationships she forges with her activist counterparts in
the Philippines compel her to commit all the work to fighting "in the
belly of the beast." Through these relationships Mangaliman becomes
more acutely aware of the relative privilege she enjoys as a resident
in the United States and how that privilege can have the effect of making her complacent about the struggles of people in the Philippines,
but the direct connections made with people on the ground serve to
keep her motivated to sustain her work.

Pyxie Castillo, GABRIELA USA, shares her exposure program experience in the Philippines: "The experience of traveling to and inte-
grating in the Philippines gave me a deeper understanding of the
history of the Philippines. Having a heritage of resistance and revolution was no longer theories and words in a book but has become lived
experience. I became more committed to doing as much as I could to
address the root problems of the suffering of the Filipino people and
made a promise to tell the stories of those on the ground in the Philippines organizing every day, risking their lives to change things."[9]
Here Castillo is impacted not only by her firsthand experiences of the
three basic problems but by her personal involvement with the liberation movement. As she puts it, "Resistance and revolution . . . have
become lived experiences."

The relationships forged and stories shared between Filipino activists from the United States with Filipino activists in the Philippines
are not only important in ensuring that members of BAYAN USA gain
a deeper political and social understanding of the radical organizing
work done by BAYAN; they also maintain and strengthen the organizational relationships of the alliances across the Pacific. Perhaps

most important, the relationships forged with their counterparts in the Philippines offer US-based activists a sense of inspiration and hope. This was true of Jhonry Delacruz of Migrante Youth Fort Washington, who states: "It gives me so much hope, inspiration, and energy to see the vibrant mass movement and different forms of community building and engagement back home, which I can try to rebuild and replicate here. The resources, campaign materials, and stories shared really inform how I conduct my organizing and political work here in the United States."[10]

Terrie Cervas of GABRIELA USA, however, is not only inspired by her counterparts in the Philippines but also outraged by the fact that many activists risk the possibility of losing their lives for the work they do. She shared her observations:

> During my ten-month-long exposure trip with Kilusang Mayo Uno, I spent time on picket lines and learned about how unions are formed and collective bargaining agreements.[11] I saw firsthand the hardships that workers and peasants faced and the injustices done to them when they were unjustly exploited and taken advantage of. I met some union leaders and other activists who were later murdered because of the organizing they were doing. Witnessing these things changed me, and I felt a responsibility to tell their stories and to be involved. I also decided to get involved because I agreed with the analysis of the movement—that the basic problems of the country must be solved and that there must be national industrialization and genuine agrarian reform to achieve national democracy in the Philippines. I saw the power of the workers and peasants when they collectively banded together to fight and assert their rights. I learned how the National Democratic movement in the Philippines organizes the most oppressed and exploited people in the country and fights for national liberation, and I felt I found the cause that I wanted to be committed to for the rest of my life.[12]

Among the interviews there is a common thread, in which the interviewees explain a sense of responsibility in needing to share the stories of the people and communities they've encountered while on exposure programs in the Philippines. Storytelling is key in the reportbacks that the organizations host following exposure programs in

order to share the experiences of the participants and, more important, the stories from the communities they visited. Jennelle Barajas,
with GABRIELA Portland, shares some of her most memorable
experiences:

> There was a cultural sharing night at the Alternative Learning
> Center for Agricultural and Livelihood Development [ALCADEV]
> when I went in summer 2019. It was raining so hard, and the stage
> covering was aluminum, so the rain beating down was deafening,
> but the show didn't stop. The people's voices rang so loud, and
> they sang in a cadence I never heard before. Someone explained it
> to me later—that since they're connected to their land, their
> singing lilts like the changing of the seasons, the sowing and the
> harvest. There was another woman whose brother and nephew
> were just killed by the Armed Forces of the Philippines [AFP] as
> they were farming abaca. I remember she was explaining to us
> what they did to them, and she put her wrists together and showed
> us how they shot them and bound their hands with the abaca
> they were farming. I have that image burned into my memory.
> The tears in her eyes, her hands raised up wrist to wrist. She was
> looking straight into my eyes. She just wanted her story to be
> told.[13]

These stories are connected to the overall issues in the Philippines
and in particular to three basic problems and the National Democratic
movement. By conducting report-backs, in which exposurists share
their experiences in the Philippines to community members in their
local areas, a wider audience is exposed to the issues in the Philippines through the real-life stories and experiences of the exposurists,
typically through cultural song, dance/movement, theater, video, and
photos. The aim is to encourage the audience to take action by joining the organizations or enrolling in the next exposure program to
the Philippines.

In the United States there are a variety of Filipino or Philippine-
specific organizations and nonprofits that Filipinos can choose to participate in. Through our interviews we gained insight into why people
decided to join our National Democratic organizations. We found that
members gravitated toward the political issues happening in the Philippines and felt the desire to do something about it. Many of them

experienced a certain type of politicization in our organizations that connected them to their homeland, the Philippines, and some of them were involved in political issues based in the United States and then got introduced to our organizations.

Another striking dynamic about Filipino Americans' experience while in the Philippines in exposure and integration programs is that they come to develop a deep sense of belonging and home while there. Several describe their experiences of being marginalized in American society as immigrants or people or color while growing up and how involvement in BAYAN USA organizations and going back to the Philippines give these activists the feeling that they have a legitimate claim to the Philippines as their homeland. Pyxie Castillo describes her politicization in college and how she connected to the Philippines:

> For me, even growing up in the diaspora, the Philippines was always painted as "home." I didn't analyze my relationship with the Philippines as my personal "homeland" until I was in college with other Filipinos who grew up with their Filipino identity estranged or seen through a more white and/or Western lens. Now, in college, they were now afforded the opportunity to learn more about themselves, as they might not have had the ability to grow up knowing themselves as part of the land of the Philippines and thus were estranged from it. I also connect to the Philippines in understanding that if my family was not forced to migrate, due to the lack of national industrialization and available jobs, the Philippines would have been my physical home.[14]

Jill Mangaliman explains how she got politicized through issues in the United States and then was exposed to the Philippine National Democratic movement and organizations that then connected her to Philippine politics and community building:

> I became politicized in 2008 due to the US presidential elections and later the Occupy movement. At the time I had little knowledge of or connection to my Filipino heritage or identity. All I knew about being Filipino was around food and culture. There was something different about the National Democratic organizations that I met. They had a goal to liberate the Philippines from US

imperialism, and I was excited to learn more and to do more. It was not only educational, but it was fun. We would hang out and tell each other stories about our lives, eventually to become part of each other's lives. It felt good to belong to something and have people I could rely on while working on very important work.[15]

The process for Sharlyn Santiago was also similar in that she was engaging in issues primarily happening in the United States and through attending those mobilizations and actions met an Anakbayan chapter: "I was getting more politicized by seeing the Standing Rock and Black Lives Matter movement. I saw Anakbayan was the only Filipino organization really standing in solidarity. Then I learned about our own struggle, and it confirmed all the feelings I felt growing up here in the States. It made me feel the connection to home I've been longing for."[16]

A particular way that Filipinos in the United States become politicized is through investigation into their own family migration story, and in joining our organizations, they are able to link the reasons why their families had to leave the Philippines to the basic problems that persist in Philippine society. Nina Macapinlac, BAYAN USA, makes this connection within her own story:

I got involved with organizing in 2013, when Anakbayan New Jersey was engaged in a campaign for the New Jersey Dream Act. I was a student at Rutgers University at the time and saw the struggle of undocumented youth in my own story. I did not consider myself an activist and was more interested in academic research, but I went to meetings and supported the campaign. Anakbayan New Jersey was in a coalition of youth organizations pushing for the bill, and I was naturally drawn, as I'd never seen a progressive Filipino organization so involved in immigrant rights for undocumented people. I chose to join Anakbayan New Jersey because they were on the ground fighting a campaign that I cared about. I saw that they were doing work in the community while also providing comprehensive political education. Learning about forced migration and imperialism contextualized my own life in a way I'd never been able to articulate before. The analysis Anakbayan provided also landed on a concrete way to take action—to continue serving the people.[17]

Many of the stories shared in these interview excerpts show multiple pathways that people found that led them to join one of our BAYAN USA organizations. Some of them did not consider themselves to be activists or connected to Filipino activism, but ultimately, many of them realized that underneath they were looking for an organization that was both political and Filipino. Whether they were politicized through college or through joining US-based issues, in the end they found one of our organizations and eventually joined because they wanted to be part of a Filipino activist organization that was connected to issues in the Philippines.

SOLIDARITY BUILT FROM THE GROUND: BAYAN USA PEACE MISSIONS

In addition to Philippine exposure programs for its members, BAYAN USA wanted to engage non-Filipino solidarity allies in an exposure program to the Philippines. We wanted to build on the positive experiences of previous generations of US-based activists on their trips to the Philippines. For example, Yuri Kochiyama details how she became involved: "We were invited by Bayan, which has a membership of 1.5 million people and twenty-one different organizations. GABRIELA, the women's group, comes under it and there are about five different college organizations. The press people, reporters, come under it. Even the religious orders. I couldn't believe it, but we even met with the Catholic nuns and other sisters. We met with the street sweepers, the jeepney drivers, the fishermen, the farmers, the unemployed. They all came under BAYAN, and BAYAN also has a couple of very revolutionary groups."[18]

The kind of admiration for the Philippine liberation struggle that Kochiyama expresses here is something we hoped to inspire in newer generations of solidarity allies. In 2014 we formed the BAYAN USA Peace Mission to the Muslim Mindanao areas of the Philippines that focus on the impact of US-backed counterinsurgency and military presence in the region. Being situated in the United States, BAYAN USA also has a certain duty to convey the realities of the political situation in the Philippines to solidarity allies from non-Filipino communities and organizations while also engaging in solidarity on issues allies are working on. Rhonda Ramiro, chairperson of BAYAN USA, explained, "Our peace missions have been one of the most effective and lasting ways that BAYAN USA has been able to generate tangible solidarity with the movements for self-determination of Moro and Indigenous people of Mindanao—two of the movements most viciously under attack by the US-Duterte regime."

The peace missions welcome Filipinos and non-Filipino solidarity allies to learn about the struggle of Moro (Muslim) and Indigenous people facing extreme poverty, land grabbing, and state violence. During the first peace mission, US-based activists spent time with Moro communities in Cotabato City and Maguindanao. Ramon Meiji, US Iraq war veteran–turned–peace activist reflected on his experience: "As a former US Marine, I can say that the only objective of US militarism is to pursue hegemony, that is what the Obama administration's so-called Pivot to Asia is about. The EDCA is not going to ensure protection for the Philippines, nor will it modernize the Philippine military. Securing US military control over the Philippines is strategic to the drive for US hegemony in the Asia-Pacific region, and it will come at a grave social cost for the Filipino people." He continued: "We are concerned over the conditions of abject poverty and human rights abuses we saw the Moro people suffering from on their own ancestral domain. We fully support their right to self-determination, including the right to fight to economically uplift their lives."[19]

Juyeon Rhee, US-based activist and member of Nodutol, an organization based in New York City composed of first- through fourth-generation Koreans living in the United States, describes his experience on a peace mission: "As active peace activists in the US, we came to hear the stories of a people facing increasing US intervention and witness their struggles to fight for their basic rights. And we will take these stories back to better inform the US-based peace movement of what is happening on the ground in the Philippines. There are problems inside the US that need to be resolved—unemployment, homelessness, lack of access to education, and affordable health care. We need our tax dollars to be directed toward solving these problems, not for US intervention in countries like the Philippines."

In 2019 John Prysner, from Los Angeles, joined the peace mission in Lianga, the location of a Lumad school and a resource-rich region in Mindanao, and wrote about his experience meeting Indigenous families impacted by militarism and state violence:

[We] asked Lumad villagers in Lianga about the effect of this state terrorism on children. We were told, "There is extreme fear among the children. Some start screaming in the middle of the night. Some refuse to go to school." We were also told that two infants have died from extreme stress as a result of bombings and violence (these deaths are not included in the direct extrajudicial killings statistics). Villagers in Lianga spoke about the importance of international solidarity for their struggle: "Brothers and sisters from another country, we are grateful you are here to help us in our struggle, and you are in the US, which is the most oppressive country to us. We are happy you are there to fight."[20]

Past participants included delegates from Veterans for Peace, Nodutol for Korean Community Development, the Palestinian Youth Movement, the Coalition of Anti-Racist Whites, the School of Americas Watch, the Party for Socialism and Liberation, People Organizing for Philippine Solidarity, and the International League of People's Struggles. The successful mission trips have deepened solidarity and understanding between groups united in the fight against a common enemy, US imperialism.

Filipinos in the United States continue to play an integral role in educating, organizing, and mobilizing their local communities to contribute to advancing the national liberation movement in the Philippines. Filipinos residing in the United States are driven to connect to their history, culture, and homeland through community organizing and educational exposure trips to the Philippines with the most oppressed sectors of Philippine society, particularly peasants, workers, and Indigenous people. The BAYAN USA exposure programs are essential in teaching young activists, US-born and Filipino immigrants, and non-Filipino solidarity activists the concrete conditions of Philippine society that have driven many families to migrate across the world and even gain inspiration and lessons on how to organize youths, women, workers, artists, health workers, teachers, and professionals. Their experiences have helped activists to find a sense of purpose and responsibility in organizing communities in the United States to support the National Democratic movement, connect their local issues to a national and international level, and in some cases even move to the Philippines. So long as there is a neocolonial relationship between the United States and the Philippines, activists will continue to struggle for a brighter future and toward revolutionary change.

Jill Mangaliman helps to sum up the purpose of this chapter in answering the importance of Filipino transnational activism in the United States and the need for Filipinos in the United States to go on Philippine exposure programs:

> To participate in the National Democratic movement is to be "Happy and Determined." To find joy in taking up the everyday struggles of the masses, to serve the people and be with them and to fight with them. To be so resolute that the way to victory is when the people all rise up together to overthrow US imperialism, the comprador landlords, and the bureaucrat capitalists. To want to never give up (and when I do feel like giving up, *kasamas* ["comrades" in Filipino] are there to help bring me back and vice versa). Just as I had wanted to feel happiness for myself to go home, I want that and more for the whole of the Philippines, the Lumad who are losing their ancestral lands, the urban poor who are being gunned down by Duterte's death squads, and the families who are losing loved ones in this rotten system. I hope we can muster every bit of strength, resources, and creativity to organize more and more migrant workers here in the US, more youth and women, so that they too can take up the call to struggle and fight for a truly sovereign Philippines.[21]

NOTES

1 Antonio Tujan Jr., "Role of Diaspora in the Struggle for National and Social Liberation," *IPE Journal* (October 2019), https://iboninternational.org/download/ipe-journals-october-2019.

2 Rene Ciria Cruz, Cindy Domingo, and Bruce Occena, *A Time to Rise: Collective Memoirs of the Union of Democratic Filipinos (KDP)* (Seattle: University of Washington Press, 2017), 9; Estella Habal, *San Francisco's International Hotel: Mobilizing the Filipino American Community in the Anti-Eviction Movement* (Philadelphia: Temple University Press, 2007), 180.

3 In order to be part of BAYAN, you must be part of a member organization. Individuals typically cannot join the alliance.

4 Despite nominal independence granted in 1946, the Philippines is considered semicolonial in that it remains a neo-colony of the United States, exercising control of the Philippine economy, politics, culture,

military, and foreign relations, particularly through unequal policies and support from the Armed Forces of the Philippines. The Philippines remains semifeudal in character because of the uneven development of the country, in which the main mode of production remains feudalism dominated by rich landlords and foreign monopoly capitalists. Amado Guerrero, *Philippine Society and Revolution* (Hayward, CA: Philippine Information Network Service, 1996).

5 This is not a full list of BAYAN Philippines member organizations, but among the major ones are Kilusang Mayo Uno (KMU, May First Movement Labor Center); Kilusang Magbubukid ng Pilipinas (KMP, Peasant Movement of the Philippines); Anakbayan (youth and students); League of Filipino Students (LFS); Student Christian Movement of the Philippines (SCMP); GABRIELA (National Alliance of Women's Organizations); Kilusan ng Manggagawang Kababaihan (KMK, Women Workers' Movement); Amihan (peasant women's association); Samahan ng Malayang Kababaihang Nagkakaisa (Samakana, urban poor women's association); Health Alliance for Democracy (Head); Ecumenical Movement for Justice and Peace (EMJP); Alliance of Concerned Teachers (ACT); Pambansang Lakas ng Kilusang Mamamalakaya ng Pilipinas (Pamalakaya, fisherfolk association); Confederation for Unity, Recognition and Advancement of Government Employees (COURAGE); Promotion for Church People's Response (PCPR); Kalipunan ng Katutubong Mamamayan sa Pilipinas (Kamp, National Minorities'Association); Migrante International; and First Quarter Storm movement. There are also other organizations that may not be member organizations of BAYAN Philippines but are supportive of the National Democratic movement.

6 As part of BAYAN's eight-point program, the member organizations are united in wanting to build a self-reliant and progressive economy by dismantling the imperialist and feudal stranglehold of the economy and carrying out national industrialization and genuine land reform.

7 "The International League of Peoples' Struggle (ILPS) is an anti-imperialist and democratic formation (see ILPS Charter). It promotes, supports, and develops the anti-imperialist and democratic struggles of the peoples of the world against imperialism and all reaction." https://ilps.info/en/about-ilps/, accessed January 20, 2020.

8 Jill Mangaliman, personal interview, October 13, 2019.

9 Pyxie Castillo, personal interview, October 9, 2019.

10 Jhonry Delacruz, personal interview, October 11, 2019.

11 The Kilusang Mayo Uno (KMU), formed in 1980 in the Philippines, is an independent labor center promoting genuine militant and patriotic trade unionism. The KMU is a member organization of BAYAN.

12 Terrie Cervas, personal interview, October 11, 2019.

13 Jennelle Barajas, personal interview, October 13, 2019.

14 Castillo, personal interview, October 9, 2019.

15 Mangaliman, personal interview, October 13, 2019.

16 Sharlyn Santiago, personal interview, October 11, 2019.

17 Nina Macapinlac, personal interview, October 14, 2019.

18 "Yuri Kochiyama: With Justice in Her Heart," *Revolutionary Worker* 986, December 13, 1998, https://www.revcom.us/a/v20/980-89/986 /yuri.htm.

19 BAYAN USA Statement, "US Iraq War Veteran Warns of Drones in Mindanao, Pacification, and EDCA," August 7, 2014, http://bayanusa .org/us-iraq-war-veteran-warns-of-drones-in-mindanao-pacification -and-edca.

20 John Prysner, "Eyewitness: US Tax Dollars Fund State-Run Terrorism in the Philippines," *Liberation News*, July 10, 2019, https://www .liberationnews.org/eyewitness-u-s-tax-dollars-fund-state-run-terrorism -in-the-philippines.

21 Mangaliman, personal interview, October 13, 2019.

PART 3

POLITICAL EDUCATION
AND RADICAL PEDAGOGY

CHAPTER 7

POLITICAL EDUCATION AS REVOLUTIONARY PRAXIS

MAY C. FU

> The object in presenting these considerations is to defend the
> eminently pedagogical character of the revolution.
> —PAULO FREIRE, *PEDAGOGY OF THE OPPRESSED*

POLITICAL EDUCATION IS A PILLAR OF REVOLUTIONARY PRAXIS.
Unlike traditional forms of education that cherish hierarchy and
reward conformity, political education is grounded in guiding principles that produce a pedagogical theory and practice of individual and
collective liberation. It emerges from aggrieved communities as a
response and antidote to hegemonic forms of education that function
to delegitimize their ways of knowing and being in the world. As
such, political education develops locally, organically, and out of necessity. Community organizers, educators, and social theorists like Glenn
Omatsu, Yuri Kochiyama, Madonna Thunderhawk, Ella Jo Baker, and
Bob Moses understand that liberatory education plays an indispensable role in movements for community self-determination.[1] They recognize the transformative power of ordinary people coming into
awareness as active participants in the making of history, as change
agents with the capacity to theorize complex systems of oppression in
everyday terms to deconstruct state violence, interrupt intergenerational dispossession, form new societal relations, and in the words of
activist-philosopher Grace Lee Boggs, "become more human human

beings."[2] This chapter examines key principles of political education and explores how three grassroots organizations—Providence Youth Student Movement (PrYSM), Hai Bà Tru'ng School for Organizing (HBT), and Adhikaar—utilize various forms of political education to transform community members, workers, and youth and build community power from the ground up.[3]

Political education, as defined by Paulo Freire and Ella Jo Baker, embodies important principles that lay the foundation for liberatory curriculum and learning. In the forms of political education analyzed in this chapter, several key features emerge. *Horizontal learning* encourages a nonhierarchical exchange between facilitators and participants based on mutual respect. Characterized by deep listening and engaged dialogue, horizontal learning rejects unequal power dynamics between facilitators and participants, upsetting hierarchies that cast the facilitator as more knowledgeable and correct than the participant. *Process-oriented education* challenges traditional pedagogies that focus solely on goal-oriented learning and conceptualizes education as an ongoing, cumulative experience that deepens our relationships to ourselves, others, and the world. *Collective wisdom* proceeds from the premise that perspectives are partial and that the most powerful revelations about how power operates are those generated in shared dialogue with others. It means that every person has valuable insights to exchange and learn, not just those who are most educated or most assertive.

Lived experience values everyday experiences as legitimate sources of information and political direction. It respects the knowledge that arises from navigating the social, economic, political, and emotional structures that define our lives. *Relevant education* holds the expectation that education should not only reflect and engage with our complex realities but also provide the tools to transform it. Social justice curricula, for example, center the voices of aggrieved groups whose eyewitness accounts produce an intimate knowledge of systemic abuses and shape the strategies needed to address community needs. *Authentic dialogue* invites us to have honest, thoughtful, and hopeful exchanges with others. Sometimes challenging and always humbling, it values the viewpoints produced in and through dialogic exchanges with others. In the words of Paulo Freire, dialogue requires a "profound love for the world and for people . . . [and] faith in their power to make and remake, to create and re-create, faith in their vocation to be more fully human."[4] *Critical thinking and action* value reflection, self-reflexivity, and informed action. It analyzes the root causes of injustice and situates experiences within concrete historical, social, and structural contexts rather than isolated and individualized viewpoints in order to produce incisive strategy and movement for social change. Shaped by these principles, political education is a deeply relational and dialectical praxis.

Grassroots organizers have long utilized political education as a strategy and method to educate, mobilize, and organize local people. In the 1960s community-controlled education emerged from an urgent need to nurture and empower disenfranchised youth, adults, and elders in accessible, affirming spaces that equipped them with the critical skill sets needed to address their communities' most urgent issues. The American Indian Movement Survival Schools, the Student Nonviolent Coordinating Committee Freedom Schools, the Highlander Folk School Citizenship Schools, the Young Lords Party's liberation schools, and other grassroots programs impacted generations of students with political education curricula that centered communities of color within their own histories, deconstructed US racial capitalism, forged interracial solidarity, and most important, cultivated individual and collective self-efficacy.[5] Asian American Movement history overflows with formal and informal educational spaces, from the nearly daily workshops offered by revolutionary organizations headquartered at the International Hotel in San Francisco to the intergenerational political discussions held in cozy apartments by Asian Americans for Action in New York City to the collective study groups of the Asian American Political Alliance in Detroit and the Union of Vietnamese in the United States in Los Angeles. These vibrant, homegrown programs tapped into people's resentment of their marginalization within mainstream education and nourished their deep desire to learn. Across the country numerous community-run classes and study groups—such as those hosted by movement organizations, unions, political collectives, worker cooperatives, and *escuelas*—served as autonomous sites of learning and grassroots action.

By the 1980s nonprofit organizations primarily dedicated to revolutionary theory, organizing, and direct action began to form. The School of Unity and Liberation, the Center for Third World Organizing, the Highlander Research and Education Center, and other organizations produced a constellation of alumni who went on to become movement organizers and leaders; however, the neoconservative backlash to leftist organizing, limitations of grant-reliant nonprofit organizations, and steep cost of living increases challenged the proliferation of similar organizations.[6] Always at the forefront of movement organizing, grassroots community groups continue to offer political education and organizing trainings to deepen their members' political analyses, sharpen skills for their campaigns, and nurture future leadership. Three community organizations—PrYSM, HBT, and Adhikaar—illustrate how political education acts as both strategy and method that situates local problems within broader structural and historical context, demystifies political hegemony, amplifies voices of the oppressed through transformative storytelling, and builds movements led by those who are most impacted.

FROM EDUCATION TO ABOLITION: CAMBODIAN YOUTH ORGANIZING IN THE PROVIDENCE YOUTH STUDENT MOVEMENT

In November 2001 Southeast Asian (SEA) teenagers, college students, and queer and trans folks formed the Providence Youth Student Movement to address the Cambodian gang violence occurring in their community.[7] Three months later PrYSM launched its first community campaign in response to a repatriation agreement signed by the United States and Cambodia that authorized the forced deportation of Cambodian refugees and state-sanctioned family separation. As the only SEA and queer youth of color–led organization in Providence, Rhode Island, PrYSM quickly became a community activist and organizing base for gang members, single parents, queer and trans youth, and middle, high school, and college students.[8]

Two decades later PrSYM has emerged as a powerful youth-led prison abolitionist organization that seeks to dismantle systems of oppression and build a society with "no prisons, no police, and no borders."[9] The organization is composed and led by mostly queer and trans SEA middle and high school students and a small staff, who, according to the group's website, center "youth, female, queer, and people of color leadership in [their] campaigns, organization, and [communities]."[10] PrSYM organizers recognize that queer and trans people and youth of color have, in the words of co–executive director Steven Dy, worked "with us, for us, and have paved the foundation" by leading a movement that believes that "our liberation is tied to the liberation of Black folks here in the US and freedom fighters in Latin America."[11] The organization embraces a liberatory and intersectional politics that is committed to addressing deep-seated community needs and creating necessary, healthy alternatives. The group's website states: "PrYSM must work toward transforming our community by building safe spaces that foster accountability, healing, and dialogue. Social justice, community organizing, and institutional change must be rooted in community passion and unity. Love for ourselves, our families, and our communities must guide PrYSM's work, actions, and collective vision" (figure 7.1).[12]

"Peace, Love, and Power" are central tenets in the work of PrYSM, says Dy, and are the "moral reasons that we stand by and organize by." These principles anchor PrYSM's abolitionist politics and shape an organizational culture that is as much an expression of their political education pedagogy as their programs. Members are committed to being with each other, supporting each other, building with each other, and being willing to "practice, practice, practice" becoming the community they wish to see. Dy explains that through critical dialogue and wholehearted care, members "try however we can, with whatever we have, to sharpen and hone and deepen our analysis."[13] Members and their families are survivors of US militarism in and forced migration from Cambodia, Laos, and Vietnam as well as state surveillance and local police harassment, which generates instability and violence within their homes. Seeking to end cycles of violence and patriarchy, PrYSM practices the values of "Peace, Love, and Power" as intentional responses to these layered histories.

Political education lies at the crux of this youth-led organization. New student members from local middle and high schools participate in a political education program that takes place over two weekends. Every meeting opens with youth-generated "community agreements," collectively authored and agreed-upon guidelines that create the conditions for respectful and loving interaction.[14] Agreements are different from—and better than—rules. They embody an ethos of co-creation, accompaniment, and group accountability, rather than authoritarian discipline and control. For SEA, queer, and trans youth whose lives are structured by punitive rules not of their making, community agreements create a participatory democratic space in which their voices matter. Community agreements include Safe Space, Brave Space; What Is Said Here Stays Here, What Is Learned Here Leaves

FIGURE 7.1. Providence Youth Student Movement youth engaging with community members at the Annual PrSYM Block Party in August 2019. Photo courtesy of Steven Dy.

Here; One Diva, One Mic; Move Up, Move Down; Don't Yuck My Yum; and W.A.I.T. (Why Am I Talking?).[15] These deceptively simple agreements acknowledge the risks that people take to be vulnerable and define listening as an intentional, spacious, and self-aware practice. More than communication techniques, community agreements help students recognize that their attitudes, words, and interactions produce their organizational culture and manifest the political education principles that they seek to convey.

PrYSM's political education is composed of foundational workshops, including Systems of Oppression, SEA History, and Queer Justice, which introduce students to the historical conditions and power relations they navigate every day. The Systems of Oppression workshop defines critical terms such as *heterosexism, classism, ableism, racism, sexism, ageism,* and *anti-immigrant system* in order to build a shared language and critique of structural discrimination. Former and current PrSYM members act as facilitators who ask youth to consider each term and share examples from their own lives for the group to hear, reflect, and discuss together. In an exercise called Pyramid of Power, youth are divided into groups and handed an envelope labeled sexuality, race, gender, ability, class, or age. Inside the envelopes are slips of paper with subgroups that the youth are asked to rank according to social privilege and tape onto a large Pyramid of Power hanging on the wall. Students explain the rationales behind their rankings and placements on the pyramid, eventually exploring the dangers of oppression hierarchies and the importance of intersectional politics. Youth practice how to think relationally and comparatively, connecting seemingly disconnected identities to parallel experiences of systemic discrimination and developing solidarities based on politics.

The Queer Justice workshop invites youth to reflect on and engage gender, sexuality, and identity. The young people learn about the meaning and fluidity of gender identity, gender expression, biological sex, and sexual and romantic attraction. In an open and supportive environment, they discuss gender pronouns, the multiplicity of trans identities, and the violence experienced by queer and trans communities. Facilitators ask: "What does it means to be queer? How do we respect that? Do you think these forms of oppression occur in activist spaces? How do we build a safe space for LGBTQ* people?"[16] Safe spaces to explore gender, sexuality, and attraction are rare for first- and second-generation SEA youth who face intergenerational language and cultural barriers, but PrSYM's pedagogy provides a model for healthy, loving, and transparent discussions and allows them to establish new norms that respect queer and trans lives.

The SEA History workshop utilizes a narrative timeline and detailed maps to outline the history of French and US colonialism in Vietnam,

Laos, and Cambodia. Facilitators explain the political, military, and environmental impact of US military occupation in SEA while highlighting the rise of antiwar demonstrations and drawing attention to Dr. Martin Luther King Jr.'s iconic speech "Beyond Vietnam," which critiqued the militarism, capitalism, and racism of the American War in SEA. Although the US wars in Vietnam, Cambodia, and Laos were among the most controversial in US history, Providence's public school curriculum fails to address them with any meaningful depth. The SEA History workshop, Dy notes, is often the first time that SEA youth "know their history so they can know themselves."[17]

With these critical building blocks, PrSYM facilitators and youth leaders link histories, ideologies, and systems of oppression with issues that currently impact their communities. Dy describes how youth make the connections between the US wars in Vietnam, Cambodia, and Laos and the dispersed and impoverished "hyperghettos that our families were dropped in" that produced state surveillance and violence within their refugee communities. They see how an under-resourced and underfunded public school system disenfranchises and criminalizes youths, who are then funneled into the school-to-prison-to-deportation pipeline.[18] Co–executive director Veronica Flores-Maldonado explains: "Youth understand each part of the pipeline and how they feed into each other. They are already familiar with removal orders, how law enforcement works with each other. They know that there is database sharing between the police and ICE. They have their lived experience and know the impact."[19] Drawing from personal and peer experiences, youths already have the tools to deconstruct the school-to-prison-to-deportation pipeline as a racist mechanism that facilitates the separation of their families and destruction of their communities.

SEA youth and their families were placed in Rhode Island as part of the US refugee resettlement programs in the aftermath of the American War in Vietnam, Laos, and Cambodia, and they have struggled with the dire lack of infrastructure to support basic economic, educational, health care, and linguistic needs ever since. Over 36 percent of Cambodians and 18 percent of Laotians live in poverty, compared to 11.9 percent of the general population. Although Khmer is the state's third most used language after English and Spanish, Cambodian families live in linguistic isolation without interpreters or translators. Elders are survivors of war and refugee migration, but their mental health needs are unmet; over 70 percent of refugees who receive mental health services are diagnosed with post-traumatic stress disorder. In addition to high rates of unemployment, refugees are hesitant to civically engage with local politics and struggle with US cultural values, gender norms, and queer and trans sexualities.[20] Despite these challenges, first- and second-generation SEA youths serve as multitalented, multitasking, bilingual, and bicultural interpreters, translators, advocates, cultural bridges, and critical resources for their families; however, institutional support systems for SEA youth are abysmal and fail to address high rates of school truancy and absences, low graduation numbers, and needs for mental health, academic counseling, tutoring and after-school activities, and employment. Further, the Rhode Island Department of Education does not disaggregate data about "Asians," so specific statistics about Cambodians, Laotians, and Hmong are unavailable and therefore unaddressed.

In 2006 PrYSM took matters into its own hands by training seventeen members to design, conduct, and analyze a sixty-question youth survey. They waited outside of middle and high schools, door knocked, walked in SEA neighborhoods, and asked SEA merchants about their experiences with Providence public schools, police, racial profiling, gangs, and violence as well as collected demographic data. They completed 365 surveys by hand, which accounted for 16 percent of the entire fourteen- to twenty-eight-year-old SEA population in Providence. Their cutting-edge research revealed that 58.9 percent of Laotians and 38.1 percent of Cambodians ages eighteen to twenty-four and 38.1 percent of Hmong did not graduate from high school; the national average is 19.2 percent. In addition, 75 percent of SEA youth skipped school, and 66 percent of that group did so more than once a month; a whopping 64.5 percent of them ditched school several times per week.[21] These absences, they found, correlated with the heavy burden of family responsibilities shouldered by young people, low after-school participation, and high dropout rates.[22] The compelling report also revealed staggering statistics regarding Providence police abuse and misconduct, racial profiling, and criminalization as well as intergenerational conflict, gender violence, and the need for queer and trans resources.

After many group discussions, the youth developed campaigns to address directly the needs voiced by their communities. They listed the most pressing issues, developed strategies, identified points of intervention, organized public actions, and built citywide alliances. In 2012 PrSYM partnered with Direct Action for Rights and Equality, Olneyville Neighborhood Association, and the American Friends Service Committee to author the Community Safety Act (CSA), a community-centered city ordinance that addressed policy accountability, banned racial profiling, and created a protocol for police interaction with Providence residents. PrYSM organizers planned forums for and by youth that asked about their encounters with police and collected recommendations for best practices for police-youth interactions. PrYSM worked closely with a community attorney to draft the ordinance's sections on youth privacy and the right for young people to be informed of their registration on the city's otherwise confidential "gang list" of alleged gang members. Youth organized direct actions that packed Providence City Hall with hundreds of people and met with elected officials to share testimonials about police harassment and violence.[23] In June 2017 the city passed the CSA, which was widely recognized as one of the most progressive municipal police reform laws in the country. Directed by the analyses of its queer, trans, and SEA youth members, it was also PrYSM's first policy win.[24] In July 2019 PrSYM filed a federal lawsuit against the city of Providence for "violating local and federal law by using broad 'association' criteria to list people in a gang database." The ongoing lawsuit alleges that the Providence Police Department violates the CSA and "tramples fundamental constitutional rights" in its gang database policy, which enables racial profiling, harassment, and the violation of youth privacy. Local journalists Julia Rock and Lucas Smolcic Larsen conclude that "the city was put on notice" by the young people of PrYSM, who continue to hold the city accountable to queer, trans, and SEA youth and residents of color.[25] This policy victory was also pedagogical. Youth practiced direct organizing, speaking out, and treating themselves as equal to those in power. They learned how the system works and used that knowledge to improve the conditions in their community. Confronted with the failure of municipal policing, these young people know that the problems they face are systemic and structural and that fighting for reforms is a step on a path toward revolution.

As a queer-, trans-, and youth-centered and led abolitionist organization, PrYSM is fiercely loyal to the needs and vision of its members.

Lack of employment opportunities, little to no resources for SEA families, housing instability, rising costs of living, and an incompetent school system mean that one of PrYSM's biggest challenges is, Dy points out, "keeping students around through their issues related to time, work, school, and family issues." It also means that PrYSM directly challenges entrenched state institutions that create and exacerbate the violence and disenfranchisement experienced by SEA communities. "Being a radical and revolutionary abolitionist organization creates a lot of enemies, such as school systems, police, and courts," says Dy, "but it's also what attracts folks to the organization. Police are not going to police themselves. Only we can save ourselves. Revolution is more important than reform."[26]

REENVISIONING REVOLUTION: DECENTERING VIETNAMESE ANTICOMMUNIST NARRATIVES IN THE HAI BÀ TRƯNG SCHOOL FOR ORGANIZING

In 2009 several Vietnamese grassroots organizers in Southern California started meeting to share their experiences in the Vietnamese community. Each of them were longtime organizers who had worked with queer and trans youth, youth of color, Asian American, and Vietnamese communities in Los Angeles and Orange County in Southern California, the San Francisco Bay Area, Portland, New Orleans, Biloxi, and New York City. After a year and a half of relationship building, they began to explore their capacity to organize Vietnamese communities in more concerted ways. Community organizer thuan nguyen remembers: "We were starting to meet and come across more and more folks who had similar questions and critiques about the Vietnamese community's conservatism, critiques about US involvement in Southeast Asia. There just weren't enough spaces or opportunities to explore these questions. . . . Yes, there was a significant aspect of the community that was conservative, anticommunist, pro-US, etc., but we didn't want to just react to that condition. We wanted to be able to create opportunities and spaces for us to be more visionary in terms of what our politics were beyond that."[27] A year later the organizers convened the first statewide gathering of progressive Vietnamese organizers, academics, and artists at the Vietnamese American Arts & Letters Association (VAALA) building in Santa Ana, California. Entitled "Beyond 35: Building a Vision for Social Justice in the Viet Community," the two-day gathering was attended by about fifty Vietnamese organizers from Southern California, the San Francisco Bay Area, Portland, New Orleans, and New York City.

Organizers addressed Vietnamese histories of war and migration, US occupation in Southeast Asia, and the political challenges of organizing the Vietnamese community, especially noting the entrenched post-1975 anticommunism and political conservatism of Vietnamese communities. Progressive Vietnamese organizers, many of whom are second- or third-generation and shaped by international anticolonial liberation movements and their experiences as youth of color in the United States, are often accused of being communist sympathizers who disrespect the harrowing experiences of those who fled post-1975 Vietnam and experienced significant hardship and trauma after the country was unified. Anticommunist sentiment is so pervasive within Vietnamese American communities that, as nguyen relates, "discussions that did not strongly condemn the Communists and NLF were not allowed."[28] In fact, any expression of curiosity or sympathy for the National Liberation Front that opposed US military occupation, for former North Vietnamese prime minister and president Hồ Chí Minh, or for the Socialist Republic of Vietnam resulted in hostile public opposition that included fire bombings, physical violence, and sometimes death. From 1981 to 1990 at least seven Vietnamese Americans were murdered in these incidents; five were journalists who published newspapers, wrote or republished North Vietnamese news, or critiqued Vietnamese anticommunist forces in the United States. All of these homicide cases remain unsolved.[29]

That the statewide gathering was held at the VAALA space was not lost on the group. On January 9, 2009, VAALA hosted the opening of *F.O.B. II: Art Speaks* [*Nghệ Thuật Lên Tiếng*], a nine-day exhibit that highlighted the work of over fifty visual and performances artists across the Vietnamese diaspora.[30] The exhibit, which included images of the national flag of the Socialist Republic of Vietnam and Hồ Chí Minh, sought to reconsider refugee politics, sexuality, and Vietnamese identity formation through the arts.[31] The reaction from the Vietnamese community in Orange County was swift. VAALA and the curators were immediately besieged by criticism, obscene phone calls, and threats of a protest by members of the Vietnamese community. As the days passed, the art exhibit galvanized many groups from around the world to demonstrate against our art show—there were as many as eighty signatories on the internet discussion forum.[32]

Anticommunist protesters went so far as to vandalize some of the art, while others held signs with sexist slurs that proclaimed, "commie collaborators" and "'thương nữ bất tri vong quốc hận,' a phrase that roughly translates as 'businesswomen who are unaware of the people's resentment that the nation has been lost.'"[33] Hoping to ease community tensions and under pressure by city officials and local politicians, exhibit organizers closed the show early.

The organizers of "Beyond 35" deliberately held the gathering at VAALA as a way "to reclaim the space and offer some healing." They wished to honor the original vision of the exhibit, which sought a nuanced contemplation about the arts, homeland politics, and Vietnamese diasporic identity formation. They hoped to "decenter the logic of a white liberalism that would champion what is perceived as our leftist, procommunist stance or critique of an older generation, who are unable to let go of the past" while acknowledging that anticommunism is a "pedagogical" site of diasporic Vietnamese memory making and mourning.[34] Based on these critical conversations, the participants of "Beyond 35" went on to create documentary videos about Vietnamese experiences, organized "common ground" open mic events in Santa Ana, California, and a year later launched the Hai Bà Trưng School for Organizing (HBT).

In 2011 HBT organized its first weekend training program for Vietnamese organizers and activists to explore Vietnamese history and politics and build more capacity for Vietnamese community organizing. Participants were given a rare opportunity to explore revolutionary Vietnamese American identity, learn basic organizing theory and skills, and connect to a growing national network of Vietnamese activists and organizers. Since its inception HBT has been held at least once a year in Los Angeles, Oakland, Westminster, Philadelphia, or New York City and has over two hundred alumni. The program addresses the critical need for Vietnamese organizers to have a supportive space in which to explore the key issues facing their community: the legacy of US war in Vietnam, Laos, and Cambodia; an entrenched culture of South Vietnamese refugee and immigrant gratitude for US benevolence; and staunch anticommunism in US and diasporic Vietnamese communities. Because these tensions have structured intergenerational relationships and complicated the formation of a radical Vietnamese politics in the United States, HBT emerged as one way for organizers to rethink hegemonic narratives and imagine alternative possibilities.[35]

Utilizing political education as a principle and strategy, HBT coordinators carefully crafted their curriculum. On the first day of the weekend training, participants are asked to reflect upon their identities from a critical, historical, and collective perspective. What does it mean to be Vietnamese? How do you experience your Vietnamese identity? What is your relationship to your family, history, culture, and community? What does it mean for us be in the United States as a result of US intervention in Southeast Asia? What is our vision as radical Vietnamese Americans, and where are we headed (figure 7.2)?

Out of those dialogues emerged the need to center queer, trans, and femme gender identities and experiences in Vietnamese radical politics. Around the same time that HBT was forming, Vietnamese LGBTQ+

FIGURE 7.2. HBT members participate in a workshop during an August 2016 training in Southern California. Using movement and dialogue, this group activity allowed participants to explore their relationship and resistance to systems of power and oppression. Photo courtesy of Hai Bà Tru'ng School for Organizing.

community members were excluded from participating in the annual Little Saigon Tết Parade in Westminster, California, prompting critical discussions about ongoing discrimination and exclusion experienced by LGBTQ+ members of the Vietnamese community. As HBT grew, so did conversations about the need to center those issues in its curriculum so participants could formulate a politics that envisioned queer and trans liberation as co-constitutive of radical Vietnamese politics. HBT organizers who are queer, trans, femme, and nonbinary engaged in ongoing dialogues about what it means to "take on a revolutionary framework that integrates queer, trans, and femme identities and politics. What does it mean to be Vietnamese and use that as a baseline to explore and critique revolutionary history? How does the curriculum need to be updated?" Through horizontal learning and authentic dialogue, organizers trust that their collective process will continue to develop an intersectional foundation for what nguyen describes as a "left Vietnamese American politics that is grounded in a transnational, internationalist, and intersectional perspective that embraces an anti-imperialist, anti-capitalist, and anti-oppression politics."[36]

Inspired by the Zapatista movement in rural Mexico and Black, Indigenous, and Latinx liberation movements in the United States, HBT coordinators invite participants to examine hidden legacies of anticolonial liberation in their homeland. HBT itself, organizers explain, is named after Trưng Trắc and Trưng Nhị, two sisters who led Vietnam's first rebellion against Chinese colonial occupation in 40 CE. After overthrowing the Triệu Dynasty in 111 BCE, China colonized Vietnam and carved the country into districts that were overseen by appointed Vietnamese generals, who reported to the local Chinese governor. Trưng Trắc and Trưng Nhị were born to one of these generals in the rural district of Giao Chỉ in northern Vietnam and raised under the harsh rule of Chinese governor Tô Định, who exploited Vietnamese labor and punished, imprisoned, or executed dissenters. Throughout their lives they witnessed the suppression of traditional Vietnamese matriarchal family structure by Chinese colonial patriarchy. When Tô Định implemented a harsh and unfair tax, Trưng Trắc's husband, Thi Sách, himself a general of a neighboring district, confronted Tô Định. In one version of what followed, Thi Sách was executed for his defiance, prompting Trưng Trắc and Trưng Nhị to avenge his death; in another retelling Thi Sách was not killed and went on to support Trưng

Trắc's reclamation of women's leadership. In both accounts Trưng Trắc and Trưng Nhị organized the peasants into a powerful eighty thousand–person army composed mostly of women and led by several dozen women generals. Riding into battle on a herd of elephants, the Trưng sisters and their army revolted against the Chinese, overthrowing sixty-five fortresses and driving the Chinese out of Vietnam. Known as the Hai Bà Trưng sisters, both women ruled a sovereign and independent Vietnam for three years before being ousted by the Chinese. HBT organizers honor Vietnam's two thousand–year history of feminist, anticolonial, and liberatory struggles for self-determination by linking their training program to a revolutionary legacy of Vietnamese love and resistance.

HBT organizers also developed a timeline activity for participants to reconsider Vietnamese organizing in the United States within a longer history of Vietnamese radicalism and anti-imperialism. Along the walls of the room, facilitators tape a large timeline marked with key events, images, and captions from Vietnamese, Vietnamese American, and US history, including the Geneva Accords, the history of the National Liberation Front, the Gulf of Tonkin incident, the life of Hồ Chí Minh, the Paris Peace Accords, and the 1980 Refugee Act. Participants are invited to write important moments from their family histories onto sticky notes that they can insert into the timeline. Placing their personal lives into the timeline produces a multilayered, even contradictory, historical narrative for the participants. Some share the discomfort of seeing images of North Vietnamese figures or the mixed emotions that arise when considering Hồ Chí Minh and the National Liberation Front as anti-imperialist freedom fighters or when casting Vietnamese national reunification in a positive light. Facilitators realize that deconstructing and demystifying taboos is challenging work, so discussions are conducted in a spirit of love and nonjudgment that acknowledges the difficulties that arise when questioning long-held narratives. For many participants this timeline activity is the first time they had ever participated in an open, non-reactionary conversation with other Vietnamese Americans about Vietnamese radicalism, the US war in Vietnam, and homeland politics.

Insights from these dialogues are carried over to the skills training portion of the weekend, during which participants learn fundamental community organizing skills, such as conducting one-on-one conversations, mapping the political landscape of the Vietnamese community, and completing a power analysis. With each training HBT aims to partner with local organizing efforts to give participants a fieldwork opportunity to put their organizing skills to practice—some for the very first time and others who are building on their previous experience. HBT participants have done fieldwork related to the gentrification of local businesses in Los Angeles's Chinatown with Chinatown Community for Equitable Development; occupational and reproductive safety among nail salon workers and owners in Oakland, California; anti-deportation campaigns with the Dorchester Organizing and Training Initiative in Dorchester, Massachusetts; and assessing attitudes of community members around anti-Blackness and anti-deportation efforts in Orange County, California.

Organizers, however, realize several limitations to their program. As a stand-alone three-day training, HBT is not connected to a long-term campaign or organizational vision, nor is it a pathway for members to develop their political and leadership potential other than referring them to existing groups. Sustaining HBT's programming is also challenged by a lack of consistent funding. While participants may emerge from HBT more ready to organize, there have been few formal avenues to continue exploring radical Vietnamese politics and identities with other Vietnamese organizers and even fewer paid opportunities within organizations that are willing to publicly engage leftist frameworks and strategies. As a result, many HBT alumni are scattered across the country in various Asian American and social justice nonprofit organizations, informal political collectives, university graduate programs, and arts organizations; however, they strive to maintain relationships with one another by creating informal and experimental networks.

HBT organizers are currently exploring ways to connect with past and future participants and for the past decade have worked with groups and activists from around the country to support organizing efforts and build infrastructure for ongoing movement work. These efforts have evolved into the Việt Solidarity & Action Network (VSAN), a "network of Việt organizers and activists committed to strengthening a progressive/Left vision and strategy" through solidarity, community organizing, and long-term movement building." VSAN became public in June 2020 in solidarity with the Movement for Black Lives and the uprisings sparked by the deaths of Breonna Taylor, George Floyd, and Tony McDade.[37] VSAN is guided by collectively authored

Points of Unity that include working in solidarity with other communities and movements to bring about social change, embracing the intersectional identities of its members, and moving beyond Cold War politics in the exploration of Vietnamese political identity.[38]

TESTIFYING FOR CHANGE: IMMIGRANT WOMEN'S STORYTELLING IN ADHIKAAR

Its name meaning "rights" in Nepali, Adhikaar is a women-led community and worker center in Queens, New York, that serves and organizes the Nepali-speaking immigrant and refugee community on workers' rights, immigrant rights, access to health care, and language justice. Founded in 2005 by four women of color "with $500 and a vision of justice," Adhikaar is the only grassroots movement organization addressing workers' rights and economic justice for Nepali-speaking immigrants in the United States.[39] Nepali-speaking immigrants, many of whom are on Temporary Protected Status (TPS), are asylees or refugees or are undocumented; they constitute a relatively new and rapidly growing community in the United States. New York City houses the nation's highest concentration, with an estimated 12,000 residents. Adhikaar's staff and members are almost entirely first- and second-generation, working-class, women and women-identified, Indigenous, nontraditionally educated, and considered lower-caste in their country of origin.[40] They labor in what executive director Pabitra Benjamin describes as some of the "most unprotected, underpaid, and undervalued" industries in the city as domestic workers, nail salon workers, restaurant workers, and taxi and Uber or Lyft drivers.[41] Located at the intersection of race, gender, caste, class, and immigrant status, they are especially vulnerable to labor exploitation, sexual harassment, and trafficking in the workplace as well as in their daily lives.

On April 25, 2015, a severe 7.8 magnitude earthquake shook the city of Gorkha located fifty miles northwest of the Nepali capital of Kathmandu. Dozens of relentless aftershocks and landslides followed, affecting over eight million people, closing down hundreds of health care facilities and thousands of schools, and devastating densely populated neighborhoods and villages, leaving an estimated three million people homeless.[42] Two months later Adhikaar successfully campaigned for the designation of Temporary Protected Status to Nepali immigrants under the Obama administration, granting them a temporary stay against deportation back to their disaster-stricken home country. Although TPS holders were ineligible for Social Security or public assistance, they were granted work permits, social security numbers, health insurance, and the ability to cross borders. Adhikaar quickly became a central hub for the Nepali TPS community to receive services, seek legal resources, and organize for further protections. In 2019 the Trump administration terminated the program for Nepal, but the TPS membership that Adhikaar has developed continues to fight for permanent status and protections through an ongoing federal lawsuit and bill that passed the House of Representatives in 2020.[43]

Adhikaar has organized mostly immigrant women domestic and nail salon workers from its inception, firmly believing that all workers deserve safe working conditions, fair wages, and to be treated with dignity and respect, regardless of documentation. In 2010 the state of New York passed the Domestic Worker Bill of Rights, which provided housekeepers, nannies, and home health aides with a minimum wage, overtime pay, sick leave, safe and healthy working conditions, and a discrimination-free workplace; however, it was not until they received TPS that workers felt empowered to advocate for their labor rights in greater numbers.[44] For the first time Adhikaar was able to expand its campaign work in New York City and into New Jersey while also becoming an important voice in national immigrant rights coalitions. Aware of the multilayered discrimination based on race, class, gender, caste, class, and immigration status faced by their constituents, Adhikaar organizes its members through the political education that is woven into their strategies and programs.

Adhikaar's work is defined by a "theory of change" that links direct services, political education, community organizing, and leadership development.[45] All programs are determined and directed by the everyday needs and realities of the immigrant community. Most workers first step into Adhikaar's office for services such as TPS legal support, nail salon licensing, nanny training, or English for Empowerment language classes. All of these services are integrated with a political education curriculum that introduces workers to a critical framework that connects their immediate needs to a structural analysis of racist immigration laws, unfair labor practices, sexual harassment, and trafficking while generating critical dialogue and practical solutions at every stage.

Central to the organization's work are the storytelling and spokes-person trainings, two- to three-hour workshops that are held one-on-one or in groups. Workers are asked to reflect on the ways that stories are used to silence working women's voices, instill shame and lower self-worth, promote complacency, and in the words of director of campaigns and communications Prarthana Gurung, "maintain an untrue status quo." Facilitators, she explains, ask workers: "What stories did you grow up with? What did you hear about undocumented, low-wage, immigrant work? What lessons did those stories hold? . . . You have an experience. It is true. No one can take that away. Your story is as factual as data reports, numbers, and research. Your story is legiti-mate."[46] Storytelling can be cathartic and therapeutic for any group, but it is especially powerful for people who have been systematically shunned or silenced. Adhikaar members are encouraged to reconsider the stories they have heard throughout their lives and trust the insights produced by their lived experience. These trainings provide the space for immigrant women workers to articulate and compose personal nar-ratives and make their crucial labor visible. These otherwise silenced testimonies upend narratives about the disposability of immigrant women's work and reclaim the dignity of their labor by calling out the wage theft and other injustices that they confront on a daily basis.

Part of the difficulty in mobilizing workers is the stigma of associ-ating oneself with low-wage work, but as former organizer Tsering Lama observes, these workshops "empower workers to identify as domestic workers. It is not about shame and labeling. There is a stigma about being a low-wage domestic worker in the United States and Nepal. Migrants themselves had domestic workers in Nepal, so there is class disidentification."[47] Adhikaar's program, which include English for Empowerment classes, nanny trainings, TPS trainings, and nail salon licensing classes, encourage immigrants to see themselves as skilled workers worthy of respect and dignity. Through sustained, critical dialogue that centers the collective wisdom of their lived expe-riences, members understand that all workers deserve a living wage and safe working conditions, regardless of race, gender, sexual orien-tation, and immigration status. They recognize their experiences as important sources of insider knowledge that not only emboldens them to negotiate for wages, meal breaks, and overtime compensa-tion with employers but also positions them as indispensable leaders of Adhikaar's organizing campaigns. As Benjamin observes, "Dialogue radicalizes our work."[48]

In an effort to make visible the essential labor of low-wage immigrant women, Adhikaar staff collaborated with New York–based art museums and venues to create public platforms for workers to articulate their testimonies. In the spirit of the Free Southern Theater and Teatro Campesino, which transformed theater performances into political education classrooms for worker empowerment, Adhikaar partnered with the Rubin Museum of Art in 2013 to produce plays about labor trafficking that were written, directed, and performed by Adhikaar members themselves.[49] In 2016 domestic worker trafficking survivors participated in "A Letter to Home," a writing workshop in which they penned letters to family members in Nepal about their everyday lives and read them aloud in collaboration with The Moth, a nonprofit organization dedicated to the art and craft of storytelling. In December 2019 and January 2020 domestic workers and trafficking survivors worked with Project Luz, an audio and photojournalism organization for Mexican youth, to produce a stunning photography exhibit at the Queens Museum. They learned photography, layout, and publication skills as part of the process and were tasked with taking photos of their everyday lives to uplift the value of their work (figure 7.3). While labor organizing advocated for the visibility and equity of women's labor, these creative collaborations enabled the same workers to become artists, writers, and performers. "Worker experience is very nuanced," explains Lama, illuminating the importance of accessing various artistic mediums and cultural spaces in which immigrant workers can express and expand their intersectional identities as immigrant workers, family members, survivors, and organizers.[50]

Through monologues, role playing, pair-share activities, and performances, Lama continues, Adhikaar's members practice how to "use their voice, tell their story, converse with each other, and openly share their story" with audiences at public demonstrations, journalists, and especially elected officials.[51] They have shared their stories in more than sixty meetings with members of Congress, district officials, and state representatives in efforts to lobby for worker rights. They have also collaborated with the National Domestic Workers Alliance, traveling to Albany to advocate for the historic passage and current enforcement of the New York Domestic Worker Bill of Rights. Passed

FIGURE 7.3. Adhikaar's domestic worker leaders engage in a yearlong project with artist Sol Aramendi called Project Luz that mixed photography, art, cultural tradition, and storytelling to bring forward domestic worker stories through popular art mediums. The artwork was presented to the public through a series of public exhibitions across New York City in 2019. Photo courtesy of Adhikaar.

in 2010, the statewide bill was the first of its kind to be passed in the country and the first act to formally define domestic workers, outline an eight-hour workday with paid overtime for full-time employees, include paid vacation days, and provide grievance protocols. The bill changed the game for Adhikaar's immigrant members. According to Gurung: "We win because we testify. This is what stories do. . . . Storytelling gives [workers] an analytical base. It helps workers think critically and develop strategy with that self-generating knowledge. Stories define the agenda. Stories can win policy."[52]

As Lama puts it, "The power of our campaigns is in worker stories."[53] These experiences have increased workers' confidence, demystified the political process, and encouraged them to engage with confidence in the political system. They disrupt the traditionally male-dominated culture of organizing and advocacy within communities by developing an expanded capacity for long-term women's leadership. Stories and other forms of collective wisdom are practical tools for freedom.

Political education and personal transformation, however, is a slow, nonlinear, and time-consuming process. Like many grassroots organizations, Adhikaar's biggest challenges are the need for more time and more funding. Gurung explains: "It takes time. It takes time to develop. We are not engaged in the hot sexy thing. Political education requires more depth, but [the daily pace of work] is quick and is not conducive to the deep work that is needed." Workers themselves, as Lama points out, have limited capacity as well: "Workers leave their families to work five or six days a week and have one day off. It's hard to commit time to organize. Too many trainings affect retention, and the women are also dealing with patriarchal expectations at home."[54] The organization cannot "fund-raise at the rate of the work," states Benjamin, so "it is a challenge to balance being effective and being efficient."[55]

PrYSM, HBT, and Adhikaar illustrate how political education operates as both a strategy that advances organizational goals as well as a method guided by democratic participatory principles. PrYSM utilizes workshops to decenter the criminalization of SEA communities and invites youth to build an alternative culture in which all participants are valued and respected. Knowing their histories empowers PrYSM's young people to locate—and liberate—their families within a web of US empire, transnational displacement and everyday anti-Asian discrimination that ensnares them in a school-to-prison-to-deportation pipeline. HBT's school for organizing disrupts long-standing frameworks that have discouraged the formation of a Vietnamese American Left. Through intentional conversations and horizontal learning, HBT participants unravel an intergenerational silence about the Vietnamese revolutionary past in order to question the staunch anticommunism in their communities and open new possibilities for radical Vietnamese political identities. Revelatory storytelling workshops encourage Adhikaar members to see the collective wisdom of their lived experiences as crucial interventions in US immigration and labor reform. Nepali-speaking immigrant women workers participate in authentic dialogue that has produced oral testimonies, theater performances, and photography that bring otherwise elided voices to the forefront of public culture and policy.

From the passage of the Community Safety Act to the ongoing enforcement of the Domestic Workers Bill of Rights, these community organizations demonstrate how political education and direct organizing are shaped by the experiences of those most impacted. They remind us that political action is itself a form of political education and an expression of process-oriented education in which people learn by doing. Investigating community problems, conducting surveys, posing solutions, making demands, crafting speeches, door knocking, staging demonstrations, visiting public officials, and speaking to the press are all ways to educate members inside a group as well as those outside of it. The outcomes of these struggles teach us how to build power from the ground up and underscore political education as indispensable to liberatory praxis.

NOTES

I am grateful to the amazing organizers at the Providence Youth Student Movement (PrYSM), Hai Bà Tru'ng School for Organizing, and Adhikaar for teaching me about political education as strategy and method. Their clarity of heart and mind are guiding lights for all of us, especially in these times. I also thank Diane Fujino, George Lipsitz, and Steve Louie for their wonderful feedback on earlier drafts of this chapter.

1 Glenn K. Omatsu, "Freedom Schooling: Reconceptualizing Asian American Studies for Our Communities," *Amerasia* 29, no. 2 (2003): 9–33; Glenn K. Omatsu, "The Movement, Then and Now," keynote lecture for the 27th Annual Asian Pacific American Awareness Conference, University of California, Irvine, Asian Pacific Student Association, January 28, 2012, http://apsauci.wordpress.com/2012/01 /30/glenn-omatsu-apaac-keynote; Yuri Kochiyama, *Passing It On: A Memoir by Yuri Kochiyama* (Los Angeles: UCLA Asian American Studies Center, 2004); *Warrior Women*, directed by Elizabeth Castle and Christina King (Lincoln, NE: Vision Maker Media, 2018), DVD; Charles Payne, *I've Got the Light of Freedom: The Organizing Tradition and the Mississippi Freedom Struggle* (Berkeley: University of California Press, 1995).

2 Grace Lee Boggs, *Living for Change: An Autobiography* (Minneapolis: University of Minnesota Press, 1998), 255.

3 Scholarship on the Asian American Movement has historically addressed East Asian American communities and organizations disproportionately, especially those located in California and elsewhere along the West Coast. The organizations in this chapter were intentionally selected for their diverse geographic locations and focus on Southeast and South Asian American immigrant, youth, and refugee communities. These organizations also present different models for how to creatively engage political education in community organizing.

4 Paulo Freire, *The Pedagogy of the Oppressed* (New York: Continuum, 1996), 70–71.

5 *Warrior Women*; Payne, *I've Got the Light of Freedom*; *The Young Lords: A Reader*, ed. Darrel Enck-Wanzer (New York: New York University Press, 2010).

6   See the School of Unity and Liberation website at http://www
.schoolofunityandliberation.org; the Center for Third World Organizing at http://ctwo.org; and the Highlander Research and Education
Center at www.highlandercenter.org.

7   "Southeast Asian" is used here as a transnational and political identity
for those affected by the American War in Laos, Cambodia, and
Vietnam. Author interview with Steven Dy, February 20, 2020.

8   Kohei Ishihara, Paul Pasaba, Davide Gnoato, Reza Clifton, and Jane
Wang, *For Justice and Love: The Quality of Life for Southeast Asian
Youth"* (Providence, RI: Providence Youth Student Movement, 2010);
Bill Ong Hing, "Deporting Cambodian Refugees: Justice Denied?"
Crime & Delinquency 51, no. 2 (April 2005): 265–90.

9   See PrYSM website, https://www.prysm.us.

10   PrYSM website.

11   Author interview with Steven Dy.

12   PrYSM website.

13   Author interview with Dy.

14   Author interview with Dy.

15   PrYSM, "Queer Justice," PowerPoint presentation, n.d.

16   Author interview with Dy; PrYSM, "Queer Justice."

17   Author interview with Dy.

18   Eric Tang, *Unsettled: Cambodian Refugees in the NYC Hyperghetto*
(Philadelphia: Temple University Press, 2015; Paul Jung, Gregory
Cendana, William Chiang, Ben Wang, Eddy Zheng, Monica Thamma-
rath, Quyen Dinh, and Katrina Dizon Mariategue, *Asian Americans &
Pacific Islanders behind Bars: Exposing the School to Prison to Deportation
Pipeline*, report (Washington, DC: National Education Association, 2015).

19   Author interview with Veronica Flores-Maldonado, February 16, 2020.

20   Ishihara et al., *For Justice and Love*, 22.

21   Ishihara et al., *For Justice and Love*, 17–19.

22   Ishihara et al., *For Justice and Love*, 20.

23   Author interview with Dy.

24   Martha Yager, "How One Community Succeeded in Making Police
More Accountable," American Friends Service Committee, July 22,
2017; "Key Points of the CSA," *Providence Community Safety Act*, blog,
https://providencecommunitysafetyact.wordpress.com/about, accessed
February 22, 2020.

25   Julia Rock and Lucas Smolcic Larson, "Providence Police Gang
Database Policy 'Tramples Fundamental Constitutional Rights,'"
Appeal, January 10, 2020.

26   Author interview with Dy.

27   Author interview with thuan nguyen, January 10, 2020; Kim Tran,
"Healing Trauma, Healing Justice: A Conversation with Thuan
Nguyen," *NSN*, February 12, 2013, http://nsnjournal.wordpress.com
/2013/02/12/healing-trauma-healing-justice-a-conversation.

28 Author interview with thuan nguyen.

29 "FBI agents came to believe that the journalists' killings, along with an array of fire-bombings and beatings, were terrorist acts ordered by an organization called the National United Front for the Liberation of Vietnam, a prominent group led by former military commanders from South Vietnam. Agents theorized that the Front was intimidating or executing those who defied it, FBI documents show, and even sometimes those simply sympathetic to the victorious Communists in Vietnam. But the FBI never made a single arrest for the killings or terror crimes, and the case was formally closed two decades ago." See A. C. Thompson, "Terror in Little Saigon," *ProPublica*, November 3, 2015.

30 My-Thuan Tran, "Vietnamese Art Exhibit Puts Politics on Display," *Los Angeles Times*, January 10, 2009; Richard Chang, "Protestors Shut Down F.O.B. II Exhibition," *Orange County Register*, January 16, 2009.

31 Lan Duong and Isabelle Thuy Pelaud, "Vietnamese American Art and Community Politics: Engaged Feminist Perspective," *Journal of Asian American Studies* (October 2012): 241–69.

32 Duong and Pelaud, "Vietnamese American Art and Community Politics." The incident was reminiscent of a 2009 incident in which thousands of protestors denounced the Vietnamese owner of Hi-Tek video store who had displayed a picture of Hồ Chí Minh in the front window in the nearby city of Westminster.

33 Duong and Pelaud, "Vietnamese American Art and Community Politics," 249, 247.

34 Duong and Pelaud, "Vietnamese American Art and Community Politics," 242, 251.

35 Author interview with thuan nguyen; Thuy Trang Nguyen, "Hai Ba Trung School for Organizing," in *Many Bridges, One River: Organizing for Justice in Vietnamese American Communities*, ed. thuan nguyen and Vy Nguyen (Los Angeles: UCLA Asian American Studies Center, 2019), 127–33.

36 Author interview with thuan nguyen.

37 On March 13, 2020, Breonna Taylor was a Black medical worker who was killed in her apartment by police officers in Louisville, Kentucky. On May 25, 2020, George Floyd, an avid church volunteer and youth mentor, was murdered by the Minneapolis Police Department upon suspicion of using a counterfeit twenty-dollar bill. Two days later, Tony McDade, a thirty-eight-year-old transgender man, was murdered by an officer from the Tallahassee Police Department. Their deaths, along with so many others, prompted national outrage and inspired hundreds of demonstrations against anti-Black racism and police brutality.

38 The Việt Solidarity & Action Network (VSAN) was formerly the National Progressive Viet Gathering (NPVG), a group that grew out of the 2010 statewide gathering held at VAALA. For VSAN's mission and

points of unity, see https://www.facebook.com/groups/705073 853588041.

39   See Adhikaar website, www.adhikaar.org/our-story.

40   Author interview with Pabitra Benjamin, January 23, 2020; author interview with Prarthana Gurung, February 11, 2020.

41   Author interview with Benjamin.

42   John Washington, "'I Used to Wonder What My Karma Was That I Had to End Up in a Place Like This,'" *Nation*, September 18, 2019; Pearl Bhatnagar, "Nepalis Fight for TPS," *Asian American Writers' Workshop*, April 19, 2018.

43   See Bhattarai v. Nielsen, U.S. Citizenship and Immigration Services website, https://www.uscis.gov/humanitarian/temporary-protected -status/update-bhattarai-v-nielsen, accessed February 14, 2020; American Dream and Promise Act of 2019, H.R. 6, 116th Cong. (June 10, 2019), https://www.congress.gov/bill/116th-congress/house -bill/6/text, accessed February 14, 2020.

44   Ahdikaar currently reaches 12,500 Nepali-speaking immigrants in New York City and has a robust worker program with over 550 active members. Author interview with Benjamin.

45   Adhikaar's "theory of change" closely aligns with the Community Transformational Organizing Strategies model utilized by Asian Immigrant Women Advocates in Oakland, California. See Jennifer Jihye Chun, George Lipsitz, and Young Shin, "Intersectionality as a Social Movement Strategy: Asian Immigrant Women Advocates," *Signs: Journal of Women in Culture and Society* 38, no. 4 (2013): 917–40.

46   Author interview with Gurung.

47   Author interview with Tsering Lama, February 12, 2020.

48   Author interview with Benjamin.

49   Thomas Dent, Richard Schechner, and Gilbert Moses, *The Free Southern Theater, by the Free Southern Theater: A Documentary of the South's Radical Black Theater, with Journals, Letters, Poetry, Essays, and a Play Written by Those Who Built It* (New York: Bobbs-Merrill, 1969); Beth Bagby and Luis Valdez, "El Teatro Campesino Interviews with Luis Valdez," *Tulane Drama Review* 11, no. 4 (Summer 1967): 70–80.

50   Author interview with Lama.

51   Author interview with Lama.

52   Author interview with Gurung.

53   Author interview with Lama.

54   Author interview with Lama.

55   Author interview with Benjamin.

CHAPTER 8

"ORGANIZING WHEREVER YOUR FEET LAND"

Reconceptualizing Writing and Writing Instruction in the Legacy of Asian American Activism

KATHERINE H. LEE

THE RICH PRESENTATIONS AND DISCUSSIONS THAT TOOK place at the Contemporary Asian American Activism symposium at UC Santa Barbara in January 2019 and the closed-door deliberations among the participating organizers and activist-scholars became the foundation for this anthology.[1] Over the next year, as the authors wrote their chapters, I continued working closely with them as an interlocutor and editor, witnessing how they conceptualized and practiced what it meant to engage in collaborative and collective forms of analysis, thinking, and dialogue in order to develop written histories and tools for social transformation with and for their fellow Asian American activists and allies. Here I offer a critical analysis and reflection about the ways that the process of writing unexpectedly became an organizing space and what it meant for me, as a former college writing instructor and graduate student researching how university writing instructors work toward racial and social justice in their classes, to learn how to reconceptualize writing through my conversations with Asian American activists as they wrote. This chapter examines how Asian American activists have reenvisioned the work of writing in order to foster and strengthen the intergenerational connections and collaborations that are crucial for social change.

Pam Tau Lee, a long-standing Asian American Movement and environmental justice activist, delivered a powerful keynote address for the Asian American Activism symposium. Using her own experiences of growing up working class in San Francisco Chinatown, witnessing environmental racism in garment factories, and developing into an activist with I Wor Kuen, Pam highlighted the rich history of Asian American radicalism and environmental justice organizing. During the Q&A session a graduate student invited Pam to comment on "how students can be actively engaged in sustainably building change across systems" when facing the seeming disconnect between their desire to change an oppressive system through activism and the prospect of facing a life of employment or underemployment in a system designed to preserve the status quo.[2] To the crowd of students, faculty, staff, and community members sitting in the seats and aisles of the standing room–only theater and in the adjoining overflow room, Pam responded with a story:

I have a friend, a young person who is a chemist, and she studied under one of the great green chemists globally. And then after participating in and understanding the political situation, she wants to get involved in legal work and policy. And you know what I said to her? I said, "Girl, we need green chemists!" A lot of young people, they have these different passions around the environment and other things, and I say, wherever your feet land, you can organize. Wherever your feet land, there are other people with like minds. Come together as a group. Study together and analyze the situation and decide what needs to be done, wherever your feet land, and be that in the workplace, in your communities. But if you are fortunate enough to find a space, a job opening, go for it. Do it. But please, encourage your students. Where did you come from? What is your passion? What is your skill? And we have one person who transformed . . . she came to CPA [Chinese Progressive Association] and organized workers, but you know what her passion is? Comics. She is changing the world through comics.[3]

The principle of "organizing wherever your feet land" became one of the central issues that Pam wanted to focus on as she began writing her contribution to this anthology. This story was just the first of many that she and her husband, Ben Lee, would share with me over the next twelve months as we discussed how Pam wanted to develop her ideas. In each of their stories about the young people they are working with and organizing with who are changing the world by practicing the principle of "organizing wherever your feet land," Pam and Ben's messages have been clear: building the kind of world and communities we envision and making the kinds of changes we want to see in society require people organizing, doing political analysis, and working toward social transformation in and across different systems, areas of specialty, and spaces. By refusing to restrict activism and organizing to particular groups or disciplines and by instead conceptualizing them as practices that are needed everywhere and that can thrive when connected to an individual's passions, Pam and Ben have challenged young people to begin building their own visions and practices of what it means to organize. Their efforts and encouragement have meant that the youths with whom they organize bring not only their political analysis to their work but also their unique strengths, passions, backgrounds, and visions so they can develop new spaces for and ways of responding to what they see as the most pressing issues facing their generation.

As a former college writing instructor and doctoral student studying writing instruction, I have struggled with the reality that the field in which I work is deeply tied to and invested in maintaining the very practices of standardization, conformity, and outcomes-based instruction that have historically marginalized students and communities of color through linguistic racism and deficit models of education. The stories Pam and Ben shared with me and the ongoing conversations Pam and I had as she wrote her chapter have inspired and pushed me to think seriously about what it means to organize wherever your feet land when it comes to writing. University writing courses have long maintained an ongoing investment in seeing students adopt mainstream ways of analyzing and writing that ignore, and in many cases denigrate, the many innovative ways of thinking, doing, and seeing that students of color bring to the classroom. There is a rich history of students and faculty of color protesting and building cross-racial movements to challenge the racially unjust approaches to writing instruction in colleges and universities, but their efforts to make education more relevant to the needs and experiences of their communities have quite literally been rewritten and suppressed by what Carmen Kynard calls the "master script" of writing studies. This narrative has problematically rewritten history to name white compositionists, not student of color activists, as the leaders who helped transform writing studies from a field that marginalized students of color to one that better served their needs.[4] This narrative subsequently repositioned the student of color activists who wrote ethnic studies courses and curricula and who practiced new forms of literacy that were grounded in their fight for social transformation as the supposedly "underprepared" students in remedial writing courses.[5]

In this context, then, writing instructors and students face significant challenges when organizing in spaces in which students are taught to use writing as a tool for individual advancement within existing academic and social structures rather than as a tool that can benefit the masses. It is not common for students to see academic writing classes as spaces where they can build the skills they need to change oppressive structures or to transform the dominant assumptions and practices that underlie them. Haivan Hoang importantly reminds us that although writing played a critical role in the Asian American Movement, Asian American students did not write about their activism in mainstream university writing classes. Instead, they turned to literary and cultural production outside of the academy by creating their own, self-sponsored publications, such as *Gidra* and the Asian American Political Alliance newspaper, and by launching community-based efforts to fight for bilingual education.[6] In effect, they built their own spaces where they could practice new forms of literacy, write about key issues affecting the Asian American community, connect their struggles to international and Third World liberation movements, and control the written representation of Asian American consciousness and politics.[7] None of this was possible within the curricular and pedagogical constraints of traditional university writing classes, as evidenced by the long history of the fight by the UC Berkeley Asian American Studies program (originally called the Asian Studies Division) since the late 1960s to develop, house, and teach its own academic writing courses.[8] Within this context, then, figuring out what it means to organize where my feet have landed in academic writing programs—to find other people with similar politics and figure out what needs to be done—has not been easy. Most of the models for organizing around writing instruction in the university either have been rewritten or suppressed in the dominant historical narrative of the field itself or these models have presented writing as a tool capable

of advancing student-led organizing efforts only when the writing process takes place outside of the classroom.

Through my work with Pam and by watching how she and other
Asian American activist-scholar contributors to this anthology have
used writing to advance their movements and work, I have observed
what it could mean for Asian American writing instructors like myself
to ground our work with students more meaningfully in the principle
of organizing wherever your feet land. Academic writing programs
have continued to struggle to make themselves relevant to students of
color and social movements despite their attempts over the past fifty
years to become more sensitive to the needs and backgrounds of communities of color. Through my work over the past year, I have come
to believe they have much to learn from looking to some of the basic
principles and experiences that inform Pam's and other Asian American activists' approaches to writing—principles that enable the work
and praxis of writing to evolve into something much more profound
than simply mastering the standard skills, forms, or genres agreed
upon by university faculty and administrators.

Pam writes in her chapter, for instance, about the importance of
Asians "work[ing] together and reimagin[ing] what it means to find
solutions that work in the spirit of 'all my relations.'"[9] This practice of
deepening relationships, working in solidarity, and creating connections with one another within the environmental justice movement
has been central to Pam's approach. Her writing has never been done
in isolation: whether with Ben, her activist colleagues, her friends, or
me, Pam was constantly in dialogue with others about the issues she
wanted to write about for this book. She shared her writing with them,
reworked her piece based on their conversations, and constantly refor-
mulated and reorganized her ideas in response to the discussions and
shared experiences with her colleagues that were critical to the points
she wanted to make. Though it may be tempting to see her piece as
pure memoir, Pam repeatedly noted as she was writing that it is a collection of "radical love stories" to and about the many people she has
organized with, dialogued with, listened to and learned from, shared
meals with, and built community with over the years. The long and
collaborative processes of both documenting the stories and long histories of these relationships, acts of mutual appreciation, and ongoing
work and political analysis she and her colleagues have built together
over time (in many cases decades) are what I have come to understand

as the heart of Pam's work: over the past year her writing has brought people together in new ways and opened opportunities for them to work toward "all my relations." Her practice of writing as a cocreated process that emerges from and strengthens these existing working relationships offers an important example of how writing can be a vehicle to highlight the voices of others while also deepening the rich connections and important dialogues Asian American activists have built with their communities and colleagues over time. In these ways Pam's writing process is reminiscent of the kinds of transformative pedagogies at work in the notion of accompaniment, which sees the difficult process of working, analyzing, discovering, and struggling together across our individual differences over time as a productive site for cocreating new ways of knowing, doing, and being. As a process that is fundamentally collaborative in nature, accompaniment brings into being relationships and ways of working with each other that are "rooted in freedom, justice, and humane social relations."[10]

In academic writing courses we are trained to help students identify which audience(s) they are writing for, to think about the purpose of their writing, and to think about how they will rhetorically build their arguments for their audiences in the most powerful and persuasive ways, all in a matter of a few weeks. Yet when looking at these academic approaches in the context of activist writers like Pam, whose writing is never done in isolation but who instead uses writing as a way to deepen the working relationships she has built with her colleagues over the span of decades, conventional academic approaches to writing using a formulaic toolkit of methods seem inadequate for building the kinds of relationships that are at the core of how Pam organizes and writes toward social change. Academic writing courses often problematically ask students to *imagine* relationships—to write to and for hypothetical audiences, to think about but never know for sure what these imagined audiences might need to be persuaded of, and to consider how their audience might think about and respond to their work without ever speaking with or building real experiences with the people to whom or with whom they are supposedly writing. Much of the work of these writing courses thus forces students to work in hypotheticals under artificial time restrictions and, by extension, encourages them to work in spaces in which their writing is structured based on requirements and learning outcomes to be fulfilled within the neoliberal university. In these contexts writing is rarely shaped or driven in real time by the real-world issues, material realities, and relationships they are meant to reflect on, draw from, and work toward. Pam's interlocutors and the many people whom she consulted as she wrote—all activists with whom she has organized in the environmental justice movement—offered feedback, reminders, explanations, timely updates, encouragement, and more, which were all reflective of their deep expertise as well as the trust they have built with Pam over the years through shared experiences, struggles, and study. The co-creation of knowledge that their long relationships and shared commitments to environmental, racial, and economic justice have made possible reflect what it means both to practice the notion of accompaniment over an entire lifetime of organizing and movement building and to carry this practice of accompaniment over to the process of writing as well.

As I observed how these conversations and relationships shaped Pam's work, I began to understand more fully what a profound disservice we, as writing instructors, do to students when we operate under the assumption that they will become better writers when they write on topics we have chosen in advance for them or when we structure writing around the mastery of technical forms and skills that force students to conform to dominant norms. When we teach writing as a structured task centered around meeting performance targets and learning outcomes, we overlook the importance of giving students the space to build their own projects, in which they can write about issues that are not only meaningful to them but for which something important is at stake. Pam's work makes visible the great potential writing has to contribute to social and material change in people's lives and ways of engaging with each other when it emerges organically from and in response to the work people are already doing and the critical analysis that they are already generating together on the ground as they work collectively toward social change. In these ways writing is not merely the task of *reporting on* or *writing about* issues, but instead, it becomes a process through which people can *problem solve* and *design* together. The collective and intersubjective forms of analysis and understandings that Pam and her colleagues have cocreated over time and across contexts reflect what it means to connect the work of writing to the work of building the deep relationships necessary for solving urgent social problems. Pam and her colleagues offer a model of writing that is premised on discovering and creating together through struggle and through the shared experiences of working together on urgent social issues. As their decades-long collaborations show, the stakes of their collective work—and thus the stakes of their writing—are real and are always meant to lead to material change.

Part of the transactional, product-driven nature of academic writing has to do with the decontextualized form of academic essays—the fact that writing instruction in the neoliberal university is structured around demonstrating the mastery of skills, form, and genre rather than advancing a larger movement that will contribute in meaningful ways to material change. Students are expected to reach performance targets and a standard of writing that will ensure their ability to analyze and write across academic disciplines and contexts successfully during their time at the university, which often means developing critical thinking, reading, writing, and communication skills that are highly specialized for academic purposes and genres. This opens opportunities for individual advancement within academic structures but does not necessarily contribute to grassroots movements or effect change for the masses outside the university. My discussions with Pam and with another symposium speaker, Eddy Zheng, have reminded me that as much as these academic forms of writing are useful to learn, they do not necessarily prepare students for writing as part of a larger movement for social change. When writing classes no longer focus solely on rewarding individuals for mastering disciplinary frameworks and skills, writing can instead be used to give voice to and advance the larger visions and goals that communities are working toward collectively while simultaneously documenting the long histories of grassroots struggles from which their work emerges. Writing that is connected to movement building and Asian American activism can become an intergenerational process and space in which activists, young people, and communities can come together to discuss the complexities of the issues they are working on while also situating themselves within the larger lineages of Asian American activism and movement building for social, economic, and racial justice. Pam's writing, for instance, has evolved into a dialogue with and call to action to the young people with whom she works and who will read this anthology. Her writing thus links the experiences, visions, movements, and forms of analysis of her generation to the visions, movements, and analysis of future generations. In doing so, her work encourages all young people to see themselves as holding important insights that are critical to the continuation of the movement for environmental justice.

Eddy Zheng's writings reflect his experiences as a former prisoner who grew to political consciousness fighting for ethnic studies and Asian American studies in San Quentin State Prison and who later helped to found the Asian Prisoner Support Committee with Yuri Kochiyama. He speaks to the importance of writing the histories of Asian American activism that have been buried or ignored in mainstream curricula so that Asian American communities can learn about their histories and understand how they can continue the activist work and unanticipated movements their elders began.[11] Through my discussions with him as he began to write about his history as an activist and his work with students across the country, Eddy has shown me that it is through our ability to locate ourselves within the long histories of Asian American struggles and resistance that we can begin to see ourselves as part of and vital contributors to this rich and ongoing legacy of Asian American activism and cross-cultural movement building. For Eddy, as demonstrated in the book *Other: An Asian & Pacific Islander Prisoners' Anthology*, the process of writing these histories of Asian American struggle and resistance for others to see and point to plays a crucial role in allowing for moments of self-understanding and self-expression, historical documentation, and cross-cultural political education that inspire individual activism, collective action, and sustained movement building.[12] Pam, Eddy, and the other contributors to this anthology have shared with me and with each other their hopes about what they believe their chapters offer and why they believe it is critical to bring these issues to light through writing. Their work illustrates the great potential there is when writing is conceptualized as contributing to a larger movement, meant to spark critical discussion and inspire collective action as it encourages Asian Americans to look to their roots and situate themselves in the present to figure out where we need to go in the future.

The ongoing processes of working and speaking with Pam and Eddy as they wrote and being able to see firsthand how they conceptualize and practice writing have made visible to me the importance of recovering the histories of Asian American activism through writing. Their collective and consultative writing processes offer a model of writing grounded in the understanding that writing for social change is most powerful when it emerges from real relationships built through experiences of shared struggle over time: in these moments writing opens spaces for collaboration and discussion that are deliberately intergenerational and invested in sustaining a larger movement for social transformation. Pam's and Eddy's practices of writing as an intergenerational, movement-based, and collective process not only reveal the problematic assumptions that underlie traditional academic writing pedagogies and assignments but, importantly, make visible what is possible if Asian American writing instructors such as myself begin to recover these histories in order to rethink our approaches to and practices for teaching writing in the spirit and legacy of Asian American activism through writing.

Eddy, Pam, and Ben have each reminded me in different ways that we have a responsibility to understand our history and roots in order to figure out how to build the kinds of relationships and collaborations over time that will help us move forward in our work toward accompaniment and social transformation. For me, as a writing instructor and graduate student seeking to challenge conventional approaches to teaching writing, this responsibility entails seeking out and documenting these histories and lineages of how writing has been reconceptualized and practiced by Asian American activists both in and outside of the university so they will not be forgotten, overlooked, suppressed, or rewritten.[13] The histories I have learned about and conversations I have been able to have with Asian American activists and writing instructors as a result have helped me to appreciate what their movement-based writing and writing processes envisioned and have made possible. Yet they also underscore the implications if we fail to write down these stories about writing or, worse, when we fail to search actively for these histories or believe they do not exist because they have not been asked about, written down, or acknowledged by mainstream narratives, curricula, and publications.

The other part of this responsibility entails figuring out where to go from here—how to, as Pam and Eddy have done, use writing as part of my efforts to begin connecting the work and the visions of previous generations of Asian American activists and writing instructors with the visions and futures that my generation and future generations of Asian American writing instructors and students want to bring into being. In 1970 the UC Berkeley Asian Studies Division had already begun its ambitious and groundbreaking project to reformulate the teaching of academic writing as a political project that would emerge from and work in service of the Third World Liberation Front's visions of self-determination, social transformation, and economic and racial justice for the larger Asian American community. The writing instructors in the Asian Studies Division sought the input of Asian American students, faculty, community organizations, parents, and educators across all levels of the California education system as they designed their proposal for a new series of academic writing classes.[14] Their new vision for academic writing was thus intergenerational, collaborative, and meant to emerge from and serve the community from the start. Against this backdrop student activist Floyd Huen wrote that "learning research and paper-writing is essential to gaining an understanding of what is being done, *and from there, we can construct what needs to still be done*."[15] Huen's words and the UC Berkeley Asian Studies Division's community-based efforts to reenvision academic writing speak powerfully to the ways that writing, when used to work toward social change and when conceived of as part of a larger political project, always allows us to reformulate, reconceptualize, and build new ways of doing and working with others so we can respond directly to the evolving realities of people's lived experiences as we simultaneously document the past. Writing, as practiced and conceptualized in the legacy of Asian American activism and as reflected in both Pam's and Eddy's work and writing processes, always has the potential to be a collective, collaborative process in innovation—always working to build new approaches based on the dynamic and evolving relationships and dialogues that drive sustained movement building and political consciousness. These approaches offer clear models for how we can ground our work in our Asian American activist roots and deepen intergenerational relationships while always seeking to "construct what needs to still be done" in order to bring new possibilities into being. I hope they will continue to inform and inspire new visions for how writing both in and outside of the university can work to advance the visions and work of Asian American activists.

NOTES

1 I was involved as the event coordinator and graduate student researcher for the symposium and anthology project.
2 Pam Tau Lee, Q&A for "The Struggle to Abolish Environmental Racism: Asian Radical Imaginings from the Homeland to Our

Frontlines," UC Santa Barbara, Santa Barbara, CA, January 24, 2019, https://www.asamst.ucsb.edu/community/activism.

3 Tau Lee, Q&A.

4 For a discussion of how the student-led movements for ethnic studies and open admissions as well as the Black Arts movement shaped writing instruction and challenged problematic approaches to writing instruction in higher education, see Carmen Kynard, *Vernacular Insurrections: Race, Black Protests, and the New Century in Composition-Literacies Studies* (Albany: State University of New York, 2013); Haivan V. Hoang, *Writing against Racial Injury: The Politics of Asian American Student Rhetoric* (Pittsburgh, PA: University of Pittsburgh Press, 2015). For information regarding efforts by the UC Berkeley Asian Studies Division and students in the Afro-American Student Union to transform writing instruction in the late 1960s and early 1970s, see Elaine H. Kim, "English and Asian American College Student," *Education and Urban Society* 10, no. 3 (May 1978): 321–36; Colin Watanabe, "Self-Expression and the Asian American Experience," *Personnel and Guidance Journal* 51, no. 6 (1973): 390–96; UC Berkeley Asian Studies Division, "A College-Level Reading and Composition Program for Students of Asian Descent: Diagnosis and Design," March 23 1971, University Archives, Records of the Office of the Chancellor, University of California, Berkeley, 1952– (CU-149, box 119, folder 5), Bancroft Library, Berkeley; Katherine H. Lee, "'We Can Construct What Needs to Still Be Done': Reformulating the Politics and Pedagogies of Academic Writing Programs in Higher Education" (PhD diss., University of California, Santa Barbara, 2021).

5 Irene Dea Collier, "The Strike Is Not Over," in *Mountain Movers: Student Activism and the Emergence of Asian American Studies*, ed. Russell Jeung, Karen Umemoto, Harvey Dong, Eric Mar, Lisa Hirai Tsuchitani, and Arnold Pan, 57–72 (Los Angeles: UCLA Asian American Studies Center Press, 2019); Hoang, *Writing against Racial Injury*; Kynard, *Vernacular Insurrections*.

6 Hoang, *Writing against Racial Injury*.

7 Karen L. Ishizuka, *Serve the People: Making Asian American in the Long Sixties* (Brooklyn, NY: Verso Books, 2016).

8 Kim, "English and Asian American College Student"; Watanabe, "Self-Expression and the Asian American Experience"; UC Berkeley Asian Studies Division, "College-Level Reading and Composition Program"; Lee, "'We Can Construct What Needs to Still Be Done.'"

9 Pam Tau Lee, "The Struggle to Abolish Environmental and Economic Racism: Asian Radical Imagining from the Homeland to the Front Line," in this volume.

10 Diane C. Fujino, Jonathan D. Gomez, Esther Lezra, George Lipsitz, Jordan Mitchell, and James Fonseca, "A Transformative Pedagogy for a Decolonial World," *Review of Education, Pedagogy, and Cultural Studies*

40, no. 2 (2018): 69–95. For more information about work of accompaniment, see Barbara Tomlinson and George Lipsitz, "American Studies as Accompaniment," *American Quarterly* 65, no. 1 (March 2013): 1–30; Barbara Tomlinson and George Lipsitz, *Insubordinate Spaces: Improvisation and Accompaniment for Social Justice* (Philadelphia: Temple University Press, 2019).

11 Eddy Zheng is an activist-poet and coauthor of several publications, including *Asian Americans & Pacific Islanders behind Bars: Exposing the School to Prison to Deportation Pipeline* (Washington, DC: National Education Association, 2015), and coeditor, with Ben Wang, and the Asian Prisoner Support Committee, of *Other: An Asian & Pacific Islander Prisoners' Anthology* (Oakland, CA: Asian Prisoner Support Committee, 2007). He is featured in the documentary *Breathin': The Eddy Zheng Story*, directed and produced by Ben Wang (2016), and recently founded the New Breath Foundation.

12 Zheng, Wang, and Asian Prisoner Support Committee, *Other*; Eddy Zheng, "Prison-to-Leadership Pipeline: Asian American Prisoner Activism," in this volume.

13 Lee, "'We Can Construct What Needs to Still Be Done.'"

14 UC Berkeley Asian Studies Division, "College-Level Reading and Composition Program."

15 Floyd Huen, "A Clarification of the Proposal for an Educational Technique Seminar," 1970; emphasis added. University Archives, University of California, Academic Senate, Berkeley Division Records 1869– (CU-9, box 150, folders 70–72), Bancroft Library, Berkeley.

CHAPTER 9

HOW DOES IT FEEL TO BE ON THE PRECIPICE?

ChangeLab, A Racial Justice Experiment

SOYA JUNG

IN 1903 THE GREAT SOCIOLOGIST AND HISTORIAN W.E.B. DU Bois wrote in *The Souls of Black Folk*, "How does it feel to be a problem?" It was a description of the certainty of Black difference and abjectness, of white normalcy and benevolence that laid thinly veiled in questions that white people would ask of Black people. A full century later, in a nod to Du Bois, historian Vijay Prashad would ask of South Asians, "How does it feel to be a solution?"—a provocation for segments of South Asian and other populations racialized as "model minorities" to think critically about their presumed success and its weaponization against Black Americans. This chapter now asks of all Asian Americans, "How does it feel to be on the precipice?" Here in this volatile moment it invites us to think not about *what* we are in the white gaze but *where* we are in the arc of history.

I was asked to write about how and why we formed ChangeLab as an experimental limited liability company (LLC) and not as a nonprofit, to describe our work, and to share lessons learned—in particular to address why ChangeLab sounded the alarm fairly early on the threat of fascism. How could we have predicted a decade ago that something like Trumpism was coming? It has to do with the particular conditions of the Pacific Northwest, where we cut our political teeth. In the 1970s, having lost a battle over civil rights, white nationalists began eyeing the Pacific Northwest region as a new white homeland through the *Northwest Territorial Imperative,* or *The Butler Plan,* so named after Aryan Nations founder Richard Butler.[1] One need only look to the morass of political violence that has taken place over several months in Portland, Oregon, to see the impact of the antidemocratic Far Right's long investment into that region. Our encounters with white nationalist, Christian Evangelical nationalist, and antigovernment paramilitary groups as we organized on a range of issues during the 1980s and 1990s deeply influenced our approach to politics.

It now feels worn-out and late in the hour to declare that we live in unprecedented times. In this period of upheaval, forces from all political tendencies are vying to narrate the breakneck changes we are witnessing, to become the heroes of what will surely be an epic story. This perfect, existential storm includes crises that have been familiar to the majority of the world for at least the last fifty years—austerity policies, rising state violence, deregulation of capital, the weakening of unions and the public sector, all justified via appeals to order and progress. It now also includes a devastating pandemic that has saturated the world with loss, albeit unevenly. At the time of this writing, the SARS-CoV-2 virus has claimed nearly 2.5 million lives, including 490,000 lives in the United States, with disparities mapped along pathways of vulnerability by race, class, and zip code. Changes to the media and information environment, driven by the rise of largely unregulated technology capital, have intensified political polarization and contributed to a fragmented sense of reality, such that facts are in constant politicized dispute.

In order to weather this storm, the US racial justice movement needs organizational experiments to facilitate thinking, risk-taking, and knowledge sharing by those whose political experiences may once have been considered niche but who may now be able to offer insights and lessons learned for navigating the multiple, layered crises we face. We stand on a historic precipice laden with danger and opportunity. Now is the time to share everything we know.

WAY BACK WHEN IN 2010

In the wake of President Barack Obama's first election in 2008, racial politics were shifting in seismic ways. The election of the first Black US president solidified a narrative of "post-racialism"—the assertion that America had finally transcended race such that it no longer mattered.[2] This made the work of racial justice advocates ever more necessary and difficult while playing to the fears of racially anxious whites. US demographic projections drove media headlines declaring that the nation would no longer be majority white by 2050. Studies showed that a majority of white people believed that they were the primary victims of racism.[3] Right-wing authoritarian movements found new political leverage in the story of demographic change and in President Obama's election and used it to drum up white fear and support. Tea Parties, militias, and white nationalist groups were on the rise.

This period marked the fastest rise of white nationalist organizations since 1995, when they were driven underground following the bombing of the Alfred P. Murrah Federal Building in Oklahoma by domestic terrorist and antigovernment conspiracist, Timothy McVeigh. While underground, white nationalists were not dormant. They continued to operate through websites such as Stormfront, which became the first major online hate site in 1996, formed by former Ku Klux Klan leader and white supremacist Don Black. They were not lying down. They were preparing.

TAKING THE LEAP

Against this backdrop my longtime colleague and dear friend Scot Nakagawa and I found ourselves at a crossroads. We had both spent decades working in community-based, government, social movement, and philanthropic organizations. We had occupied nearly every level of work in these sectors—as volunteers, direct service providers, administrative staff, organizers, trainers, writers, executive directors, legislative staff, grant makers, and nonprofit consultants. But on a personal and professional level we were struggling in the late aughts. Our families were reeling from economic losses from the 2008 recession and other life ruptures. We lost jobs, homes, relationships, pets, and frankly, overall clarity and resolve about our role in movement building nearly all in the course of a single year.

So, we did what many people in similar situations do. We became organizational development consultants, seeking to make a living while sharing our accumulated skills. However, while we had honed those skills out of necessity, our hearts resided elsewhere. We hungered for space to explore deep questions about the role of racial politics in the future of society and democracy, amid breakneck and paradigm-shifting economic, technological, and cultural change.

As significantly as our personal lives had shifted, the political air was also changing. The post-racial story line ignored the endurance of racism in US society and the growth of right-wing authoritarian movements, on top of decades of austerity policies. We were witnessing unprecedented wealth inequality; global and domestic displacement by war, climate, and gentrification; the widening gap between education and labor demands; rapid technological innovation; and increasing political polarization. Together this led us to suspect that a firestorm of danger was coming. Worse, to paraphrase historian Carol Anderson, everyone seemed to be ignoring the kindling—the bureaucratic violence that kept race so central to American life and that had long animated US politics.[4] Scot and I felt in our bones the need for new organizational forms and a break from business as usual, for progressive forces to prepare for a novel, manifold crisis.

It was in this context that we took a leap out of familiar waters and formed ChangeLab in 2010. Our greatest asset was our broad and deep set of relationships built over decades, which spanned sectors and issue areas. We wanted to create space for these superb thinkers and doers to dig into thorny societal problems, to assess the moment, to think deeply about where we were heading, and to formulate strategy together. All of this seemed impossible to do within the constraints of the nonprofit sector. Even the best foundations were fundamentally risk averse. The philanthropic model continued to expect individual organizations to analyze problems, create solutions, and predict outcomes despite rapidly shifting political, economic, and cultural terrain, with no acknowledgment that this required significant time and space away from day-to-day mission-related tasks. Without funding and support for movement-wide thinking and planning, how could we possibly compete with the robust, decades-old infrastructure of right-wing think tanks, foundations, political strategists, media outlets, and more?

We formed ChangeLab as an LLC. In an enormous stroke of luck, we found a values-oriented investor who was willing to take a chance on us and very likely to incur losses over a period of years, which is not novel in the private sector. Start-up investors put down capital in exchange for *equity*, meaning a portion of ownership in the startup with rights to its potential future profits. We learned that experimentation and failure are norms in the private sector. Investors know that *90 percent of start-ups fail* and that it typically takes seven to ten years to see any profit. We pushed ourselves to lean into this approach, a far cry from the nonprofit-philanthropy mentality of expecting results in impossibly short funding time frames. We were also stunned at how easy it was to form an LLC. You do not need a board of directors. You *do* need to amass resources but from investors and clients rather than from donors, which changes the way you think and work. You can do, say, and risk much more, and vision deeply matters.

LLCs offer freedom from much of the bureaucracy of corporations while still protecting any owner's personal assets—car, home, bank accounts—from liability if the business is ever sued or incurs debts. Members contribute to, draw from, and manage the corporation's assets, with each member's equity valuation based on her or his ownership share. One of the drawbacks of the LLC structure is that investors *can* have control over the mission and work of the organization, but this depends on the operating agreement. With the right kind of values-driven investor, it is possible to structure an LLC to designate percentage ownership and roles for each member. The profit or loss of the company accrues to each member's equity according to their ownership share, and you can name the principals who make decisions and drive the work in the operating agreement. Obviously, there is no getting around the politics of money, so even if the main investor is a minority owner and not a principal, they have to believe in the work in order to continue investing. But to us this seemed like a no-brainer, given the constraints of philanthropy and the nonprofit sector. The LLC is a legitimate option for movement experiments.

Our hypothesis was that if we created ChangeLab as a space free from foundation and nonprofit constraints to study, think, and analyze conditions across issue areas, geographies, and constituencies, we could help social movement actors generate a more robust understanding of our times, bolder ways of doing our respective work, and readiness for what we believed would be ever more difficult times to come.

THE NEW WATERS

As an LLC, ChangeLab has been able to experiment with an iterative process, meaning that we repeated certain steps—inquiry, analysis, practice, synthesis, and back to inquiry—and adjusted as we went. Our *practice* was not on the front lines of political struggle but, rather, in conversation and partnership with leaders and influencers of those struggles—organizers, policy advocates, scholars, researchers, trainers, funders, and cultural workers. In this way we functioned like a movement think tank.

INQUIRY AND ANALYSIS

As anyone who has been a paid organizer, executive director, or practically any kind of full-time movement worker will attest, when you are in the thick of it, there is little time to study and reflect on the conditions surrounding and shaping your political struggle. This is not to say that no one in social movements studies or reflects, but nonprofit organizations, the primary vehicles for our struggles in the political economy of the last half-century, rarely provide workers the ability to do so as part of their work. Workers become so saturated in *doing*—campaign planning, field work, leadership development, fund-raising, board development, reporting and due diligence (which amounts to risk management), media advocacy, administration—that we have no room for *thinking.* Even in processes like strategic planning, the level of thinking we do rarely crosses issue areas and sectors or accounts for overarching social, political, and economic conditions to help us build movements rather than individual organizations.

Free from these constraints for the first time in our adult lives, Scot and I began by asking racial justice leaders about gaps in the movement and how ChangeLab could be of use. They described the limitations of contemporary approaches to anti-racism in leading to deep structural change, the political implications of demographic change, the absence of public discourse about Asian Americans that both concealed and deepened the impacts of the model minority myth on racial politics, a lack of awareness of the role of right-wing movements in shaping our politics, and more. We listened deeply, then decided to focus on how demographic change and growing right-wing movements were changing the political terrain, with a strategic emphasis on Asian Americans and the prospect of multiracial democracy.

In our initial research project, we conducted in-depth interviews with ninety-seven primarily but not exclusively Asian American racial justice advocates and leaders to explore the relationship between Asian Americans and the racial justice movement. We published two reports on our findings: *Left or Right of the Color Line? Asian Americans and the Racial Justice Movement*; and *The Importance of Asian Americans? It's Not What You Think: Future Directions in the Racial Justice Movement.* A year later we also published *Asian Americans on the Sunday Shows: What They Talk about When They Talk about Us*, a report based on six months (130 episodes) of programming on the Big Five Sunday cable news shows that revealed an absence of media coverage on Asian Americans and race.

In addition to research, ChangeLab gave Scot and me the opportunity to read more books, articles, and research papers and to talk with more experts on theory and philosophy than we ever had before. We were surprised to find that theory had advanced in ways that rang true to us but that were largely not reflected in anti-racism pedagogy or movement strategy. On the flip side, much theoretical writing lacks direction or insight into practical, dialectical applications on the ground, with real people in struggle. This is why ChangeLab has spent significant effort to draw scholars and activists together, to delve into both theory and application.

We discovered historian Dr. Ellen Wu's book, *The Color of Success: Asian Americans and the Origins of the Model Minority* (2013). The book disentangles the model minority myth from surface-level discourse about stereotypes and Asian American complicity to locate its deeper origins and purpose. Beneath the hand-wringing over individual Asian American privilege lies an ideological project. The myth is historically rooted in a number of global phenomena starting in the 1930s: US imperial ambitions in Asia and the Pacific; post–World War II Cold War politics; the proliferation of third-world liberation movements, including the Black Power movement; as well as deep changes in the global economy. It is the creation not only of media but of state actors, philanthropic institutions, and academics. Dr. Wu became a close colleague, and we came to understand that because of the breadth of its impacts in concealing structural racism and the impacts of global politics, dismantling the model minority myth was not an Asian American burden but a movement-wide imperative.

We also discovered historian Dr. Khalil Gibran Muhammad's book, *The Condemnation of Blackness* (2019), which chronicles how actors within and beyond the state weaponized statistics to legitimate and cement Black criminality as a central logic behind urban development and social policy. This strategy shaped not only the lives of Black people but the lives of all people as a result of a wide range of social and economic policies enacted since the turn of the twentieth century. We came to view the myths of Black criminality and the model minority as two sides of the same coin, different but closely related processes of race making in service to economic and political elites rather than to any particular racial group. This is just one example of how inquiry and analysis sharpened our thinking. We wanted to help people see that the model minority myth and Blackness did not describe distinct groups of people but, rather, closely intertwined political agendas that were doing harm to a majority of people across racial lines.

PRACTICE AND SYNTHESIS

Our practice has taken the form of writing, testing ideas, convening people, and pursuing specific interventions. Our convenings—called Race Labs—are inspired by a private sector practice in the field of innovation that brings people together who would not normally be in the same room to invent solutions to big problems. In the private sector this might look like physicists, microbiologists, technologists, political leaders, and small-scale agricultural producers in conversation to solve a problem such as the safe transportation of milk within and between villages in the Global South. In our work it looks like convening people across issue areas and sectors to assess movement conditions, to identify thorny problems, and to create interventions. Race Labs are relatively small and are curated based on admittedly subjective assessments of issue expertise and interest. At times we have included and learned a great deal from people in the private sector. One lesson learned is that we do our movements an immense disservice when we presume that all private sector actors are our adversaries, uncritical defenders of the racial capitalist order. We have found strong values alignment with people who see their role as people who can shake up the old capitalist order and build new economic principles and experiments that address capitalism's failures.

Our first Race Lab took place in 2013. We shared the findings of our research and invited longtime organizers Steve Williams and N'Tanya Lee to share findings from their seminal "Ear to the Ground" project.[5] The lab was broad in scope. We asked participants to present on what we called "the good, the bad, and the ugly" taking place in their respective sectors: government, philanthropy, science and race theory, media/culture/technology, gender and sexuality, national security and criminalization, low-wage worker organizing, pan-Asian community organizing, and global movements. It was unlike any gathering that we had ever attended, let alone convened. Because of its focus on cross-sector analysis and the absence of funder or organizational expectations, there was more incentive to pursue knowledge than to perform.

Subsequent Race Labs addressed more specific topics such as the historical construction of the model minority myth (2014), the connections between Black and Asian American racialization (2015), the movement implications of artificial intelligence and robotics (2015), the threat of Trumpism and fascism (2015), and more. We synthesized the discussions during these labs into notes; captured the innovations that emerged from them; tested ideas on our blog, *RaceFiles*, and elsewhere; and took action where we could. For example, the model minority lab led to testing #ModelMinorityMutiny as an offering to replace complicity or penance with active resistance, to supporting the launch of a permanent scholar-activist space within the Association of Asian American Studies, to publishing a pilot discussion guide called *Model Minority Myth-Busting: A Racial Justice Imperative*, and to various forms of largely behind-the-scenes work with grassroots and national Asian American and AAPI organizations.

Our inquiries into the state of right-wing movements kicked off in earnest with a 2011 gathering in partnership with longtime colleagues in fight-the-right work. We did not call this a Race Lab because ChangeLab was one of several conveners. The goals were to develop a broad, shared view of the configuration and strategies of the US right wing and to identify strategies that progressives could use to thwart right-wing gains. Outcomes of the gathering emphasized the need to educate more leaders in those movements being heavily targeted by the right wing (for example, immigration, criminalization, and reproductive justice) to help them craft effective strategy, including the inoculation of diverse communities against right-wing appeals. This led to articles on *RaceFiles* and other platforms, to the creation of a discussion guide called *A Little Thought Exercise about the Right Wing and the Political Culture of Our Times*, to various trainings and presentations, and to much behind-the-scenes support for a range of movement organizations, especially leading up to and following the 2016 elections. One important intervention has been to lift up the central role that anti-Semitism plays in animating white nationalism—an aspect of right-wing politics that is dangerously (and intentionally) little known—and partnering with progressive Jewish organizations such as Bend the Arc on political strategy.

Another intervention has been research into the growth of conservative Chinese immigrant–led groups in the United States. Partnering with Alex Tom and other longtime organizers, ChangeLab conducted research into a small yet highly networked and vocal set of political actors known as the "Chinese Tea Party"—so named for their use of Tea Party–style aggressive and inflammatory tactics. They have actively opposed progressive policies on policing, affirmative action, data disaggregation, sanctuary cities, Muslims, and homelessness at local and national levels. They have ties to right-wing institutions such as the Koch brothers–backed Libre Initiative, the Heritage Foundation, the Federalist Society, and the Republican Party. At the local level they have worked with groups further to the right, such as the Proud Boys.[6] Much of their organizing takes place online through WeChat, a global platform with over one billion users, and mobilizes Chinese immigrants in suburban areas where civil rights institutions typically don't have a strong presence. They have established local and national infrastructure. The Chinese American Alliance, for example, claims to have nineteen thousand registered members in forty-one states.

In our research we placed the emergence of the Chinese Tea Party into political context—for example, changes to US immigration policy favoring highly educated and wealthy immigrants and changes in the economy of the People's Republic of China such that today nearly half of all Chinese immigrants in the United States arrived in 2000 or later. These recent arrivals tend to be wealthier and more conservative than their predecessors and are being organized by the Chinese Tea Party in order to dismantle civil rights protections. Again, our aim has been to focus on the implications for political analysis and strategy.

Another form of intervention has been the creation of political education tools. One example is *A Different Asian American Timeline*, an interactive online resource that covers nearly six hundred years of history. It begins with the early Atlantic slave trade in the fifteenth century, traces the rise of modern nation-states, and covers events that have affected not only Asians in the Americas but people across racial boundaries. It arranges history by periods of crisis and by the logics of white supremacy—labor, land, and empire. It is an intervention that argues that there is no such thing as Asian American history apart from the systems of power that organize society.[7]

This brings me to one of our core findings—that most people, even within the racial justice movement (and including Scot and me at earlier points in our lives), have misunderstood race to be a set of distinct human groupings. Because of this, we often mistake solidarity to be a constellation of such groupings based on mutual political commitments. But if we understand race to be a construct that upholds an unjust economic and social structure, then this is backward. Instead, we should look for those who have the greatest interests in transforming that structure and identify and forge political alliances accordingly, in spite of those racial groupings. In this time of the COVID-19 pandemic, massive uprising to defend Black lives, profound economic dislocation, and the mounting threat of fascism, this could look like organizing essential workers, people with disabilities, survivors of state-sponsored and vigilante violence, people who have been structured out of the economy—in short, those who have been harmed by the system or who are otherwise ripe for agitation—against Trumpist authoritarianism and for broad democratic principles and a new economic vision.

FACING THE PRECIPICE

In writing this chapter, I am struck by how many prescient moments took place over the first decade of ChangeLab's work. Participants in our 2013 Race Lab spoke to the need for the racial justice movement to understand and address class as race and vice versa in order to close a gaping political vulnerability through which the Right could advance—a prediction that Trumpism proved true. Incisive assessments from that lab of trends in sectors from government to the media haunt me in these days. I am reminded of the words of my colleague, dear friend, and mentor Suzanne Pharr, who once said that prediction is not prevention. It is hard in hindsight not to regret our inability to do more, sooner.

The reality is that pursuing the interventions that emerged from our Race Labs at scale would have required much more capacity than ChangeLab or our movements had. It would have required investments into other, similar kinds of experimental spaces, into the infrastructure needed to implement new ideas, to build narrative power, to coordinate, and to aggressively develop a deep bench of leaders ready to organize in unorganized, strategic sectors. This requires risk-ready funders and investors. I know they exist, especially now, but we need to find and organize them.

The other day a friend and colleague joked with me that ChangeLab should adopt the slogan "Spreading the good news since 2010!"—a gallows humor dig at the fact that over the last decade we have worked to draw attention not only to the centrality of race in US politics but also to the very real, frightening, and present threat of authoritarianism. We have paid special attention to Asian American politics but often found ourselves misunderstood in this respect. Rather than singling out Asian Americans for particular castigation or praise (we, like others, have been criticized for both), we believe Asian American racial politics is an area of deficit *and* of strategic importance to the overall racial justice movement and thus to the project of inclusive multiracial democracy. White nationalism and allied right-wing movements will seek out and exploit any vulnerability, any issue or constituency left up for grabs, and thus effectively ceded to them by the progressive Left. For this reason we need new strategies and structures to bring yet unorganized, contested constituencies into the broad struggle for genuine democracy.

Doing so has never been more urgent. While right-wing "grasstops" figures and institutions have been influential in US politics for decades, until Trump's presidency, never in our lifetimes had we seen such emboldened, visible, unapologetic, and scaled-up moves by grassroots right-wing organizations, often directly backed and/or legitimated by state power. At the same time, an extraordinary level of anti-racist resistance has flourished, led by forces ripened over generations to fight not only for Black lives but for, in the words of Black feminist Barbara Smith, "a place on this globe that is fit for human life." Spurred by the vicious police killing of George Floyd in Minneapolis in May 2020, protests took place in at least two thousand cities and towns across the United States. In response, the Trump administration deployed armed federal agents to several of those cities. Those agents—unidentified and in unmarked vehicles—arrested peaceful protesters without cause.[8] The insurrection by thousands of pro-Trump seditionists at the national Capitol during the electoral vote count on January 6, 2021, was the unsurprising outcome of our current set of conditions.

In this volatile moment more people have awoken to the possibility that we are sliding into fascism. Throughout 2020 mayors appealed to Congress; protests grew out of moral outrage, with mothers and veterans turning out to defend our democratic rights. Black-led, multiracial, feminist movements threw down in the 2020 presidential and down-ballot races throughout the US South and delivered a clear, though notably not overwhelming, electoral defeat of Trump.[9] Asian American forces were critical in this effort. This cooperation has opened democratic space in the terrain of struggle ahead, in terms of civil liberties and legal and institutional leverage, to continue the fight for racial justice and inclusive democracy. As undergirded by violence as our democratic norms and institutions have been to date, there is simply no democratic space under fascism or autocracy.

Yet electoral defeat is not absolute. As I mentioned at the start of this chapter, right-wing authoritarian forces were preparing during the 1990s, underground. They are practiced at building their ranks and their strategies *as opposition forces*, when they perceive themselves to be underdogs, rebels. Having won and then lost the presidency (unfairly, in their estimation) at the ballot box, they will likely turn to other, less democratic means. We should be ready, by continuing to build multiracial bases of pro-democracy forces able to demonstrate the power of our convictions through local organizing and governance for tangible social and economic justice and for inclusive civic participation. This is how we will construct life- and community-affirming alternatives to the deadly pathways of both neoliberalism and fascism.

So far, ChangeLab's hypothesis appears to be true. The creation of space free from nonprofit and foundation constraints can result in robust analysis and bold ideas, but we need far greater resources to test those ideas. The ever more difficult times that Scot and I saw on the horizon ten years ago are taking shape today, but we are still in the foreshocks. To draw from the late writer and activist Grace Lee Boggs, the hour is late on the clock of the world, but there is time to act—not only to prevent (and prepare for) full-scale authoritarianism but also to plan for a different, more feminist and care-centered world. I deeply believe that those of us who find white nationalism and authoritarianism abhorrent are the majority, despite the political differences among us. We need to fight like hell to prevent white nationalists from winning the state while also building the democracy and freedom that we so fundamentally need and deserve, including an economy that works for all of us. In short, we need to finish the work of Reconstruction and pursue the new roads that it would offer.

So, how does it feel to be on the precipice, and what will we do? For me, being on the precipice feels deeply, soul-achingly, gut-sinkingly uncomfortable and frightening. But with every step we take to build and behave like a multiracial majority that yearns for an inclusive, care-centered society, we build new ground beneath our feet. With every breath we take to replace the racial tropes and retributive politics we've been tricked into seeing as our only options with genuine curiosity and compassion, we transform fear into hope. Since June 2020 we have witnessed the largest mass mobilization for racial justice that I have ever seen in my lifetime. Let's turn that mobilization into institutional leverage, into actual governing power.

And let us never forsake our basic, fundamental commitment to real solidarity. They cannot come for any of us without going through all of us. Hearts open. Fists up.

NOTES

1   "Richard Butler," Southern Poverty Law Center, https://www.splcenter
    .org/fighting-hate/extremist-files/individual/richard-butler, accessed
    February 23, 2021.
2   Kimberlé Crenshaw, "Martin Luther King Encounters Post-Racialism."
    Kalfou 1, no. 1 (Spring 2014); Eduardo Bonilla-Silva, *Racism without
    Racists* (Lanham, MD: Rowman & Littlefield, 2003).
3   "Whites Believe They Are the Victims of Racism More Often than
    Blacks," *TuftsNow*, May 23, 2011, https://now.tufts.edu/news-releases
    /whites-believe-they-are-victims-racism-more-o.
4   Carol Anderson, *White Rage: The Unspoken Truth of Our Racial Divide*
    (New York: Bloomsbury, 2016).
5   N'Tanya Lee and Steve Williams, "More than We Imagined: Activists'
    Assessment of the Moment and the Way Forward," *LeftRoots*, August 2,
    2013, https://leftroots.net/more-than-we-imagined-activists
    -assessments-of-the-moment-and-the-way-forward.
6   Angela Poe Russell, "Nationalist Group 'Proud Boys' Linked to Oppo-
    nents of Washington's Affirmative Action Measure," King5.com,
    October 17, 2019.
7   "A Different Asian American Timeline," *ChangeLab*, https://aatimeline
    .com, accessed February 23, 2021.
8   "Federal Officers Use Unmarked Vehicles to Grab People in Portland,
    DHS Confirms," *NPR*, July 17, 2020, https://www.npr.org/2020/07/17

/892277592/federal-officers-use-unmarked-vehicles-to-grab-protesters
-in-portland.

9 Mike Baker, "A 'Wall of Vets' Joins the Front Lines of Portland Protests," *New York Times*, July 25, 2020, https://www.nytimes.com/2020
/07/25/us/a-wall-of-vets-joins-the-front-lines-of-portland-protests
.html.

PART 4

ON MOVEMENT BUILDING

Shaped by the Past, Creating New Futures

CHAPTER 10

ON MOVEMENT PRAXIS IN
THE ERA OF TRUMPISM

ALEX T. TOM

SPURRED BY MOUNTING OPPRESSION AND INEQUALITIES aggravated by the global pandemic, racist police killings, and massive unemployment, grassroots communities of color showed up in full force to defeat Trump and stem the slide toward authoritarianism. These movements were rooted in the radical traditions of the Southern Freedom Movement, decades in the making, and a Black-led, multiracial united front. We have also seen an emboldened right wing and white nationalist movement. While we advance our struggles for justice, we work with a sober assessment that it will take decades to undo the harm and decimation to our democracy and communities. Even with Trump out of office, the ongoing impacts of Trumpism continue in ways that are demoralizing and disheartening. And yet I truly believe self- and social transformation is not only possible but necessary in the twenty-first century. We need a "movement of movements" to win the hearts and minds of millions.[1] Across the country and around the world, young people, especially working-class, women, disabled, queer and trans people of color, are already leading the way in bold and inspiring ways. The key is supporting and sustaining this work toward a vision of collective liberation. In this struggle, deepening our movement praxis is critical.

Praxis is the application of theory into practice. In *Pedagogy of the Oppressed* Paulo Freire, the Brazilian Marxist, defines *praxis* as "reflection and action upon the world in order to transform it."[2] In the movement there is a false dichotomy between theory and practice. Some get stuck in theory and ideas, while others get immobilized by practicing and doing the work.

As Mia Mingus, a community organizer for disability justice and transformative justice, said: "Practice yields the sharpest analysis. Practice is one of the most effective teachers. If theory alone could have gotten us free, it would have already happened." Praxis is the constant process of applying theory into action toward our long-term vision.[3]

This chapter reflects on the process and politics of movement building, based on my years of organizing and study, primarily with the Chinese Progressive Association (CPA) in San Francisco and the Seeding Change Fellowship. Our collective liberation is not only possible; it is necessary. It is also a long journey. We must deepen our movement praxis toward a long-term vision and strategy. The first section are my observations of the time, place, and conditions of our times. I see three dangerous trends in the movement, which include pessimism, perfectionism, and purism. In the second section I share ten movement practices that have helped me as an organizer and activist over the last couple of decades. These practices are based on a deep desire to transform self and society toward our collective liberation. In the final section I share three key opportunities to deepen our praxis in these urgent times: calling in and out the right wing in the Asian American community, especially the rise of the new Chinese American Right; combating Trumpism on local, national, and international levels; and (3) practicing long-term self- and community care.

The ideas in this chapter emerge from many years of conducting trainings for the Seeding Change Fellowship, a national summer fellowship for young Asian Americans interested in community organizing.[4] Every summer the program provides training and support to twenty to twenty-five fellows who are placed in grassroots organizations across the country. In particular, my focus has been on *how* to organize in these times within the myriad of contradictions from capitalism and other systems of oppression as well as challenges within our own community and movement. It was also an immense privilege for me to learn from and better understand the needs of young organizers and activists.

For nearly thirty years I "grew up" in the youth and labor movement, in the 1990s, and the progressive 501(c)(3) nonprofit organizing sector, in the 2000s and beyond. As a cis-gender, middle-class, Chinese American man, I was fortunate to have access to political education and organizing trainings at a young age. In 1992 I was trained in high school youth programs in San Francisco and the broader Bay Area, such as the Encampment for Citizenship, which is an anti-oppression program that trained and developed thousands of young people since the 1940s.[5] Then I attended the University of California, San Diego, and spent nearly ten years organizing in the San Diego US-Mexico border region with the Center on Policy Initiatives, Students for Economic Justice and Youth Organizing Communities.[6] There I cut my teeth during the reign of California governor Pete Wilson, which I thought would be the most xenophobic and racist time period in my life. This was later proved wrong with the election of Donald Trump. Finally, I spent fifteen years at the Chinese Progressive Association in San Francisco, including ten years as the executive director, where I learned about the radical legacy of Asian American activism and the power of intergenerational grassroots community organizing.[7]

I faced several challenges when I started organizing at CPA. Coming out of the youth sector and organizing primarily Black and Latinx high school—and college-aged youths, I saw how our identities are often siloed in the movement. When I started organizing garment and restaurant workers, I realized young people were part of a larger movement and that I was organizing the children of these adults. Also, workers are often also tenants, mothers, and/or caretakers. I learned that the basis of community organizing is to work with people across generations, with all their identities.

Also, I realized early on that most of the community organizations like CPA had political education and skill trainings for working-class grassroots community members; there were few, if any, programs for young Asian Americans. Often students are seen as too "privileged"; however, there are many first-generation and working-class students who are often "invisibilized." Not to mention, youth and students have historically played a critical role in all movements. We started the Eva Lowe Fellowship Program and the Seeding Change Fellowship Program as an intervention to ensure that young people had the mentorship, support, and tools to engage and organize in the community.

The movement is where I found my inspiration, joy, and purpose; it was also an extremely lonely and difficult place. I spent years challenging my privilege and guilt by overworking myself for multiple cycles of burnout. I fell into the pitfalls of martyrism without even knowing it. Each time, I became more aware of my needs and limits and slowly learned how to ask for help. I was also lifted up by the good people around me. I feel immense gratitude for the love and support I received for nearly three decades.

I'm especially grateful for the movement elders at CPA who listened, mentored, and shared their own experiences. Eva Lowe, who cofounded the Chinese Worker Mutual Aid Association in the 1930s was nearly one hundred when I met her in 2007. She shared the incredibly rich history of the transnational role of Chinese leftists and progressives during the Japanese aggression against China and of organizing unemployed worker councils in the Chinatown during the Great Depression. Pam Tau Lee, a cofounder of CPA, was the board chair for over ten years and a leader in the labor and environmental justice movement. I will always cherish the inspiration, mentorship, and friendship she provided me in some of my most difficult times. Ben Lee, a cofounder, was one of the best movement storytellers. He could always provide humor as well as historical and ideological insights grounded in the community and movement. Warren Mar, a cofounder who was also a community and labor leader, always had some real talk and solid perspectives on the Chinese immigrant community and the broader working class. Francis Wong, a former board chair and world-renowned artist and community leader, always had profound reflections on how to take care of each other and sustain the movement long term. Mabel Teng, the former board chair and member of the Board of Supervisors and Assessor in San Francisco, had such an important role in the Chinese immigrant community in the 1980s and 1990s. Her insights on the community and political strategy were invaluable. Gordon Mar started as a student volunteer in the 1980s and then became the first paid staff member of CPA in 1991. He is currently serving as a supervisor for District 4 Board of Supervisors in San Francisco. I have much to thank for his leadership and the foundation he built at CPA in the 1990s and 2000s. Finally, Qi Wan Pan, who passed away in 2017 at the age of ninety-six, was a longtime member of CPA since the 1980s. She was the first generation of revolutionaries in China in 1949 and a teacher. I will always remember the time she spent with me analyzing community issues and contradictions. She was patient, kind, and full of wisdom. There are so many more to name, but these are some movement elders who kept me grounded and helped me keep my eyes on the prize.

Now in my midforties, I am a proud "yelder" (young elder) and understand my role is to be a steward for the current and next generation of young leaders. It is indeed a daunting task, but as Happy Lim, one of the cofounders of the 1930s Chinese Worker Mutual Aid Association,[8] a mass organization that fought for the rights of unemployed Chinese immigrant workers during the Great Depression, said: "Those revolutionary-minded youths who were advanced in thinking had an unshakeable determination and faith. They provided a solution to transform the social services of the Chinese community, to fight against poverty, and to answer 'the problem of starvation. . . . I will follow the advanced youths of today and keep on fighting.'"[9] Yelders are a critical bridge between generations. Through the years young people would ask deep and profound questions about what to do with their lives, how to deal with burnout, and how to be in solidarity with other oppressed communities. "Should I go to law school, graduate school, or become a teacher or community organizer?" "How do I do this work without burning out?" "How do we fight anti-Black racism and show up for Black folks without re-centering Asian Americans?"

Most organizers grapple with these questions, and there are usually no simple answers. Soon I realized that it was less about giving the "perfect" answers and that the act of revealing my personal journey, challenges, and lessons was powerful in it of itself. Organizing is a journey and a dynamic process with constant ebbs and flows. In this heightened stage of capitalism, many who are doing this work feel "stuck" in contradictions and fear failure and making mistakes. Through the decades I've seen too many people leave the movement or tear each other apart because of these doubts and contradictions. This is exactly what the system wants us to do. Instead, how do we stay centered despite these contradictions and move toward our collective liberation? We can build a strong and vibrant movement in which we all have the capacity to take care of ourselves and each other while changing the material conditions of our community toward our collective liberation.

This chapter is my contribution to deepening our movement praxis. I have been humbled by so many movement organizers and activists, the young and the young at heart. Much of what I share comes from my own experiences and the wisdom of others. In particular, some of the most grounded praxis comes organically from struggle within grassroots communities that are the backbone of our resilient movements. Deepening our collective movement praxis is not an easy task, but it is critical, especially in these times.

To be clear, there are many roles in the movement. Since my experience has been mainly in paid and nonpaid organizing and activism in the Chinese immigrant community and Asian American Movement, this is the particular focus of this chapter. We need expertise in all areas, including caregivers, doctors, service workers, storytellers, social workers, economists, healers, teachers, engineers, farmers, spiritual and religious leaders, activists, and organizers, to name a few.[10] Recently, however, I've seen that many have conflated paid organizing in progressive 501(c)(3) nonprofits as the entire work of the movement. In actuality progressive 501(c)(3) nonprofits are part of a much larger movement. Organizing, in fact, is a value, and everyone needs to organize in their perspective fields. It is also a profession and a craft that fails to be understood clearly enough, which has led to some dangerous trends.

THE 3 PS: DANGEROUS TRENDS IN THE MOVEMENT—PESSIMISM, PERFECTIONISM, AND PURISM

Even before Trump, capitalism, sexism, heterosexism, transphobia, ableism, ageism, and other systems of oppression were alive and well in the United States. At its core capitalism breeds isolation, competition, fragmentation, and alienation. Over the last few years the right wing has become emboldened by white nationalism, white supremacy leaning toward neofascism. The system creates conditions that prevent us from uniting and achieving our collective liberation. How do we stay grounded and keep our eyes on the prize of building a world based on interdependence, mutuality, and love?

Antonio Gramsci, an Italian Marxist of the early nineteenth century, provides a useful tool for understanding this dynamic. He saw that Western capitalist societies maintained their power not only through force and coercion but also through the consent of the working class. He believed that the system maintained its hegemony through institutions in civil society such as media, education, and government, to name a few. Therefore, he asserted that our role as revolutionaries is a "war of position," which is resistance to domination with culture, rather than physical might, as its foundation.[11] Countering hegemony and organizing people to build an alternative within society is a long-term strategy in the twenty-first century. Some of the most toxic symptoms of US hegemony are pessimism, perfectionism, and purism. Here I offer my observations of these dangerous trends.

PESSIMISM

It is understandable that people feel demoralized in the face of overwhelming power. But let's be clear, negativity is a symptom of capitalism. The system needs us to be cynical about change and transformation. Many want change but do not believe it is possible. This is especially true among Asian immigrants and refugees in the United States who have largely had painful experiences in communist and socialist experiments in their home countries. When I started at the Chinese Progressive Association in 2005, we took on worker exploitation in San Francisco Chinatown. Even though many believed in the values and ideals, we were told by community members: "That's a nice idea. We tried this in China, but we will never change Chinese culture and the minds of Chinese people."

This is how hegemony works. It is not necessarily coercive and physical but achieves its dominance through culture and ideas. It takes years of listening, education, and organizing to develop people's capacity to believe that change is possible. Worker exploitation continues to exist, but now wage theft and wage exploitation are broadly seen as "bad" across the Chinese immigrant community, whereas before they were seen as normal.

Similarly, pessimism also deeply impacts our strategic orientation. For example, some may not believe that radical change is possible in these times and think that change can only happen through short-term policy and electoral fights. Historically, however, the most strategic movements have had bold visions and have used the policy and electoral arena as part of the long arc of radical change.

PERFECTIONISM

Perfectionism is also pervasive in the movement and leads to overthinking, overprocessing, and ultimately stagnation and inaction. The #BlackLivesMatter movement, started in 2014, inspired a new generation of Asian Americans who wanted to show their solidarity with the Black community. However, as a new and emerging movement, there was no twenty-first-century "blueprint" for solidarity. Many Asian Americans continued to ask, "How do we show up without re-centering Asian Americans?" Many Black leaders saw how Asian Americans were being used as a wedge to maintain white supremacy and the racial hierarchy. They called on Asian Americans not to overthink and to take action by "putting their bodies on the line."[12]

Across the country Asians showed up in solidarity for Black lives and began to counter anti-Black racism within their own communities.[13] Some already had been building long-standing relationships for decades, and some were just beginning to build new relationships. Regardless, nothing was "perfect," but the solidarity built in real time was dynamic and beautiful. It was within this ongoing practice that solidarity and "co-conspiring" were defined and sharpened.

The allyship also unraveled deeper questions of solidarity within the Asian American community. Organizers in the Southeast Asian community "called in" East Asians, who were so ready to support non-Asian people of color while offering little to no support to Southeast Asians, who were also facing police and state violence, not to mention to members of the Arab and Muslim community. This process sparked honest conversations and started to deepen our movement praxis and solidarity within the Asian American community. How to build solidarity within continues to be an important question for the Asian American Movement.[14]

As we strive toward our collective liberation, we need to remember not to get immobilized by perfectionism. There is no perfect person, no perfect idea, no perfect space, nor is there a perfect plan. Instead, we can create a movement that can embrace and learn from all our imperfections.

PURISM

Purism is another symptom of capitalism and can be extremely toxic to our ability to develop a long-term visionary strategy. In some cases purism can be harmful and reactionary. It seeks to have pure ideas that are not grounded in our current conditions of contradictions among people, relationships, the community, and the movement. This does not mean we accept all contradictions. It means we need to understand the core contradictions based on the time, place, and conditions and understand that transformation is a dynamic process.

As Paulo Freire says in *Pedagogy of the Oppressed*, achieving our collective liberation is not a guarantee; it is a process of navigating the complex set of contradictions: "The contradiction between the oppressors and the oppressed, and how it is overcome; oppression and the oppressors; oppression and the oppressed; *Liberation: not a gift, not a self-achievement, but a mutual process.*"[15] Some of the worst forms of purism appear in the "call out" culture, in which some use oppression as a weapon against others. It often comes from a place of fear, anger, and rage and ultimately becomes reactionary.

Purism creates a false dichotomy between "long termism" and "short termism." Long termism appears to be more visionary and transformative but also smaller and weaker, while short termism seems to be more impactful and scalable yet is very transactional. However, the two approaches are not mutually exclusive. For example, many radicals avoid electoral work because it tends to be dominated by short-term thinking and winning the next election or policy; however, it is also critical for young radicals to engage. Not only do we have the threat of an emboldened right-wing and white nationalist movement; it is a time in which we have the attention of millions of people who are seeking change. Without young radicals, the field will remain nothing but transactional and short term. We need to learn how to engage in the short term and develop a bold strategy toward our long-term vision.

Although pessimism, perfectionism, and purism are so pervasive in the movement, visionary movements have also emerged in these times. From movement moments such as Occupy Wall Street, Standing Rock, Black Lives Matter, and Mauna Kea to winning on local and national levels such as the Fight for 15, Indigenous communities stopping the Keystone XL Pipeline, and disability justice activists staving off attacks on the Affordable Care Act (ACA) as well as the fight against deportations, and the climate justice movement, there are new leaders and organizations emerging across the country.[16] In 2020 movements have pushed forward bold and visionary policy platforms such as the BREATHE Act, Green New Deal, and People's Charter.[17] The key question is how to sustain this, grow our movement, and win the hearts and minds of millions.

DEEPENING OUR MOVEMENT PRAXIS: TEN MOVEMENT PRACTICES

We often forget that "another world is possible and necessary" because capitalism is unstable and unsustainable and will eventually implode. But what will the next system be, and who will define it? If we truly desire another world that is based on mutuality, interdependence, and love, we need to deepen our praxis and prepare to govern toward our long-term vision.

While there have been inspiring wins, we are facing unprecedented attacks and it will only get worse. In the post-9/11 world the role of the surveillance state has intensified. Although social media created the scalability of movements, they have also been strategically used by right-wing forces to spread misinformation and diffuse movements.[18] Social media is an important organizing tool, but we need to remember that movements now and historically are built upon trust and relationships and ongoing organizing on the ground. Finally, in these intense times organizers, activists, and our communities overall are more traumatized than ever before. Even with Trump defeated, the conditions that gave rise to his election and to Trumpism will not disappear, and it will take decades to undo the harm and destruction Trumpism has caused.

Here are ten practices that have helped deepen my own praxis. At the core they are based on transforming self and society toward our collective liberation.

1. Think dialectically. Capitalism is quite nimble yet pushes us to think rigidly. Dialectic thinking is the practice of analyzing and holding multiple contradictions toward the long-term vision. Instead of an "either-or" framework, we will need a "both-and" framework to navigate these complex times. It should not be mistaken for indecisiveness; it is an approach that allows for greater precision in the path forward.

2. Develop strategy grounded in time, place, and conditions. The path to our collective liberation requires a short- and long-term strategy that is based in a sharp and sober assessment of the time, place, and conditions. Too often, strategies do not match the actual circumstances and can lead to inaction. Knowing that conditions are complex and rapidly changing, we need to

be willing constantly to assess and reassess them on a micro and macro level.

3. Be a "fighter, thinker, and healer." Drawing from the late revolutionary general Gordon Baker Jr. aka General Baker, organizers and activists need to assess their own strengths and weaknesses and grow in new areas. For example, some people are good "fighters" in campaigns, some are good "thinkers" and writers, and some do a lot of emotional labor as healers. In the end everyone needs these skills and more. It is the only way we can grow a leaderful movement in which we are able to rotate roles and take turns.

4. Be a unity builder. To counter the fragmentation and alienation of the times, we need to become stronger unity builders. Concretely, we need to learn to struggle alongside other people with love and compassion, especially within the community and movement. This will not happen overnight. It will require ongoing practice of self-awareness, listening, and reflection.

5. Prepare to govern. As a movement, we need to believe that through every action we are preparing to govern. Too often, governing is seen as just the work of the government; however, we are also governing every day in our relationships, families, the community, and the movement. We need to govern at all levels for the present and the future and cannot do one without the other. We can also learn a lot from Indigenous communities whose members have a long-term vision of governance and have been governing for thousands of years. Regardless of whether you are a lawyer, academic, teacher, or community organizer, there is a role for everyone. We need people everywhere, and, more important, organizing is needed everywhere.

6. Practice self and community care. "Self-care" has been misunderstood and mischaracterized within the movement. For a full transformation of self and society, we need to balance the individual and collective needs of the movement. However, this requires us to be aware of our needs and stronger systems of community support. The tendency in these times is to isolate and wait until burnout hits to call for support. Unintentionally, without fully considering the needs of the people around us, self-care can lead to "selfish care." Under capitalism this will

not change anytime soon, but how do we counter isolation until it is eventually not necessary?

7. Build a political home. Many confuse their paid work in the community as their only political home. This may be more the case with a growing number of progressive nonprofit organizations. However, the role of the community organization is primarily a space for community members to develop their ideas and vision.[19] Organizers also need time and space to reflect on their community work, develop their vision, and practice working with others in different ways.[20]

After volunteering at CPA and becoming the campaign coordinator in 2005, I was so excited to breakdown capitalism and imperialism to grassroots community members. I was quickly humbled and learned that community organizing was actually a transformative process of *building relationships*, *listening* to people, and *being in dialogue* with each other over a long period of time. As mentioned earlier, many in the community already understood the systems of oppression but did not believe change was possible. CPA was a political home for them to tap into their own agency, individually and collectively.

But CPA did give me space to create my own political home. Since CPA was part of a rich legacy and ecosystem of radical Asian Americans, I participated in and built projects, such as the Activist Community Training (ACT), a community organizing training program for college-age youths; API Movement Building Network (APIMB), an initiative to build a national network of progressive organizers and organizations; and the WT(N)O Delegation, which was an Asian American delegation of workers, students, youths, and activists to protest the World Trade Organization meeting (WTO) in Hong Kong in 2005. More important, these political homes and activities were open to everyone regardless of if you were a paid organizer.

8. Stretch and try things on. Organizing is the process of constantly building new skills and muscles outside of our comfort zones. As we prepare to govern, we need to own our leadership in building organizations and political power. These areas are fraught with contradictions; however, if we do not deepen our

praxis, we will not be prepared to govern when the time comes. We need more leaders, and they need to be everywhere. Some say movements are *leaderless*, but really movements are full of leaders and leadership.[21]

As I mentioned earlier, I initially came out of the youth sector organizing mostly Black and Latinx high school and college-aged youths in San Diego and the US-Mexico border region. At CPA I was tasked with organizing garment and restaurant workers who were the same age as my parents. Immediately, I was confronted with my own class guilt as I organized workers to confront their employers. In fact, I was called out several times by workers: "Who do you think you are telling me to stand up to my boss? What do you have to lose? You already have a job, and you went to college." I gradually learned that organizing is not about pushing people to do things they don't want to do; rather, it is tapping into their sense of agency and supporting them individually and collectively as much as possible. This stretched me in so many difficult ways but eventually transformed my leadership.

9. Have your ear to the ground. Collective liberation will only be possible when we win the hearts and minds of people. We need to learn to listen and reflect while taking action. This can be one of the most difficult practices because there is a lot of internalized oppression and many divisions within the community and movement. Through the process we can sharpen our approach and analysis.

10. Be your best self. Capitalism is built on competition with others, which is destructive. Instead, we need to strive to be the best versions of ourselves. Doing so requires incredible self-awareness and self-compassion.

MOVEMENT TASKS IN THESE URGENT TIMES

Although our path to collective liberation is a long journey, I will share three urgent tasks to consider as opportunities to deepen our praxis. In this stage of capitalism we need to call in (and out) the right wing in the Asian American community, especially the Chinese American Right; take on Trumpism on a local and national level; and deepen practices around self- and community care.

1. Calling in (and out) the right wing in the Asian American community. With the rise of white nationalism, there is also a more emboldened ethnic nationalism, such as the "Chinese Tea Party," the new Chinese American right wing in the United States, whose members are primarily wealthy and educated. This trend is happening in some form in all communities of color. In this current moment the Chinese immigrant community has been strategically used as a wedge against other people of color, including other Asian Americans.[22] I think it's a mistake to write off this community as lacking any progressive politics, as many, including Asian Americans, have done. We recognize, too, that the Chinese American right wing has been weakened nationally with Trump's escalation against China and the Chinese community. Asian American support for Trump decreased from 37 percent in 2016 to 20 percent in 2020.[23] I believe that we need to expose the self-interests and political interests of key individuals and engage and build in new ways with segments of the new Chinese immigrant community, to encourage them to be part of the broader Asian American Movement. I believe that there is a great potential for building a cross-class and multiracial movement in the current moment with issues such as public charge rules, further limits on H1B visas, and US-China trade war tensions. CRW Strategies LLC, the WeChat Project, and Chinese for Affirmative Action offer some examples of how we can develop a new digital hub for progressive content creation to engage Chinese immigrants and counter rampant misinformation online.[24] Lastly, the Hindu Right is also a dangerous force, and building a program around countering the Chinese and Hindu right wings could prove to be very powerful.[25]

2. Taking on Trumpism on the local, national, and international levels. Even with Trump out of office, it will still take decades to repair the harm of Trumpism and of the systems of oppression in place long before Trump. We need to think about our short-term policy and electoral fights as part of the long-term strategy. We cannot wait for Trumpism's destruction of what is left of our democracy to destabilize us further into inaction. We need to see the current moment as an opportunity to practice all strategies and to build toward the transformation of the system

we want. As the Organizing Upgrade Collective wrote: "The struggle against Trumpism will last longer than any electoral cycle. . . . Defeating the political bloc that is driven by white nationalism and has captured the Republican Party is our immediate responsibility as left organizers."[26] Some great examples are the National Domestic Workers Alliance's winning $400 billion for the caregiving sector within the American Jobs Plan, Movement for Black Lives' BREATHE Act, Sunrise's Green New Deal, United We Dream's campaign for citizenship for all immigrants, and the Working Families Party's People's Charter.

3. Practicing long-term self- and community care. As mentioned earlier, the last few decades, especially the last several years, have been deeply traumatic to our communities. Many in the movement are ill equipped to address trauma and healing, especially those who are working class, queer or trans, women, disabled, and/or people of color. Trauma also shows up within the community and movement. Without clearer interventions and leadership, self-care has almost come to mean that individuals need to isolate and "leave" the movement or that the organization needs to shut down to "heal" before continuing the work. It also strongly relies on the (invisible) emotional labor of women and/or people with higher emotional intelligence. We need to redefine and "visibilize" this work more. It is hopeful that there are more resources such as Generative Somatics, Transformative Justice, and Coaching for Healing Justice and Liberation that integrate within the movement the social, personal, and political aspects of being human.[27]

As activist and writer Grace Lee Boggs wrote: "[We must] redefine our relationships with one another, to the Earth and to the world . . . about finding the courage to love and care for the peoples of the world as we love and care for our own families."[28] *How do we practice self-care and community care as a way to reimagine our revolutionary politics for the current and future?*

How do we know if we are on the right track? How do we know when and what to start? How do we stay accountable to our vision? Many, including myself, have gotten stuck here. To me it goes back to praxis, which is the applying of theory into practice, assessing and reflecting and repeat.

First, it is less about the "perfect" vision and more about having a grounded assessment of time, place, and conditions. All campaigns need to have good strategy that is grounded by assessing and reassessing our vision. Second, we need to practice learning about ourselves and how to be in community with each other. This does not mean we just practice random things or fail fast just for the sake of it. It means we practice *toward* our vision. I have practiced a lot as a martyr, and the results have been mostly reckless and about myself. Practicing with real friends and comrades and getting good at it over time will take our collective and individual power to another level. Finally, organizing and movement building are about building power and transforming the system. The idea of power has been misused and tainted. We have an automated response that power only means top-down, not grassroots; individual, not collective; scale, not depth; anger and rage, not love; replication, not transformation, to name a few. Many of us shy away from power because these binaries immobilize us. We need to redefine *power* for a world of interdependence, mutuality, and love. Simply put, power is about getting what our communities deserve.

Alicia Garza, cofounder of the Black Lives Matter Network and the Black Futures Lab, describes it well: "For me, power means getting to make decisions over your own life. Power means being able to determine where resources go, who they go to, where they don't go, and who they don't go to. . . . For me, power is about the ability to shape the narrative of what is right, what is wrong, what is just, what is unjust. But most importantly for me, power is about making sure that there are consequences when you're disappointed. When the people who you elect don't carry out the agenda that you elected them to carry out."[29]

We need everyone to be in their full power so that we can transform big and small parts of society. It will require us to deepen our movement praxis in these times. We all need each other and are counting on each other to be visionary practitioners and powerful in our own ways. This is our path to self- and societal transformation.

NOTES

1 Movements are complex, dynamic, and not prescribed. It is not only one set of individuals, nor is it just a group of organizations. I've found the term *movement of movements* useful; it was coined by Naomi Klein

in 2001 in a PBS series *Commanding Heights: The Battle for the World Economy* to describe the anti-globalization movement; also see Van Gosse, "A Movement of Movements: The Definition and Periodization of the New Left," in *A Companion to Post-1945 America*, ed. Jean-Christophe Agnew and Roy Rosenzweig (Oxford: Blackwell, 2006), 277–302.

2 Paulo Freire, *Pedagogy of the Oppressed* (1970; reprint, New York: Continuum, 2007), 51.

3 Praxis also builds on Mao in "On Practice," stressing the unity of theory and practice and the importance of practice.

4 On Seeding Change, see https://seeding-change.org.

5 On Encampment for Citizenship, see http://encampmentforcitizenship .org.

6 On the Center on Policy Initiatives, see https://www.cpisandiego.org /sej.

7 On the Chinese Progressive Association, see https://cpasf.org. On intergenerational organizing and Black-Asian solidarity in the CPA, see Alex T. Tom, "The Chinese Progressive Association and the Red Door," in *Black Power Afterlives: The Enduring Significance of the Black Panther Party*, ed. Diane C. Fujino and Matef Harmachis (Chicago: Haymarket Press, 2020), 289–300.

8 H. M. Lai, "A Historical Survey of Organizations of the Left among the Chinese in America," *Bulletin of Concerned Asian Scholars* 4 (1972): 10–20.

9 *East Wind: Politics & Culture of Asians in the US* 1, no. 1 (Spring–Summer 1982).

10 This is not a new concept. In movements, including US and international movements (past and present), everyone has a crucial role in the "popular front" toward a long-term vision.

11 Antonio Gramsci, *Prison Notebooks*, vol. 3, trans. J. A. Buttigieg (New York: Columbia University Press, 2007).

12 In the initial phase of the movement, there were hundreds of direct actions across the country on a monthly basis. There were also specific calls to Asian American activists to put their bodies on the line and to lead and follow at various times.

13 Asian Americans responded to the police killings of Eric Garner and Akai Gurley in New York, Philando Castile in Minnesota, and Mario Woods in San Francisco, to name a few. See May Fu, Simmy Makhijani, Anh-Thu Pham, Meejin Richart, Joanne Tien, and Diane Wong, "#Asians4BlackLives: Notes from the Ground," *Amerasia Journal* 45 (2019): 253–70.

14 In 2013 movement leaders from the Southeast Asian Freedom Network raised this question at the Grassroots Asians Rising (GAR) gathering in New Orleans, which catalyzed new and deeper relationship building within the Asian American Movement. In 2018 GAR integrated this

principle into its movement statement, "Building a Movement Family: Our Statement," https://www.grassrootsasians.org/2018-statement.

15 Freire, *Pedagogy of the Oppressed.*

16 For more examples of visionary movement organizations, see the Climate Justice Alliance, the Movement for Black Lives, Mijente, United We Dream, Native Organizing Alliance, Indigenous Environmental Network, Southeast Asian Freedom Network, and the Grassroots Asians Rising, to name a few.

17 Movement for Black Lives, "The BREATHE Act," https://breatheact .org; Working Families Party, "The People's Charter," https://www .peoplescharter.us/read-the-charter; Sunrise Movement, "What Is the Green New Deal?" https://www.sunrisemovement.org/green-new-deal /?ms=WhatistheGreenNewDeal%3F.

18 Emily Stewart, "Facebook's Political Ads Policy Is Predictably Turning Out to Be a Disaster," *Recode*, October 30, 2019, https://www.vox.com /recode/2019/10/30/20939830/facebook-false-ads-california-adriel -hampton-elizabeth-warren-aoc.

19 CPA was formed in 1972 to be a grassroots organization for people in the community; I Wor Kuen (IWK) was the collective for people in the community who wanted revolutionary change. There was a lot of synergy between CPA and IWK, but there were clear roles and identities.

20 Many organizers are from the community as well but need time and space to reflect in the capacity of an organizer

21 Barbara Ransy, "Ella Taught Me: Shattering the Myth of the Leaderless Movement," *Colorlines*, June 12, 2015, https://www.colorlines.com /articles/ella-taught-me-shattering-myth-leaderless-movement.

22 Chinese Americans have been used as wedges on core issues such as affirmative action, police violence, and data disaggregation, to name a few.

23 2020 Asian American Voter Survey, by APIAVote, AAPI Data, and Asian Americans Advancing Justice, https://www.apiavote.org /research/2020-asian-american-voter-survey.

24 On CRW Strategy, see http://crwstrategy.com/front-page/our-services; on WeChat, see https://www.thewechatproject.org; on Chinese Against Affirmative Action, see https://caasf.org. These entities played a crucial role in creating more educational Chinese-language content and massive distribution among WeChat groups to ensure ACA-5 (Proposition 16) got on the ballot in California. Progressive Chinese American college students who started "The WeChat Project" (https://www.thewechatproject.org) have also challenged conservative discourse on WeChat; see Zijia Song, "Can WeChat Be Woke? The Progressive Chinese Americans Countering Right-Wing Narratives," *SupChina*, October 22, 2020, https://supchina.com/2020/10/22/can -wechat-be-woke-the-progressive-chinese-americans-countering-right

-wing-narratives. The group published an open letter in response to the murder of George Floyd that went viral on the platform; see Eileen Huang, "A Letter from a Yale Student to the Chinese American Community," https://chineseamerican.org/p/31571.

25 On the Chinese Right's use of social media as an organizing tool, see Yuanyuan Feng and Mark Tseng-Putterman, "'Scattered like Sand': WeChat Warriors in the Trial of Peter Liang," *Amerasia Journal* 45, no. 2 (2019): 238–52.

26 Trumpism, El Paso and Our Responsibility as Left Organizers," *OrgUp* (blog), August 6, 2019, ("Hyperlink16","https://www.organizingup-grade.com/trumpism-el-paso-and-our-responsibility-as-left-organizers.

27 On Generative Somatics, see http://www.generativesomatics.org; on Transformative Justice, see https://leavingevidence.wordpress.com/2019/01/09/transformative-justice-a-brief-description; on Coaching for Healing Justice and Liberation, see https://www.healingjusticeliberation.org.

28 Grace Lee Boggs, "Solutionaries Are Today's Revolutionaries," *Boggs Blog*, October 27, 2013, https://conversationsthatyouwillneverfinish.wordpress.com/2013/10/27/solutionaries-are-todays-revolutionaries-by-grace-lee-boggs.

29 Leah Fessler "How the Leader of Black Lives Matter Defines 'Power,'" *Quartz*, September 16, 2018, https://qz.com/1391762/black-lives-matter-co-founder-alicia-garzas-definition-of-power.

CHAPTER 11

"PETE WILSON TRYING TO SEE US ALL BROKE"

Asian American Cross-Racial Student Activism
in 1990s California

ROBYN MAGALIT RODRIGUEZ, WITH WAYNE JOPANDA

IN THIS CHAPTER I CRITICALLY REFLECT ON MY ORGANIZING
work as an Asian American student activist working in cross-racial
solidarity spaces in the 1990s as an undergraduate in the University
of California system.[1] As I wrote this chapter, in 2020, many communities around the country were in upheaval as Black communities
along with their allies engaged in several months of protest action in
response to the killing of George Floyd by police on the heels of the
murders of other Black people by the police or white vigilantes. In the
last decade video footage going "viral" on social media platforms and
other internet outlets of white police officers or vigilantes violently
beating Black people have triggered outrage in the Black community and
other communities of color—including Asian Americans—especially
since those responsible for the violence have been left unpunished. In
some cases, as in the current period, this outrage has manifested in
outright rebellion.

For Californians who lived through the 1990s, the images from Fer-
guson, Baltimore, Minneapolis, and other cities are uncannily familiar. The city of Los Angeles erupted after the acquittal of Los Angeles
Police Department officers whose brutal beating Rodney King was
captured on video. Nevertheless, the dominant media (and even

scholarly) narratives that emerged during the riots was one of Asian-Black tensions, as some Korean American businesses were attacked by African Americans.[2] It was also true that Asian Americans and Blacks came together to challenge white supremacy in its different manifestations.[3]

As someone who teaches college students for my full-time job and also works alongside them in organizing and activist spaces, I'm especially interested in discussing lessons, based on my time educating and being educated by them, that I feel are vital for student organizers in today's political moment. First, I want to illustrate how my generation engaged in pan-ethnic organizing as "Asian Americans" at a time when the "model minority" myth seemed less of a fiction and more of a reality. We were the generation whose parents arrived after the 1965 Immigration Act was passed. Our parents were often professionals and other highly skilled Asian immigrants. Our parents benefited from the dramatic changes of the 1965 Immigration Act, which dropped the racist, anti-Asian provisions of previous laws but also incorporated new preferences for those who were already highly educated and relatively privileged in their countries of origin. Many families were solidly middle class. Our realities—though they didn't necessarily reflect all of Asian America—helped to entrench the model minority myth even more deeply by the 1990s. The entrenchment of the myth was also symptomatic of the multiculturalism that accompanied neoliberal policies of the era. Asian Americans were paraded around as examples of how truly democratic and anti-racist America was supposed to be. Though Asian Americans are a racialized minority group that has experienced extreme forms of racism over the course of their collective history (from anti–Asian immigration laws to mass incarceration during World War II), they could still "make it," so the logic of the myth goes.

Given the exponential increase in both Asian immigrants and refugees in the United States from the 1970s to 1980s, many of us would grow up in ethnic enclaves that bolstered our ethnic identities over a shared "Asian American" identity. For example, I grew up in what some scholars might call an "ethnoburb": Union City, California. The majority of our neighbors were Filipino. I had a very firm sense of myself as a "Filipino," as opposed to "Asian" or "Asian American," and if anything, I developed an affinity for Latinx folks who counted among the few non-Filipinos in our neighborhood but who worshipped with us in the Catholic church. That would change, however, as I got more and more exposed to Asian American studies in college. Detailing how I came to develop my identity as an Asian American through activism, I hope, can be helpful for those who are trying to make sense of their own identities, particularly how Asian American as an identity can be activated not simply because of an ancestral connection to the continent of Asia but as a political identity that is formed through a rejection of the model minority myth and its rootedness in white supremacy and anti-Blackness.

Second, I want to show how we struggled to do cross-racial solidarity work within a so-called post-racial context. By the 1990s we were being told that the United States was now a "multicultural" and "diverse" country; that we might even be in a post-racial context in which racism—white supremacy and anti-Blackness—was no longer as salient as in previous generations. In other words, even as we were dealing with straightforwardly conservative, and ultimately racist, policy makers like Republican governor Pete Wilson in California, we also had to contend with politicians who put forward equally racist policies yet in very "color-blind" ways, such as Democratic president Bill Clinton. Republicans and Democrats alike converged around a neoliberal agenda. How we as student organizers struggled to make sense of the emergent neoliberal, multiculturalist order—a society that passed policies that punished Black and brown people by either condemning them to a life of poverty or a life in prison while simultaneously celebrating diversity—offers important lessons for today. Reflections on cross-racial solidarity during a time when white supremacy manifested in more coded ways are vital. As I write, we now live under a Biden-Harris presidential administration. While many might feel hopeful that their election signals a (re)new(ed) shift away from white supremacy, I would caution that we maintain a critical perspective and take lessons from the 1990s. What we learned then and what continues to be important now is that some of the most pernicious forms of white supremacy are those that are not as flagrant as the forms it took under Trump.

This chapter tries to shed light on 1990s activism, which has not gotten sufficient attention as compared with the Asian American Movement (AAM). But in many ways to document 1990s activism is to illustrate the enduring significance of the AAM for our organizing. Many of us who first started organizing in the 1990s had the benefit of mentorship from AAM and other experienced radical activists. Given this volume's commitment to tracking the long reach and influence of the AAM, a discussion on the 1990s is vital, especially since the changing demographics of the Asian American community by the 1990s made pan-ethnic organizing perhaps more challenging than in earlier periods. At the same time, mentorship by AAM activists ensured that many of the AAM's orientations were at the core of our organizing efforts; that is, the internationalist, anti-imperialist and interracial solidarity politics of the AAM very much animated our work. The relationships forged between us and our 1960s counterparts were important during a time when neoliberal multiculturalism as well as the rising nonprofit industrial complex were becoming increasingly dominant.[4] The two developed hand in hand. For those of us who could benefit from mentorship by an earlier generation of radicals, we were offered a critical lens into making sense of the institutions and programs (such as affirmative action) that were created to respond to the demands of 1960s–70s radical movements but which had far more modest and limited aims. That many of my 1990s contemporaries the likes of Alex Tom (a contributor to this book), May Fu (another contributor to this book), the late John Delloro, or Kimi Lee have gone on to do vital work in Asian American activist and activist-scholar work through the 2000s and to the present suggests that the insights from the 1990s are also shaping organizing work today.

Reflecting on the intergenerational relationships and knowledges passed on between the AAM generation and so-called Gen X allows us to better understand the potential as well as the challenges for pan-ethnic Asian American organizing.[5] As a generation, many of us came out of model minority households as the daughters and sons of post-1965 immigrants who were allowed to come to the United States because they were professionals or scientists. Yet it is also true that the influx of Asian immigrants meant that there was a proliferation of more ethnic-based organizations and institutions in our communities.[6] Nevertheless, many of us would find ways to come together as Asian Americans even though we continued to work in ethnic-specific spaces.

Finally, I'm interested in thinking about my activism through the lens of specifically "student" activism because I believe that students have and can continue to play a particular kind of role in radical organizing. I want to bring to the fore how we took advantage of our status as students to organize not just around students but also around broader social justice issues. On many college campuses in the 1990s, we had organizations and programs that had become institutionalized, especially in the wake of the 1960s ethnic studies struggles, but also seemed really limited in their ability to act on issues students were facing on campus but also beyond campus. We tried to work both within those spaces and outside of them to address our concerns while participating in struggles affecting our communities more broadly. Though later I would be introduced to social movement writers who theorized explicitly about the historical role of students in large-scale social transformation, the distinctiveness of the student experience—especially the college student's experiences and how critically they can shape young people ideologically and politically— came from my own experiences in college.

California is often represented as the "left" coast, but it has long been the site of anti-Black as well as anti-immigrant policy. Indeed, if President Ronald Reagan epitomizes the rise and dominance of conservatism nationally, it must be remembered that he began his political career in California as the state's governor during the late 1960s and early 1970s, at the height of urban and campus unrest led by radical formations such as the Third World Liberation Front. Reagan actively suppressed movements led by people of color while governor and would continue to suppress communities of color, especially Black people, through a range of policies, when he was president. By the 1990s conservatism was in full swing in the state as captured by iconic rapper Tupac Shakur in his song "To Live and Die in L.A." In the song Shakur laments how California governor Pete Wilson is "trying to see us all broke." Indeed, people of color were systematically attacked not only by the governor but by highly organized conservative groups and members of the electorate as Propositions 187, 209, 224, and 227, to name a few, were all passed in quick succession. The trend in California became national, leading to the reversal of major civil rights gains, the dwindling of immigrant rights, and the further expansion of the prison industrial complex at both the state and federal levels. Often cast in color-blind and even "multiculturalist" language, the resulting laws, supported by Democrats and Republicans alike, have deeply shaped our current political landscape. They did not, however, go uncontested as communities of color resisted them in numerous ways. Indeed, this is also captured in Tupac's lyrics about "Black love, brown pride," which also extended to Asian Americans, who worked in solidarity with other communities of color during this period.

The activisms of the 1990s have not been documented to the same degree as the activisms—including those associated with the Asian American Movement—of the late 1960s and early 1970s. Even though there is still much work to be done to document the AAM, whether in the form of scholarly studies or personal memoirs or organizational reflections from groups active at the time, there has been far more writing on the AAM than on Asian American activisms in the decades that followed. Yet the 1990s was a moment of renewed sense of resolve around cross-racial solidarity. In response to the LA uprisings, the New Raza Left, the Black Radical Congress (BRC), and the Asian Left Forum, groups rooted to a great extent to the radical movements of the late 1960s, would convene to build a space aiming to draw together people of color around a leftist agenda. Meanwhile, formations such as Critical Resistance, which organizes around an abolitionist agenda aimed at dismantling the prison industrial complex and continues to work to this day, were also formed in the 1990s. This and other formations created in the 1990s have continued to have a direct impact on racial justice organizing today in ways that may yet be underappreciated. I hope this chapter can offer a bit of light on the significance of the 1990s to the current moment or at the least prompts more scholarly and activist inquiry into that era.[7]

MY COLLEGE JOURNEY

My reflections in this chapter are based primarily on my own experiences as a student organizer and thus echo the work I did with the organizations of which I was part while I was a student. I had an especially circuitous route through college. Anxious to get as far away from my very strict Filipino immigrant father and the restrictions he imposed on my life, I applied only to colleges on the East Coast. To my father's chagrin, I would end up going to Boston College right after I graduated from high school in 1991. After one year my father ceased paying for my tuition, and I was forced not only to support myself through college but to move to a college I could afford. I would end up taking a bulk of my classes at Diablo Valley College and transfer to the University of California, Santa Barbara (UCSB).

Though I was involved in a Filipino student organization while at Boston College, my student activism really commenced in 1993, when I was in the process of transferring to UCSB. I had begun doing work with the GABRIELA-Network (GAB-Net) upon my return from Boston to the Bay Area, which I would continue in my early months at UCSB.[8] At UCSB I helped to form ASIAN! (Asian Sisters for Ideas in Action Now!) and worked in ASIAN! from 1994 to 1996.[9] When I moved to the Bay Area to start graduate school at UC Berkeley, in 1996, I helped organize the League of Filipino Students and would continue my student organizing in that space from 1996 to 1998.[10] By 1998, after I had my oldest son, I would transition to different groups but would continue organizing students into the early 2000s.

THE CONTEXT: CALIFORNIA CONSERVATISM, NEOLIBERAL GLOBALIZATION, AND NEW FORMS OF RESISTANCE

The 1990s was an incredibly conservative time both in California and in the country more broadly. On one hand, neoliberal restructuring was consolidated on both a national and global scale during this period. "Trickle-down" Reaganomics was in full swing by the 1990s; meanwhile, Reagan and other neoconservative forces had all but annihilated the radical movements of the 1960s and 1970s with FBI and police repression. This conservatism would continue to characterize the politics of the Democratic Party.[11]

California, in many ways, was "ground zero" for 1990s conservatism. I don't know if we could name it yet, but I think as students we recognized that there were dynamics that seemed similar across the two political parties, despite the differences that they claimed existed between them. Successive anti-Black and anti-immigrant voter-led ballot initiatives were being introduced to the California electorate throughout the decade, albeit cast in color-blind ways. As scholar Daniel HoSang argues, these were "racial propositions": though these ballot measures were never racially neutral, and often preserved race as a defensible basis for the unequal distribution of resources and power, the electorate that embraced them also largely professed its fealty to the norms of racial liberalism. Over time these initiatives helped elaborate the dominant racial proposition of the early-twenty-first century: racial color blindness. Color blindness limits political criticism of racism almost entirely to individual actions and beliefs; wider structures of power and history become exonerated.[12]

If, on a global scale, the fall of communism meant, according to Liu et al., the undermining of "ideological frameworks and visible alternatives to the capitalist system," which contributed to the decline of the AAM, it is also true that we as a generation were also shaped by a broader cultural and global context that nevertheless helped to supply us with critical analytic tools to make sense of our lives.

Mine was (is) the "hip-hop" generation. Hip-hop was the soundtrack of our lives, giving us a language for the machinations of white supremacy as it operates on an everyday level. More than helping us to understand white supremacy, it prompted us to resist it. According to Jeff Chang, "The hip-hop generation was at least as, if not more, politically active than the civil rights generation." Like many in my generation, hip-hop—from the jams being played on the radio to the music we played and distributed through our own networks—was a politicizing force.[13] If by the 1990s conservatism had become more fully consolidated (including a brand of Asian American conservatism), those of us who identified with hip-hop were cultivating our critical consciousness and were moved to act.[14] For those of us, furthermore, with opportunities to take ethnic studies classes were able to deepen our analysis of white supremacy and racial capitalism within the United States even further as well as learn more about resistance struggles within the United States and beyond.

Indeed, as neoliberalism had become a global phenomenon, new resistance struggles would emerge in response. For example, on January 1, 1994, the Zapatista Army of National Liberation (EZLN), an armed resistance movement composed of Indigenous peoples in Chiapas, declared war on the Mexican government for its complicity in the North American Free Trade Agreement (NAFTA) championed by the U.S. president Bill Clinton. Meanwhile, struggles that predated the fall of the Soviet Union and which were critically shaped by leftist ideas would emerge victorious, such as the end of apartheid in South Africa and the election of Nelson Mandela only a few months after the Zapatista uprising. These third-world struggles offered my generation hope that social movements could successfully challenge white supremacy and global capitalism.

CULTIVATING NEW IDENTITIES

Like many other young people, I really looked forward to being able to call myself a "college student." It was an identity I actually took great pride in. I loved the prospect of taking courses of my own choosing and having more autonomy over my learning (and to some extent over my life). I looked forward to learning from college professors, whom I truly revered, as well as from my peers who came from so many different walks of life—introducing me to worlds far beyond my neighborhood. I remember looking forward to and voraciously attending programs organized by student groups: lectures of writers, filmmakers, activists, and experts in areas beyond the scope of whatever may have been offered at the college I was attending.

It was actually in spaces outside of the formal college classroom that my political consciousness would be piqued and, in the process, where I began to develop a very different sense of myself; my multiple sets of identities. It was at a lecture organized by a Filipino student group at Boston College when I heard firsthand from a former martial law political prisoner. Though I had grown up in a staunchly anti–martial law household, we never had formal discussions about martial law and its impacts on those who stood up to it. It was in college that I would get better insight into that period of Philippine history. I started to think more critically about my sense of "Filipino-ness" as it related to the Philippines and to its histories of resistance. It was at Diablo Valley College where I would befriend like-minded young women of color who were starting to make sense of our experience as racialized and gendered people. It was a friend I met in class who would introduce me to a book, *This Bridge Called My Back*, something she had been assigned to read in a different class. We would later go on to organize a kind of "book club" with other friends to do a deeper dive into the text and consider what it might mean for us to go from learning about racism and patriarchy to also engaging, resisting, and contesting those systems of power. Those sessions would prompt me to develop a sense of myself as a "woman of color" for the very first time in my life, and I would actively seek out organizations where I could involve myself with others who might be similarly identified and try to "change the world." For me identifying as a woman of color was political; to identify in that way necessarily required critical and political engagement in the world. I would initially find that kind of space in GABRIELA-Network, in some ways coming full circle, as the activist I first heard from at Boston College, Ninotchka Rosca, happened to be the same woman who helped to found the group.

LEARNING IN AND OUT OF THE CLASSROOM

It was when I transferred to UCSB that I was able to take a range of courses in ethnic studies as well as gender/women's studies. I remember the very first time I took an Asian American studies course. It was an Asian American Women and Feminism course taught by Diane Fujino, in her first quarter as a new assistant professor. In that class I not only started to develop a sense of myself as an "Asian American woman"; I would bolster my desire to deepen my understanding of issues outside and beyond the course. Diane's critical ethnic studies pedagogy encouraged us to activate our new knowledge in the classroom and commit to activism and organizing. My very first rally was one in support of Asian immigrant garment workers in Los Angeles that Diane had encouraged us to attend. A few other students and I packed into Diane's car to attend the rally. In the two-hour drive back from the rally, we collectively made the decision to form a new organization, Asian Sisters for Ideas in Action Now! (ASIAN!), and vowed to continue to deepen our study of topics we were being introduced to in Diane's course and other courses. Ethnic studies and gender/women's studies courses prompted us to start asking questions about how to make change, but those classes often failed to provide us with sufficient answers to our questions, so we pursued other forms of political education to get them for ourselves.

Political education, whether it was to do political education as a group or to organize spaces for political education for our peers, was a vital component of our work as ASIAN! We were not simply passive recipients of knowledge; we were taking leadership and initiative over what we learned. ASIAN! held regular internal study sessions for our members. Notably, our topics of study were not confined to issues or histories specific to Asians or Asian Americans. We read about the Cuban Revolution, including theories of revolution that grew out of the revolutionary struggle in Cuba by Che Guevara. Other struggles in the world that we studied included the struggle of Indigenous people in Guatemala (by reading the biography of Rigoberta Menchú). We also studied third-world revolutionary theorists such as Kwame

Nkrumah from Ghana and Mao Tse-tung in China. We studied activism (and activists) in the United States, including the Black struggle and the Asian American Movement.[15]

We also organized public education events for our peers; in the spring quarter of 1995 alone, we organized four different public events, including "Asian Women in the Garment Industry," "Asian American Labor Organizing," "Hawaiian Sovereignty Movement," and a separate film showing on the Hawaiian Sovereignty movement entitled "Act of War." It was in these forums where intergenerational knowledge was transferred to us and our peers. We brought seasoned activists to discuss their work, including David Monkawa, an Asian American Movement elder and artist who had worked on the newspaper *Gidra*, then in the League of Revolutionary Struggle, then Left Roots, and had worked as a labor organizer;[16] as well as Haunani-Kay Trask, a leader in the struggle for Hawaiian sovereignty.

As students, we were not just students—recipients of knowledge but also knowledge producers. In the early days of the internet, when it was primarily and exclusively used to send email (and not as widely used as today), many of us were producing alternative publications composed of thoughtful, well-researched pieces produced through collective processes, often meant to counter mainstream accounts and to advance political campaigns we were championing.

In ASIAN! we produced our own pamphlet on affirmative action as well. We knew we had a particular role to play in conscientizing other Asian Americans. We knew we had to directly address the kinds of narratives around affirmative action that were circulating in our peer circles, our families, and broader mainstream discourses. We also knew that we had to contest these narratives not just with alternative narratives but with evidence. We set about addressing "facts" and "myths" around affirmative action that we anticipated many of our peers might have. Among the myths we attempted to address were "Affirmative action is reverse discrimination; it gives preferential treatment to people of color and women"; "Affirmative action benefits only African Americans, Latinos, and white women"; "Affirmative action hurts whites and Asians"; and "I had a friend/brother/ sister _____ (fill in the blank) who was qualified for the job/college but didn't get it because of affirmative action." We were intentional about using evidence collected by researchers and scholars to make our arguments. In response to the myth "Affirmative action hurts whites and Asians," for example, we discussed how this myth is premised on the idea that all Asians "are success stories" (that is, model minorities) and cited a UCLA School of Urban Planning study indicating that the poverty rate for Asian Americans was three times more than that of whites to illustrate the falsity of the model minority myth and therefore the falsity of the myth that affirmative action has no benefit for our communities. For the myth "I had a friend/brother/sister," we actually cited evidence that Harvard's admissions rate for legacy admissions has ranged between 35 to 40 percent, more than twice the overall admission rate of about 15 percent. Yet there has been no attack on these types of century-old preferences based on family ties and "old-boy" networks. We ended the pamphlet with the question "What does this picture tell us now?" to engage our readers in a process of critical reflection. Though we gave readers information on the kinds of action they can engage in if they share our analysis, and ultimately hoped they would join us, minimally we hoped the pamphlet could at least leave Asian American readers questioning dominant narratives and that their interests were piqued sufficiently to ask even more. The pamphlet, much like our approach overall as an organization, was to put "ideas into action." For us that meant applying the insights gleaned from Asian American studies, ethnic studies, and other scholarship focused on race and applying it to our work in politicizing our peers. We took ethnic studies knowledge and activated it outside of the classroom.

What is distinctive about students as a sector when it comes to social justice organizing is just that: they are students. Their primary purpose in the colleges and universities where they are enrolled full-time is to study. Inasmuch as the high cost of tuition and fees as well as the high cost of living that tends to characterize off-campus (as well as on-campus) housing options mean that students may be working multiple jobs, for the more part their identities, their sense of selves, are not connected to their jobs. They are still primarily oriented toward the learning process, which includes meeting specific college and university requirements for graduation; however, the broader culture of learning of which they are part primes them for learning overall, regardless of whether the topics they are learning actually connect with their majors, graduation requirements, or even future career trajectories. This culture of learning creates opportunities for exploring topics of study in peer settings, outside of the classroom. This was certainly the experience I had.

Ethnic studies courses were especially vital in my political conscientization—that is, the process by which I became "woke." However, while ethnic studies courses gave me the tools to apply critical analyses to the world around me, these analyses became much more meaningful when I worked with others to deepen my understandings of vital social issues for the purpose of strengthening my activist work through collective study. Inasmuch as we all need to continue to fight for ethnic studies so that it can continue to do the good work of helping California's youth initiate a process of un- and relearning, we don't need to stop there. Even if there are no ethnic studies courses in specific institutions, there is something about the nature of student life that makes political education fairly easy to organize. We just have to commit to the process.

It is the kind of institutional and extra-institutional knowledge sharing—from assigned books and organized lectures, on one hand, and informal book clubs, on the other—made possible through higher education spaces that creates distinctive possibilities for students to develop their political consciousness.

AUTONOMOUS STUDENT ORGANIZING AND "INSIDE-OUTSIDE" STRATEGIES

By the 1990s both ethnic studies programs and other diversity-related student affairs initiatives were institutionalized on many campuses.[17] The organizers I worked with in ASIAN! and some of the other students of color we worked with were really suspicious of student government and other officially recognized student groups. We questioned whether they could really be spaces advancing a more radical, liberatory agenda or not. We could see, for example, how being part of a formal, officially recognized student organization that depended on funding from the university that could only be used for very specific purposes could be potentially constraining when it came to developing a more critical and radical agenda. Indeed, alongside my work in ASIAN! I was actually an officer in a Filipino American student group on campus called Kapatirang Pilipino (KP). I was the political chair, but I was sorely disappointed that my peers failed to respond to the political issues of the day despite all of my efforts to try to bring these issues to the table. The organization had become far more social in its orientation and wedded to its annual programming, which included the Pilipino Cultural Night (PCN). I participated in and tried to provide some historical content for the PCN, and I took really great pleasure in participating in it, but I also struggled in what I felt like were the constraints of the organization that I felt might be somewhat rooted in a kind of organizational culture that had developed over time partly because of its formal status as a student organization.[18]

Based on our observations of other student organizations and our own experiences in them, we were intentional about ASIAN! being an autonomous organization that would be composed primarily of students but would also include faculty and staff who supported our mission statement: "ASIAN! is a political action group devoted to uplifting humanity, with a specific focus on improving conditions facing Asian and Asian American women. We emphasize ideas in action based on the unity of theory and practice. ASIAN! is guided by an ideology that is opposed to systems of capitalism, racism, patriarchy and heterosexism."

Over the course of organizing with student government representatives and other formally organized student groups, however, I came to recognize that depending on the nature of the leadership and membership and depending on the extent to which the leadership and membership were connected to autonomous student spaces and community-based social justice groups and movements, they could in fact open up possibilities for radical analysis and action. Progressives and radicals in the Associated Students of UCSB (ASUCSB) could and did mobilize resources to help facilitate organizing and movement building. ASIAN! was part of an Affirmative Action Coalition on campus trying to organize students to oppose moves toward the elimination of affirmative action through the introduction of Proposition 209. In that space were many student government leaders from the ASUCSB and representatives of officially recognized groups. These students managed to mobilize funding through official university channels to support the work of the coalition. They were able, for example, to requisition a university vehicle so we could caravan to a protest of the UC regents in San Francisco. As noted earlier, on other campuses officially recognized student groups used their funding to produce publications to counter anti–affirmative action narratives on their campuses. Our work collectively might be thought of as "inside-outside" strategies that took advantage, on one hand, of the kinds of resources that affiliations with powerful institutions like the university can offer while, on the other hand, maintaining a connection to and cultivation of "outside" spaces that can ensure that the necessary critiques of the university are maintained.

THE PLEASURES AND CHALLENGES OF CROSS-RACIAL SOLIDARITY

What I recall with most fondness about my time in college was how much I was able to cultivate cross-racial relationships with other students of color. There have been times over the course of my life since college that I have remarked on how much my life no longer affords the same opportunities. Given the whiteness of academia and the fact that I chose to pursue a career as an academic, it was often difficult to connect with other scholars of color, especially after I graduated UC Berkeley to take a new job on the East Coast. It would take active, intentional work to reach outside of the department where I taught to connect with the few faculty members of color on the campus, and it would take work to actively make choices about where to live to ensure that my family wouldn't live in a segregated (white) neighborhood. If I had made the choice to live in the neighborhoods where most of my colleagues lived, that would have been the case. Generations of policies that not only limit the diversity of academia but limit the diversity of neighborhoods make it challenging to live the kind of life that one committed to cross-racial solidarity aspires to.[19]

There is a special distinctiveness about being a student that allows you opportunities to make cross-racial connections that I really hope young people today take advantage of. Despite the fact that affirmative action was reversed in California (despite our best efforts as student organizers to fight that reversal) and colleges and universities since then have become increasingly white (and even economically privileged Asian), these institutions have nevertheless tried to institute policies that ensure a degree of diversity that many students did not experience before getting to college and may not experience again afterward. Our communities are segregated by race and class; this is often also true of our workplaces. College and university life, however, can still offer the potential, for the first (and maybe only) time in our lives, to connect with people of very, very different backgrounds from ourselves and to learn through our relationships with them. As much as I connected with Mexican friends growing up, it was in college where I was able to cultivate far more intimate relationships with Chicanx folks as we shared the common experience of living on our own as young adults. I remember I had the good fortune of actually being neighbors with a lot of the leaders of La Mujer, a Chicana organization on campus. Our connections started with simply sharing meals together. My first lessons in learning how to cook Mexican food came from them. Those were important relationships in my life. It was in the context of friendships with La Mujer members that I developed some of my first relationships with queer women and really started to develop an emerging consciousness as a third-world woman.

Not only did we become friends and neighbors in college; our relationships were forged through shared commitments to social justice, through solidarity work (and I emphasize the importance of *work* here). Through my personal connections with La Mujer members, I got involved in supporting them, along with other compañeras and compañeros in Chicanx studies, and the Chicanx student organization, El Congreso, in their decision to go on a hunger strike to demand more resources for Chicanx studies and Chicanx students on campus. I remember being asked to serve as part of the media team to support the hunger strike. That was the first time I learned to write a press release and how to interact with media. It was intimidating, but that was the need requested to meaningfully show up for them. I needed to just figure it out. After all, my friends were putting their lives on the line.

Inasmuch as I felt a really strong sense of interracial solidarity, I recognized how fragile it could be too. In ASIAN! we knew Asian Americans were being figured—especially in the anti–affirmative action struggle—in really specific kinds of ways vis-à-vis African Americans. By being represented as model minorities, Asian Americans were being used to advance an anti-Black agenda, and we knew we had to take an immediate stand against anti-Blackness. Interestingly, the term *anti-Blackness* wasn't quite in our vocabulary in the 1990s, but between our Asian American studies and other ethnic studies courses as well as our political education work, we recognized the ways that the system of white supremacy pitted us against Blacks. Beyond the work we did in naming and critiquing that dynamic in the educational material we produced, we made every effort to actively build relationships with our Black counterparts. We attended events organized by Black students and worked to build coalitional spaces with them.

I remember, for example, the work it took to build an Affirmative Action Coalition that included faculty, staff, and students at UCSB. The coalition rested on organizational membership. In other words, though we welcomed individuals who may not have had specific organizational affiliations, most of us in the coalition agreed that to build a movement in support of affirmative action on the campus most effectively, it would require organizations—that is, groups with formal membership structures that could mobilize a base of people to participate in the actions that would be required to fight those who were rapidly gaining ground to dismantle affirmative action. Though organizational membership to the coalition was important, we also respected the autonomy of the member organizations to make decisions about whether or not to take part in specific actions that had been proposed in the coalition. We operated on a consensus basis; that is, we could not and would not move forward with a proposal if every group in the coalition was not in agreement. What that meant was that we could not move forward with events (and the advertising for them) without explicit endorsement from all the member organizations, which presumably had secured endorsement from their base. I recall one instance in which the coalition needed to wait for an official okay from the Black Student Union (BSU) before moving forward with a flyer. Though there was some time sensitivity to releasing the flyer, we also knew that some of the BSU membership was wary about their organization's participation in the coalition. We needed to give space to the BSU to make decisions in the time frame that made most sense for them. We knew that until we were certain that the BSU was fully in, we could not proceed with the flyer and the event it promoted. At the end of the day we knew it was important to center Black lives and experiences by respecting the organizational representatives, in this case the BSU, that represented their interests. Eventually, the BSU did endorse the event that had been discussed in the coalition. Though it was a drawn-out process, it was what was necessary to truly building relationships of trust and genuine solidarity across the groups.

In this set of lessons we see again the peculiarity of the student experience that makes it possible to do the work of cross-racial solidarity, not only through the interpersonal relationships made possible by college life but in the fact that so much of student life at the university is so highly organized. Despite our critiques of formally recognized student organizations, the truth is their very existence means that students have the space and the financial resources to congregate on a regular basis. If our political education sessions in ASIAN! taught us anything, it is that in societies in which large-scale transformation has successfully taken place, it has required the building of *mass* movements—that is, large numbers of people all working in concert toward shared goals. Student groups can form the basis of mass movements on campus in a way that becomes far more challenging once you graduate. As adults, organizations are few and far between. You generally do not have immediate access to groupings of people with whom you share common interest. It often takes much more work to get connected and to stay connected to groups. Indeed, even faculty and staff on universities do not have the same kind of organizational structures available to them as students do. Though many colleges and universities have unions, the labor movement has been in decline for decades in the United States at universities and across a range of workplaces. Unions may or may not actively engage their base of membership in the way that student groups do. Student groups tend to bring young people together on a very regular basis, and in the process deep bonds of connection get cultivated between them. When those bonds get activated toward social justice causes, they can be very powerful, as student movements have demonstrated historically across the world.

ON THE LIMITS OF STUDENT PERSPECTIVES AND THE VALUE OF INTERGENERATIONAL WISDOM

Despite everything I've written thus far about the wonderful possibilities that student activism opens up, I learned, too, about its limits. In our discussions of who ought to comprise ASIAN!'s membership, we were concerned about two dynamics about student life that could constrain our work. The first was the fast turnaround of the student population. In my own case, for example, as a transfer student, I would only be on campus for two years. If ASIAN! ended up being limited only to enrolled students at UCSB, I'd lose a space to exercise my commitment to social justice work, especially if I continued living in Santa Barbara after I graduated. Even for those who might enter ASIAN!

in their first year of college, the four years would ultimately pass quickly. That short time frame could have negative impacts on the organization as longer-term institutional knowledge about the university, especially if the injustices of the university were going to be among the key targets of our organizing, could be quickly lost. A primarily undergraduate membership could feel like starting anew over and over again, which could be avoided if we had the intergenerational wisdom that comes from graduate student, staff, and faculty membership in ASIAN!

Diane Fujino's membership in ASIAN! was tremendously valuable to us as students. Though we all, Diane included, recognized the power dynamic that existed between faculty and students, there was something important about having someone with more life experience and organizing experience (at the time Diane was also a member of the group Radical Women) and who occupied the university differently from us working alongside us as colleagues in collective struggle. Diane generously opened up her home to us, which provided a chance to build bonds with her that would not have been possible if we only connected in office hours, and indeed those early connections have been so durable that I find myself coediting with her the volume of which this chapter is part. Our political education sessions took place mainly in her home. Not only did we benefit from learning from Diane, but we learned from her husband, Matef, a Pan-Africanist, who often participated in our political education sessions, offering his perspectives while respecting our space as members of ASIAN! and as women (in its earliest iteration ASIAN! was an explicitly women's space).

Intergenerational wisdom coming from Diane and the nonstudent members of ASIAN! also helped orient us toward broader social justice issues and not simply those that concerned students. As an organization, ASIAN! studied and did work to raise awareness about issues that social justice movements locally, nationally, and around the world were addressing.

Beyond our relationship with Diane, we also benefited from the various publications that the AAM generation had published in the 1990s. As Diane and Kye Leung note: "What is clear is that these newer formations are aware of their connection with the past generation of radicals. It is because of the efforts of the previous generation of Asian American activists—for example, via ethnic studies and Movement publications—that the current generation knows some of its radical history."[20] We encountered some of these publications in class, but the deeper engagement with these texts was in the political education we did in ASIAN! In ASIAN! we were able not only to read these texts collectively but to think about and reflect upon the lessons offered within the context of our activism and organizing. We read these texts with the purpose of applying them.

For me the 1992 publishing of the Philip Vera Cruz biography was important.[21] In fact, Diane bought me the book as a present, and I recall how personally impactful it was for me to read a book about a Filipino American radical. Though I had learned about Filipino anti–martial law activists in the Philippines through my connections with GAB-Net, I was especially moved by Manong Philip's narrative because it spoke to the challenges of being Filipino in America, an experience that I shared. It seems not so coincidental that the 1990s marked resurgent interest in learning about the 1960s labor organizing of which Vera Cruz was a part, which led to the formation of the United Farm Workers (UFW). I recall how Filipino students on other campuses, particularly UCLA, began organizing pilgrimages to the Agbayani Village. Though I was unable to attend, it was the talk among us, prompting us to want to learn more about Filipino activism. I got plugged into a Filipino studies group that included UCLA and UCSB students that introduced me to a greater network of veteran martial law activists who were working in the Filipino American community even as they continued to weigh in on issues in the Philippines, particularly the ways US foreign policy continued to negatively impact the country. The new intergenerational relationships I was able to forge through my engagement in the Filipino studies group would have a lasting impact on my activism. Connections through that network would later facilitate introduction to other anti–martial law activist elders, most notably Vic and Becky Clemente and Mario Santos, when I returned to the Bay Area after I graduated from UCSB. I would end up devoting significant energy into founding and leading transnational organizations of Filipino Americans connected to the National Democratic movement in the Philippines (namely the League of Filipino Students and others) that would devote themselves to raising awareness about and resisting US neocolonialism in the Philippines.

While much of my organizing as a student revolved around engaging other students and addressing issues that were of particular concern to students, one thing that I learned from my activist elders was the importance of students being grounded in struggles beyond the campus as well as in struggles impacting the most marginalized—particularly workers—both on and off campus. Indeed, what many of us inherited from AAM activists who were active in fighting for Asian American studies was the idea that as students, especially college and university students, we enjoyed a set of privileges that others in our community did not and that we had a responsibility to draw on those resources to uplift and address the issues of the most vulnerable and marginalized in our communities. The following quotation by John Delloro, a well-loved union organizer who was taken from our world too soon, captures this idea best in his own reflections on student activism. John was one of the rallyists at the Jessica McClintock mobilization in Los Angeles that I participated in as a student in Diane's class. He describes how as a student at UCLA he and his peers "looked towards our campus resources to aid the workers. Through our student networks on and off campus we educated about the issue and brought it to other campuses and student organizations."[22] He also describes lessons he learned from scholar and activist elder Glenn Omatsu, who stated that "with the rise of Asian Americans entering elite universities, Asian American students have more access to resources than previous generations and can greatly help the community."[23]

My centering on student activism in this chapter is largely a result of the intergenerational knowledge I received from Filipino anti–martial law activists. I had already graduated from UCSB by the time I met them, but I remember how much they emphasized the distinctive role that students can play in social justice movement building. They themselves were students when they first joined the anti-Marcos movement in the "First Quarter Storm." They shared writings by Philippine and other third-world revolutionaries of earlier generations who theorized about the distinctiveness of that role. Those writings not only helped me retrospectively to value the organizing I had been doing at UCSB, but they helped to shape the student activism I would later lead as a graduate student. Indeed, writings on the role of students, especially university students, in social justice movement work would ultimately shape how I think about the role of university educators and have since shaped my praxis as a scholar-activist.

The major thing that makes students powerful is the fact that their job is quite simply to study. There is no other time in one's life, and this is especially true for a college student, when one can engage full-time in the study of advanced ideas in the classroom but also outside it. College is one of those unique sites in which it is possible to come together easily in space with peers to share life experiences and build bridges to people one might ordinarily not encounter in one's neighborhood (or later one's workplace) because of generations of policies that institutionalize racial and class segregation. As ethnic studies (as well as women's studies and other academic fields) have managed to survive and grow, students at colleges and universities where these courses are offered have the great opportunity to be introduced to academic knowledge by critical scholars, many of whom came from activist backgrounds or continue to work as activist-scholars, who've been trained to do deep study on issues of great importance to social justice organizing.

To study, whether formally or informally, through the classroom or political education sessions or through the exchanges of life experience, is truly powerful and empowering. The sociality of college life—the ease of being able to meet like-minded others in classes, through regularly scheduled meetings and events by student organizations, and/or through living in close proximity in dormitories—is also a unique aspect of student life. There has been only one other time in my life since college when I've been able to practically live and breathe social justice activist work. I had this chance again when I was a graduate student and lived with other organizers in a collective household, but once we all became partnered and had families of our own, it became more challenging. Though it's not impossible to create intentional communities organized around shared political commitments once you graduate, it's not always feasible in the way it can be for students. Today, in a world in which students seem to rely primarily on social media to form and sustain relationships but ones that may sometimes be fleeting, loose, and/or primarily virtual, I'm hoping that this reflection on the uniqueness of student life encourages students to consider how to cultivate deeper, more intimate relationships with their peers in space in the limited time that they have on campuses. To those reading this chapter, I can assure you that these relationships will last a lifetime and will help to sustain your political work long after you've graduated.

Another distinctive quality of students is that they're young, free from habits of thought and action that allow them to push the boundaries of their own imagination of what is possible in the world. The fact that students are generally also young people and don't necessarily have responsibility for supporting a partner or children or elderly parents (which is not to suggest that some students do not supplement household income or provide care to their families) also allows them opportunities to do social movement work in ways that become more challenging as the responsibilities of adulthood take hold and become more onerous. It is thus important for students to connect with movements beyond campus; they can serve as a vital source of energy that can bolster those movements. However, it's also important to take pause to listen and learn from elders because they offer us vital tools that can continue to be relevant in new times and circumstances.

Being students, moreover, gives you access to resources. Whether you organize through formally recognized student groups (which often have immediate access to funding) or you organize in an autonomous manner, students not only have access to funding but also gathering space and the opportunity to readily meet people from a wide range of backgrounds, things that are basic building blocks for activism and organizing.

Though this chapter has been more of a personal reflection on student activism (versus a more scholarly account), I do hope that it can prompt scholarly interest in Asian American studies to explore both the limits and possibilities of student activism. Scholars of Asian American activism have not necessarily made the category of "student activism" a specific lens through which to understand the dynamics of Asian American activism during the periods or issue-areas on which they focus. There were earlier interests in student movements among social movement scholars that can offer insight for new lines of inquiry that continue to be important to Asian American social movement scholarship.

Moreover, though I wrote this chapter primarily with my students in mind, I am hoping activists who have long been doing the work of Asian American organizing consider some of my observations here in their movement-building strategies. Even Asian American activists today, as much as they/we value cultivating a new generation of youth activists, haven't quite written about the particularity of student activism and how that activism can be harnessed for the broader community. For example, in the Asian American Racial Justice Toolkit, a wonderful resource for people organizing in the present moment that was put together by many groups that have programs specifically geared toward youth organizing, it is notable that none of the core workshops offered provides a focus on the specific issues faced by young people and/or students, nor do they provide trainings on how to organize youth or students. However, I think considering student activism as a particular form of activism with its own distinctive possibilities and potentials—unique from youth organizing more broadly—is very worthwhile.

A focus on 1990s California, a period of conservatism in what is often considered a progressive and even radical left coast state, offers important perspectives on how color-blind and liberal multiculturalist politics served to promote white supremacy and anti-Blackness.[24] In other words, "liberal multiculturalism" and right-wing, white supremacist politics work hand in hand, and the California case makes that clear. Though in Trump's America, white supremacy seems so easy to identify, it is important to understand that white supremacy has always been operating in America's institutions, even under leadership that we might not identify as "racist."[25] Though my reflection is but a small snapshot of the racial justice organizing that was taking place through the decade of 1990s, a quotation from the Black Radical Congress reflects the kinds of cross-racial solidarity many of us across communities of color were committed to building: "More fundamentally, we understand we cannot assess our enemies or allies by skin color. We recognize the struggles of Puerto Ricans, Chicanos, Native and Asian Americans and poor whites as parallel to our own. We understand the importance of struggling on multiple fronts simultaneously. The BRC is one such front. We invite support and solidarity from our sisters, brothers, and comrades around the globe."[26] As things shift in our country in the coming years under the Biden-Harris administration, we will need to be especially vigilant about the ways white supremacy masks itself just as much as we pay attention to its most virulent and visible strains.

Above all, it is my hope that this chapter challenges college students already engaged in some degree of campus organizing while inspiring those for whom activism and organizing are relatively new. I hope this reflection on the radical orientation of our student organizing offers a perspective of student activism outside of more conventional practices that dominate campus organizing today, which are often linked to cultural centers and/or diversity initiatives on campus or to some extent in student government or which focus on campus-based issues, that is, curricular reform or the expansion of student services and the like. Focusing on the radical student activism of the 1990s, I hope, can offer student activists of today new lessons on effective organizing strategies on their campuses, and ultimately in our communities more broadly, as the work of liberation will require that our struggles are linked, as Pam Tau Lee puts it, to the "greater we."

NOTES

1   In an effort to challenge notions of authorship and to make visible the labor required for work like this to be produced, Wayne Jopanda, who provided crucial support in helping to identify and incorporate relevant literature to this chapter to supplement my personal reflections, is listed as a coauthor. Wayne also played an important role in helping to bring together all of the people who contributed to this book.

2   Pawan Dhingra and Robyn Magalit Rodriguez, *Asian America: Sociological and Interdisciplinary Perspectives* (Malden, MA: Polity Press, 2014), 182. This dominant narrative of Black-Asian tension has been magnified and further assumed as a result of the media's portrayal of conflict between the two communities in 1965 Watts, 1967 Detroit, 1968 Washington, DC, and beyond.

3   Jeannette Diaz-Veizades and Edward T. Chang, "Building Cross-Cultural Coalitions: A Case-Study of the Black-Korean Alliance and the Latino-Black Roundtable," *Ethnic and Racial Studies* 19, no. 3 (1996): 680–700. One example of this solidarity work include the Black-Korean Alliance (BKA).

4   Adjoa Florencia Joes de Almeida states: "We are so trapped into hierarchical, corporate, non-profit models that we are unable to structure ourselves differently, even when our missions advocate empowerment and self-determination for oppressed communities. . . . Where are the mass movements of today in this country? The short answer—they got funded. While it may be overly simplistic to say so, it is important to recognize how limited social justice groups and organizations have become as they've been incorporated into the non-profit model." See Adjoa Florencia Joes de Almeida, *The Revolution Will Not Be Funded: Beyond the Non-Profit Industrial Complex* (Durham, NC: Duke University Press, 2017), 192.

5   Dhingra and Rodriguez, *Asian America*, 176. An example here includes the Organization of Chinese Americans (OCA) organizing around victims of racially targeted violence and discrimination, including those who were not Chinese or Asian.

6 Soya Jung, "Left or Right? Asian Americans and the Racial Justice Movement," *ChangeLab* (2014): 16–17, https://www.changelabinfo.com/research/left-or-right-of-the-color-line. "The idea of Asian American uplift, of the ability to 'rise' through hard work and intelligence, emerged amid the Black Power and other radical social movements of the 1960s. The *New York Times* article 'Success Story, Japanese American Style' first brought the concept of the model minority into popular consciousness in 1966. In it, author William Petersen lauds the hard work and values that prevented Japanese Americans from being a 'problem minority.' Against the backdrop of the 1965 Watts Rebellion the year before, the thinly veiled implication was that Blacks, and in particular, Black political resistance, were the real problem."

7 See Freedom Road at https://www.freedomroad.org/index.php?option =com_content&view=article&id=725%3Aa-very-short-history-of-our -organization&catid=171%3Aour-history&Itemid=264&lang=en; also Critical Resistance at http://criticalresistance.org/critical-resistance -beyond-the-prison-industrial-complex-1998-conference.

8 GABRIELA-Network was a solidarity organization that supported the national democratic women's alliance GABRIELA in the Philippines.

9 On ASIAN! see Diane C. Fujino and Kye Leung, "Radical Resistance in Conservative Times: New Asian American Organizations in the 1990s," in *Legacy to Liberation: Politics and Culture of Revolutionary Asian Pacific America*, ed. Fred Ho (San Francisco: AK Press, 2000), 141–58.

10 Dhingra and Rodriguez, *Asian America*, 191.

11 See Michael Liu, Kim Geron, and Tracy A. M. Lai, *The Snake Dance of Asian American Activism: Community, Vision, and Power* (Boulder: Lexington Books, 2008), 148. They argue, "While the Democrats, under the Clinton administration, regained the White House, they practiced calculated and modulated conservatism, including passing an anti-immigrant welfare reform plan, support for globalized trade and wealthy elites, and implementing fiscal austerity."

12 Daniel HoSang, *Racial Propositions: Ballot Initiatives and the Making of Postwar California* (Berkeley: University of California Press, 2010), 219.

13 Jeff Chang, *Can't Stop Won't Stop: A History of the Hip-Hop Generation* (New York: St. Martin's Press, 2007), 454. As a quick aside: Chang says that college radio stations were an especially important site from which underground hip-hop cultures were developed; I played my own part in that as a KCSB radio host with my Chicana friend Monica Lopez on our program "W.A.R.: Women in the Act of Resistance," where we always featured underground rappers from the likes of the more widely known artists such as KRS-One and Paris to local artists whose names, unfortunately, escape me now.

14 Not that I want to center this kind of work, but it is important to understand how much traction Asian American conservatives were getting during this time. For example, Dinesh D'Souza published *The

End of Racism: Principles for a Multiracial Society (New York: Free Press, 1995) and received a lot of media attention for it.

15 Ernesto Che Guevara, *Che Guevara Reader: Writings on Politics and Revolution* (New York: Ocean Press, 2003); Rigoberta Menchú, *I, Rigoberta Menchú: An Indian Woman in Guatemala* (London: Verso Books, 2010); Kwame Nkrumah, *Neo-Colonialism: The Last Stage of Imperialism*, 861–78 (New York: International Publishers, 1965); Mao Tse-tung, *Quotations from Chairman Mao* (Peking: Foreign Languages Press, 1972).

16 David Monkawa, "Out to Win!" *Left Roots* 1, no. 1 (2019): 115.

17 Nicole Ngaosi, "YES on Diversity: Three Decades of Asian American Student Activism for UCLA's Undergraduate Diversity Requirement" (PhD diss., University of California, Los Angeles, 2010). UCLA had a three-decade-long movement across generations of student organizers fighting for the current undergraduate diversity requirement, led by a mix of student government leaders, students who identified as children of Southeast Asian refugees, and student staff members of political ethnic-centered campus organizations such as Movimiento Estudiantil Chicano de Aztlan (MEChA), Concerned/Critical Asian Pacific Islander Students for Action (CAPSA), and the *Daily Bruin* student newspaper.

18 Lester J. Manzano et al., "Asian American Student Engagement in Student Leadership and Activism," *New Directions for Student Services*, no. 160 (Winter 2017), special issue on "Bridging Research and Practice to Support Asian American Students," ed. Dina C. Maramba and Corinne Maekawa Kodoma.

19 For more on segregation in New Jersey, see Robyn Magalit Rodriguez, *In Lady Liberty's Shadow: The Politics of Race and Immigration in New Jersey* (New Brunswick, NJ: Rutgers University Press, 2017).

20 Fujino and Leung, "Radical Resistance in Conservative Times," 145.

21 Lilia Villanueva and Craig Scharlin, *Philip Vera Cruz: A Personal History of Filipino Immigrants and the Farmworkers Movement* (Los Angeles: UCLA Labor Center, Institute of Industrial Relations, and UCLA Asian American Studies Center, 1992).

22 John Delloro, "Personal Is Still Political: Reflections on Student Power," in Ho, *Legacy to Liberation*, 230.

23 Delloro, "Personal Is Still Political," 231.

24 "In 2000, as California became the first large 'majority minority' state in the nation, white voters still constituted 72 percent of the electorate," Delloro, "Personal Is Still Political," 18. HoSang's quotation provides a stark difference between California's progressive masquerade of diversity versus the reality of who made up the voting bloc.

25 Delloro, "Personal Is Still Political," 219. Here we turn to HoSang's commentary on color blindness as a major tool in developing "Blue" California's political discourse: "Colorblindness limits political criticism of racism almost entirely to individual actions and beliefs; wider

structures of power and history become exonerated. Charges of racial subordination are largely inadmissible in the dominant political discourse unless accompanied by some evidence of deliberate and malicious intent. Colorblindness's command of the political discourse is so dominant that liberal political actors, even some civil rights groups, feel compelled to obey its norms in many settings," HoSang, *Radical Proposition*.

26 "What Is the Black Radical Congress (BRC)?" Black Radical Congress, June 19–21, 1998, World History Archives, www.hartford-hwp.com /archives/45a/228.html.

CHAPTER 12

THE STRUGGLE TO ABOLISH ENVIRONMENTAL AND ECONOMIC RACISM

Asian Radical Imagining from the Homeland to the Front Line

PAM TAU LEE

IT'S OCTOBER 9, 2018. I'M GATHERING MATERIAL TO WRITE this chapter when my eye catches the news announcing the findings of the United Nations Intergovernmental Panel on Climate Change (IPCC) report. I spot the Red Guard Political Platform, written in San Francisco Chinatown, February 1969. It reads: "We demand that the United States government halt the rape of the land. We believe that if greedy businessmen, with the help of the US government, do not stop destroying our land, air, oceans, and streams, the earth will become a lifeless planet of rock and dust."[1] In the midst of current environmental crises—including unprecedented fires in California, monstrous flooding in the Midwest, and the IPCC's finding that we are rapidly approaching the disastrous 1.5-degree C mark—I realize all of the Red Guard's demands remain relevant. Fifty years ago the Black Liberation movement, international struggles for self-determination, and the occupation of Alcatraz Island by the American Indian Movement awakened the social consciousness of youths of color and progressive whites.[2] Imagine where we might be if an environmental movement with similar impact had evolved.

In a recent conversation over coffee, youth activist Monica Chan asked, "What can we do about the climate?" Climate change is the crisis that threatens all humanity and living things. Her question kept me awake that night. After thirteen days of smoke from the 2018 California Camp Fire, I emailed my friend Vida Kuang, who lives in Chinatown, and asked her how things were. She replied:

It's harder to get clean fresh air in SROs [single-room occupancy units]. Especially for folks who don't have access to a window that isn't facing another wall. Windows are our only source for air circulation between shared bathrooms and kitchens. We use our rooftops to dry our clothes. We depend on clean air for everyday living. With the smoke being so thick and being told to stay indoors and close the windows, it's even harder to get *any* air. It's the lack of circulation. With spaces being tight and public spaces being our only living room—imagine your living room being polluted. Where do you go now? This isn't just about folks who live in SROs—it's also about people who are living on the streets. You end up feeling trapped. This is like a slow apocalypse—climate change won't hit us all of a sudden. It's going to be something people will slowly normalize and not question. We're walking in a cloud of smoke doing our thing, heads bent over our phones, working, commuting. People won't know what hit them because climate change is the slowest kind of poison.[3]

This chapter is my attempt to respond to Monica's query through a collection of radical love stories, using my activism as an entry into the Asian American and environmental justice movements of the past fifty years.

BECOMING AN ENVIRONMENTALIST

My journey is grounded in my family's history. I am fourth-generation Chinese American, born in San Francisco in 1948. My early years were spent in Chinatown, mainly with my maternal grandmother, Alice Jan, who took care of me during the week while my parents worked. She had earlier raised my mom and her two brothers as a single mom surviving on welfare. My maternal grandfather struggled with drug addiction and alcoholism, aggravated by the pressures of poverty and racism. We rarely saw him. Grandmother Alice herself worked at the Doh Lei garment factory on Washington Street in Chinatown, which produced overalls and jeans for Levi Strauss & Company. I spent a lot of time in this factory, as women loudly shared gossip, trying to be heard above the constant noise of fifty blaring sewing machines.

When I was seven years old, I remember sitting at the foot of my grandmother's machine and hearing a scream, followed by women rushing toward a coworker whose hand was caught in her sewing machine. As women brought paper towels to soak up the blood and dislodge her hand from the machine, the freight elevator door swung open and the boss man stormed out shouting, "Get back to work!" The women shouted back at him but gradually went back to work, the sound of the machines again filling the air. As the boss stalked the aisles to cement his authority, Grandma turned to me and asked, "Ah Guen, did you see what happened?" Pointing to the boss, she said: "Do you know who he is? Do you know why he acts like that? It's because he's mean, greedy . . . and too much soy sauce!" I had never heard my grandmother speak with such harshness. Why "soy sauce"? I believe this was my grandma telling me he had become salty and cranky from the conditions of poverty and racism that constituted Chinatown.

Chinatowns arose from exclusionary laws and racist practices that confined Chinese to segregated areas, with overcrowded, noisy, and unsafe living and working conditions. Women and men work six days a week, ten hours a day, in sweatshops that create super-profits from the super-exploitation of the labor of workers of color, especially women and immigrants. Low wages force most families to live in single-room occupancy units. These are eight-by-ten-feet single rooms, with a shared toilet, a shower down the hall, and if you are lucky, maybe one window. The lack of fresh air and adequate rest makes conditions ripe for the presence of diseases. My father had tuberculosis, as did my mother and I. This is the underbelly of the capitalist system that benefits corporations like Levi Strauss.

Etched in my mind is the violent memory of a worker's hand caught in a sewing machine. Through this event I became aware of racism and environmental justice at the same moment. As I grew older, I began to see that these events were part of daily life inside the factory. I call experiences like this my "soy sauce moments"; they transformed my consciousness and called me to action.

BLACK PANTHERS AND ASIAN AMERICAN RADICALS

In the 1960s the Black Liberation movement had a strong influence on me. In 1969 I was twenty-one, a student at Cal State Hayward. Across the Bay students at San Francisco State College were fighting for a Third World Studies College. They were demanding an education that could equip us to "change society" and envisioned a "new system of governance."[4] George Murray, an SF State instructor and the Black Panther Party minister of education, challenged students to study the root cause of war and counter white supremacy with a vision of Black Power. I was moved when Murray called for "power for all persons of African, Asian, or Latin-American descent in the United States, as well as progressive whites to change the system and overturn all power by the government to oppress."[5]

For me and so many others, "All power to the people" also meant being internationalists. When the Black Panthers came to San Francisco Chinatown to organize support to "Free Huey," they discovered a group of young, "cool" Chinese youths. Having been constantly harassed by the police, the Chinatown youths were ripe for consciousness raising. The Black Panthers soon led political study sessions with Chinatown youths and introduced them to the Panther Ten-Point Program. When these Chinatown youths asked to join the Black Panther Party, Bobby Seale replied, "No, you've got to form your own group, grounded in your own struggle." They soon formed the San Francisco Red Guards in 1969, which two years later merged with I Wor Kuen (IWK) of New York.[6]

In 1972 the San Francisco chapter of IWK became my political home. Its platform aligned with my experiences in Chinatown. IWK was a radical Asian American collective of youths inspired by the Black Panther Party and the Puerto Rican Young Lords Party. IWK was not a copy of the Black Panther Party but, rather, its own entity that centered Asians to oppose capitalism, racism, and hetero-patriarchy in the United States and the world. IWK's demands were grounded in our Asian experience, and its Twelve-Point Program provided clarity to what I had witnessed and experienced growing up.[7] The Twelve-Point platform recognized the racist oppression of communities by the wealthy, affirmed that women should hold key roles in fighting for liberation, and sought to put people's needs first through the principles of love and unity.[8]

Point 2 of IWK's program called on us to be anti-imperialist. Asian youths were being drafted into the US Army and deployed to fight in a racist, imperialist war of aggression for oil, minerals, and "cheap" labor. Point 2 exposed these problems: "We want self-determination for all Asians. Western imperialists have been invading and colonizing countries in Asia for the past 500 years. Amerikan imperialism, concentrating in Asia, is now engaged in the most sadistic [and environmentally destructive—Agent Orange] and genocidal war of aggression the world has ever seen. We want an immediate end to Amerikan imperialism."[9]

The US war in Southeast Asia was dividing the country, including families like mine. These divisions were contentious, with sectors from the white working class attacking and beating up antiwar activists. Youths from the Latinx and Black communities led the way in growing an anti-imperialist, antiwar movement. Chicanos were being killed and wounded in the war in disproportionate numbers compared to the general population. They mobilized opposition to the war. The National Chicano Moratorium Committee's assertion that "our struggle is not in Vietnam but in the movement for social justice at home" resonated with Asian youths, including those of us in Chinatowns and Japantowns and on campuses.[10]

IWK understood it was important to unite with the greater US antiwar movement. To do this, the organization helped to form the Bay Area Asian Coalition Against the War, a volunteer group of Asian radical activists who worked to expose the racist nature of US imperial wars for oil. We also wanted to call attention to self-determination for the Vietnamese people and their nine-point proposal for peace. At one planning meeting for a April 1972 rally and march, the organizers, instead of welcoming us, told us to leave, saying we were bringing in "too many -isms-isms." In that meeting we came face to face with the mainstream antiwar organizers exercising their privilege to exclude our voices and experiences. In actuality it wasn't about too many -isms; it was about race and imperialism.[11]

We returned to our communities and campuses and mobilized for the antiwar march by organizing an Asian contingent to raise our presence and consolidate our unity. On the day of the march, our contingent "snake-danced" to the stage, chanted "One struggle many fronts," and carried flags of our respective homelands.[12] Our spokeswoman, Patsy Chan, read a statement, which included: "We, as Third World sisters, express our militant solidarity with our brothers and sisters from Indochina. We, as Third World people, know of the struggle the Indochinese are waging against imperialism, because we share that common enemy in the United States."[13]

History has proven that our position was correct—the call to end the war was not just about "bringing our boys home," but it was also about exposing the racist imperialist nature of the war to gain control of Asia's natural resources; the horrors of the use of Agent Orange as a chemical weapon to kill people and destroy the land; and the massacres, such as the 1968 My Lai massacre, at the hands of the US military. Amid a country divided on the war, we as Asians had a unique understanding and perspective. It was our responsibility to expose the true motives for the war. Formations such as the Chicano Moratorium and Bay Area Asian Coalition Against the War and leaders such as Dr. Martin Luther King Jr. and Dr. Vincent Harding took radical and bold stands against the war and were critical of growing an antiwar movement that focused primarily on American lives, as in the "Bring the Boys Home" slogan, but not issues of imperialism and white supremacy.

THE FIRST NATIONAL PEOPLE OF COLOR ENVIRONMENTAL LEADERSHIP SUMMIT

The First National People of Color Environmental Leadership Summit in Washington, DC, October 24–27, 1991, was a groundbreaking event in the environmental justice movement and a major soy sauce moment for me. Those four days rocked the environmental movement by pivoting attention and action to the findings of the landmark study of the Commission for Racial Justice, United Church of Christ, titled "Toxic Wastes and Race in the United States" (1987), which highlighted the fights against environmental racism, specifically against the development of toxic facilities, landfills, and other sites of pollution where people of color live, work, go to school, and pray, including Native sacred sites.[14] I was one of thirty Asian and Pacific Islander delegates invited to participate. At the time my day job was in the field of workplace and environmental health and safety at the UC Berkeley School of Public Health's Labor Occupational Health Program. Dana Alston and Charles Lee, African American and Chinese American key conveners of the summit, respectively, invited me to submit a paper focused on workers of color and to facilitate the policy group on occupational health and safety issues.[15] This "ask" not only changed the way I understood how to be an "environmentalist" but changed my life.

The air was electric as three hundred delegates from rural areas, cities, tribal lands, the Marshall Islands, and Puerto Rico came together. Delegates spoke of the high rates of cancer, children born with birth defects, lupus, miscarriages, asthma, and a host of other health conditions. They shared frustration and anger at a myriad of issues, including health impacts from poisoned water, air, and soil; plundered land for coal, gas, uranium, and oil; and the destruction of sacred sites from logging, nuclear waste, and military toxins.[16]

On day 3 Dana Alston took the podium and delivered a speech that would have huge implications for the summit and the environmental movement. On behalf of the Planning Committee, Dana presented a redefinition of *environment* to include "where we live, work, go to school, and pray" and argued that "adults and children living in communities of color are endangered species, and environmental issues are immediate survival issues."[17] Dana challenged the 250 nondelegate participants and observers to align on this redefinition and called on the representatives from the Big Green environmental organizations in the audience to acknowledge, address, and repudiate the paternalistic behaviors their organizations practiced toward frontline communities. Her speech took courage to write and deliver. I was proud of her as she stood up and spoke truth to power. Dana risked her reputation and job on behalf of frontline communities and in the spirit of radical love and courage.[18]

On day 4 summit delegates assembled to discuss, debate, and affirm the landmark Preamble and Principles of Environmental Justice. The summit and the drafting of the preamble and principles launched the movement for environmental justice across the country and in countries around the world. I am proud to have authored the worker of color health and safety discussion paper that helped contribute to the adoption of Principle 8, which "affirms the right of all workers to a safe and healthy work environment, without being forced to choose between an unsafe livelihood and unemployment," and which also "affirms the right of those who work at home to be free from environmental hazards."[19]

The voices of millions have been affirmed because of the principles we committed to at the summit. The National Environmental Justice Advisory Committee was also created in 1993. Presidential Executive Order 12898 was issued the next year, mandating federal agencies to consider the impact of current policies and regulations on racial and ethnic communities.[20] In the late 1990s I asked longtime activist and writer Grace Lee Boggs for her thoughts on environmental justice. She replied, "I believe the Principles of Environmental Justice lays the foundation for a new constitution."[21]

BUILDING UNITY AND POWER WITHIN THE MAJORITY TO ACHIEVE JUSTICE AND LIBERATION

WORKERS AND THE COMMUNITY

Grace Lee Boggs made a statement that impacted my thinking. She chastised a group of us Asian Americans: "You are thinking like a minority, like victims. Don't do that! Start thinking and acting like a majority."[22] Her words made me reflect on an experience I'd had in the early 1990s. I was in Canada when I first met and heard Tony Mazzochi of the Oil, Chemical Atomic Workers Union (OCAW) speak. He was a visionary who was keenly aware that the reliance on fossil fuels and uranium was destroying the planet. He knew it was imperative to keep dirty fuels in the ground but that this would have a devastating impact on the men and women of his union who worked in the refineries and power plants, including my hero, the whistleblower Karen Silkwood.[23] Mazzochi refused to allow his union and workers to play into the "Jobs versus Environment" scenario. He maintained that there be both good, safe jobs and protection of the environment and proposed an early version of what people now call the "Green New Deal." He envisioned a public policy that would call on the government to set aside a "super-fund" of money to prepare workers for alternative, good-paying jobs. I was familiar with his proposal because my father was a World War II vet and qualified for the "super"-funded GI Bill. Dad felt that without this program, he could never have gone to college and moved from being a storeroom clerk to becoming an engineer. A radical love policy? Yes! An undeserved entitlement? No. I saw in Mazzochi's proposal a pathway that could unite workers and environmentalists.

A couple of years later, as a board member of the Asian Pacific Environmental Network (APEN), I was invited to meet with James Carlton and Dion Ferris, who were in the Bay Area to introduce APEN to an OCAW proposal that would center on bringing frontline worker leaders together with frontline communities to draft a Just Transition public policy for safe jobs and environment stewardship. Besides being an APEN board member, I was a workplace and environmental health and safety trainer and was brought on to be a facilitator for the project. I would assist in the long-term process of joining OCAW worker leaders with environmental justice fence line residents affiliated with the Southwest Network for Environmental and Economic Justice, Southwest Public Workers Union, Indigenous Environmental Network, and the Southern Organizing Project.

This project was a dream come true. It took hold in different geographic locations, including Alabama, Arizona, and Oklahoma, and this project gave voice and opportunity for building genuine unity and creating public policy that was place based and informed by the experiences of those who are directly impacted.[24] The story I'd like to highlight took place in McIntosh, Alabama. I remember listening to an African American worker and OCAW member describe exactly where the company had him dump PCB along the riverbanks. I sat with alarm as residents talked of being trapped on all four sides of their town by parked company trains waiting to be loaded with toxic chemical products. If a toxic explosion or other emergency crisis were to happen, the residents would have no way to escape. These company practices motivated the residents to organize an informational picket outside of the chemical plant. Predictably, this picket action angered the workers and their union. The future of the project was in jeopardy.

In response to the picket action and media coverage it generated, a series of meetings between the union were held with Connie Tucker of the Southern Organizing Project, Richard Moore of the Southwest Network for Environmental and Economic Justice, Tom Goldtooth of the Indigenous Environmental Network, Ruben Solis Garcia of the Southwest Public Workers Union, and me from the Asian Pacific Environmental Network. The union threatened to call off the project; the environmental justice organizations, on the other hand, were frustrated and angered by the union's demand that the residents cease actions against the company. But a breakthrough was achieved when the environmental justice organizations described why taking public direct action against the company was their only option for protecting the community. Hearing this, the union realized that asking residents of color not to take action against the company that was putting them in danger was like demanding their workers give up their rights to fight management and to strike. A joint statement was signed on February 14, 1997. It read in part: "Our previous struggles to protect jobs, workplace safety and health, community health, and the environment led us to each other. . . . We affirm the right of environmental justice organizations to engage in the battle for equity and fairness for those fence-line communities surrounding the toxic facilities employing OCAW workers. We affirm the right to resist corporate efforts to destroy our jobs, harm our heath, and pollute our environment in pursuit of higher corporate profits. We affirm the right to a just transition when a shift to a sustainable community and cleaner environment costs workers and communities our jobs, income, and tax base."[25]

How could this statement play out in real life? When community residents affiliated with the environmental justice groups engaged in a struggle with a company where OCAW members were employed, that environmental justice group would alert the local and national union so the union could work with union leaders inside to ensure they would not interfere or engage in conflict with the residents. This communication could open opportunities to engage in solidarity with the residents. The same efforts to inform and engage in supportive actions would hold true if workers were engaged in a struggle.

For the next ten years I was part of a team that led workshops across the country focused on building a Just Transition Movement for Jobs and the Environment that brought together workers and environmental justice residents. But because of declining union membership from refineries shutting down, OCAW was forced to merge with the United Paperworkers International Union in 1999 to become PACE, the Paper, Allied-Industrial, Chemical and Energy Workers International Union. In 2005 PACE merged with the United Steelworkers. Each merger created challenges for the project from declining interest in uniting impacted workers and communities on a grassroots level, as these grassroots efforts took more time and resources and were not "headline news–grabbing" topics of interest. Around 2006 unions were looking for more visibility regarding issues of jobs and the environment. This gave rise to the 2006 creation of a Blue Green Alliance, which relies more on the unity of labor leadership. By 2007 financial resources to the Just Transition Alliance and projects declined, and the program was shut down. I believe that the ending of the on-the-ground joint work was because of an uneasiness within the union foundations to boldly recognize and work to abolish environmental racism and the fear that the issue would divide people. The shift from abolishing environmental injustice to a focus on green jobs softens but does not eliminate the importance of addressing environmental racism.

I wish that our grassroots environmental justice policy making approach had not been pitted against other approaches. By shutting down this project, we as a society lost an opportunity to test our ability to bring people together around kitchen tables and in meetings in school auditoriums where they are exposed to each other's humanity. To be in spaces where distrust and suspicion fades and where these frontline communities, Indigenous groups, and workers uplift the issues of jobs and the environment with proposals grounded in their day-to-day experiences.[26]

INTERNATIONALISM AND SOLIDARITY AS ACTS OF RADICAL LOVE

FROM CHINATOWN TO STANDING ROCK

The fight to stop the construction of the Dakota Access Pipeline, begun in 2016, affirmed the Principles of Environmental Justice that we developed at the First National People of Color Environmental Leadership Summit back in 1991. Standing Rock exposed the evils and hazards of dirty energy. It educated non-Natives on the issues of sovereignty, destruction of sacred sites, violence against women from the pipeline man camps, human rights abuses and the lack of prior consent, and the alignment of the fossil fuel industry with the state of North Dakota, local officials, local police, and the National Guard. On April 24, 2016, Native youths from the International Indigenous Youth Council launched a historic run to stop the building of the Dakota Access Pipeline. Their act galvanized the Standing Rock Sioux tribal leaders to mobilize resistance. Standing Rock drew thousands across the country and the world to challenge the fossil fuel industry, including from San Francisco Chinatown.[27]

I was fundraising to support Standing Rock when Dallas Goldtooth, an Indigenous Environmental Network youth organizer, encouraged us to come to North Dakota. From this invitation the Chinese

Progressive Association (CPA) organized the Berta Vive Delegation to travel from San Francisco to Standing Rock.[28] On September 27, 2016, our delegation issued a statement connecting the fight for sovereignty and the protection of water, life, and community at Standing Rock with our histories in San Francisco Chinatown.[29]

To support the resistance, we brought financial aid to the camp, delivered gifts for the elders designed by artist Leon Sun, and worked under the leadership of the camp Water Protector elders. It was important to learn and honor the rules of the camp so that our actions were respectful, contributed collectively, and did not result in a burden for our hosts. Most important, we each came back with a deeper understanding of prayer and spirituality. For myself I've since strived to embrace this as a daily personal practice to decolonize and fight for justice not only with my brain and body but also from the heart.

At the Standing Rock campfire we were invited to address the elders and children who gather for the daily morning ceremony. Linda Lee from CPA shared her family's "Water Is Life" story. Linda is second-generation Hmong and grew up in Sacramento. Linda's mother is an amazingly strong and talented woman who, as Linda explains, "can grow anything." The family relies on what comes out of the garden. In 2017, in the midst of the California drought, water-use restrictions were levied across the state. Violations of the policy would result in fines and possible legal charges. The community felt scared and criminalized. Visits to water the garden became uncomfortable and intimidating. Fearing they might violate water rules, neighbors resorted to spending precious money to buy bottled water and to use the Laundromat, rather than use water from the tap. We should not be criminalizing the vulnerable communities for activities such as growing their own food. Instead, two principles should guide our work. First, in seeking to address issues such as the California water shortage, we must ensure these solutions do no harm to the community. Second, Linda recommends that people like her mother should be involved in developing protocols and policies when future climate policies are drafted and implemented. At the conclusion of Linda's story, we were humbled when the elders came and welcomed each of us into the camp with a warm handshake and hug.

On our last day Dallas Goldtooth and Kandi Mossett from IEN sent us off with much appreciation and the "ask" for us to keep up the local direct actions to stop the Dakota Access Pipeline and draw attention to the abuse, disappearance, and murder of Native women as a result of construction of the pipeline.[30] When we returned to the Bay Area, we worked with Pennie Opal Plant, Isabella Zizi, and Briana Ruiz from Idle No More and Corrina Gould from Indian People Organized for Change. Together we mobilized thousands in direct actions to shut down the populous Market Street in San Francisco, confront the US Army Corps of Engineers, and shut down Wells Fargo, CitiBank, and Chase Bank. These direct actions, which involved civil disobedience, were needed to shift the political climate and pressure the City of San Francisco to divest city funds from banks doing business with companies that engaged in dirty energy and prisons. The San Francisco Board of Supervisors voted unanimously to divest city funds and create a San Francisco Public Bank, where the funds would be deposited and

FIGURE 12.1. Gloria Ushigua Santi, president of the Sapara Women's Association of Ecuador, delivers a letter to the Chinese consulate's office in San Francisco in 2017 demanding the withdrawal of Andes Petroleum from the Amazon. The Chinese state-owned oil company was seeking to explore for and extract oil in the ancestral lands of the Sarapa Nation. The Chinese Progressive Association extended international solidarity, mobilizing a delegation to accompany Gloria Ushigua Santi as she delivered her letter. Media coverage of this exchange went viral internationally. Two years later the Ecuadorian government issued a resolution stating that Andes Petroleum would withdraw from Sapara territory. Photo by Joyce Xi.

used to serve the community. A public bank is an example of what Grace Lee Boggs meant when she said, "A revolution that is based on the people exercising their creativity in the midst of devastation is one of the great historical contributions of humankind."

FROM CHINATOWN TO THE AMAZON

Rainforests around the planet are described as the lungs of Mother Earth. All of us are dependent on tropical rainforests, but the Indigenous peoples who live there are the stewards of the land and defenders against extractive plunder and deforestation. In 2017 I learned from a representative of IEN that Andes Petroleum, a Chinese state-owned oil company, had acquired the concession to explore for and extract oil on the ancestral territory of the Sapara Nation. She informed me that Gloria Ushigua Santi, president of the Sapara Women's Association of Ecuador, tried to deliver a letter to the Chinese ambassador to the United Nations requesting that Andes Petroleum not explore for oil and immediately cancel the contract with the Ecuadorian government. She only managed to slip the letter under the door of the mission.

I was moved by our shared experiences of colonization and immediately started to think of ways to be in solidarity through concrete action. I suggested that on her way home to the Amazon, Gloria could attempt to deliver the letter to the Chinese consulate's office in San Francisco. On July 14, 2017, I helped mobilize a delegation to the Chinese consulate along with holding a press conference where local and international Chinese press were present.[31] Surrounded by supporters holding signs and chanting, Gloria led us to the door of the Chinese consulate. After a few minutes of knocking, a consulate representative opened the door. We were surprised that he was not hostile but instead listened intently as Gloria explained the situation. He then accepted the letter and acknowledged it would get to the proper authorities.[32] Media coverage of this exchange went viral internationally.[33]

We did not know the impact of these actions until 2018, when we heard that the Chinese oil company was considering pulling out. Then, on October 10, 2019, the Ecuadorian government issued a resolution stating that Andes Petroleum would withdraw from Sapara territory in response to Sapara opposition to oil exploitation.[34] While this is not yet a total victory—the Sapara Nation requested the total withdrawal from all areas designated for oil exploitation, and the resolution only references one of the two designated areas—Gloria

FIGURE 12.2. An Asian American contingent marching in the People's Climate March in San Francisco on September 8, 2018. During the Solidarity 2 Solutions week of activities, the Chinese Progressive Association hosted a Chinatown Environmental Justice tour. Pam Tau Lee has long been a leader of the national Environmental Justice and Asian American Movements. Photo by Eurydice Thomas, eurydicephoto.com.

has repeatedly acknowledged that the support received from CPA made a big difference.[35] This experience reaffirmed for me the importance of solidarity not as an isolated act but as part of international movement building.

TOWARD "ALL MY RELATIONS"

Dallas Goldtooth, an organizer for IEN's Keep It In the Ground project, always starts his presentations with the prayer *Mitakuye Oyasin*, or "All My Relations." His invocation was always a good indication of what would follow: wisdom, leadership, encouragement, connection, being in balance with Mother Earth. Every morning I wake up with the hope that I can make these words come to life in their own particular way.

In 2018 the People's Climate Movement March was held in San Francisco under the national call "Rise for Climate, Jobs, and Justice." I represented CPA at the planning meetings. In the spirit of "all my relations," this mobilization was an opportunity to deepen relationships within the Asian American community and with the broader Climate Justice movement. During the Solidarity 2 Solutions week of activities, CPA hosted a Chinatown Environmental Justice tour. The tour started at Wentworth Alley, historically known as "Fish Alley" for the mural of painted fish that were once plentiful in the San Francisco Bay and that are now threatened. We explained how pollution from toxic waste and climate change have impacted subsistence fishing in our local waters. Artist and environmentalist Leon Sun and I designed and distributed thousands of bilingual buttons in English and Chinese: "Water Is Life," "Sky Protector," and "No REDDS." For the People's Climate Movement March, I approached Leon about designing and leading a team of young people to contribute to painting the world's largest street mural. Leon and Vida Kuang created a beautiful Sky Protector design.[36]

On September 8, 2018, I was proud to play a part in mobilizing more than three hundred Asians under the banner "From our home-lands to the front line—Asians Rise 4 Climate" and initiating a joint Asian statement documenting the devastating environmental impacts of climate change and the forced extraction of natural resources across Asia as well as the racialized health and environmental impacts of white supremacy and economic exploitation on Asian communities in the United States.[37] In the spirit of all my relations and acting like a majority, the joint statement calls for Asians to work together and reimagine what it means to find solutions that work:

> The crisis of climate change has inflicted environmental disaster
> across our home-lands in Asia ranging from rising sea levels, air,
> soil and water pollution, dams bursting, typhoons, extreme
> temperatures, drought, major threats to food security and a host
> of other assaults, resulting in deaths, illness and displacement
> of millions of people. . . . In our local communities in the US,
> environmental racism, the disproportionate exposure to harmful
> environmental exposure, can also be traced to white supremacy
> and economic exploitation that has resulted in our families living
> near toxic facilities such as refineries, chemical plants, landfills,
> freeways, or in urban areas such as the Tenderloin and Chinatown.
> A toxic environment is also present when our humanity is denied,
> when our cultures, genders and ways of being are not embraced.

> We come together to oppose false solutions. . . . We come with
> solutions of our own that unite and uplift the voices of those most
> impacted by the climate crisis.[38]

It is imperative that we come together to be radical environmental justice "solutionaries," that we be aggressive in critiquing, exposing, and challenging the kinds of proposals that look like solutions but in fact enable dirty energy. For environmental justice organizations this is a challenge because many mainstream funders and environmental organizations support such market-based policies. In my search I have found only one group of funders who openly oppose funding market-based solutions.[39] We must be bold and act as the majority to halt emissions at the source, keep dirty fuels in the ground, and engage in practices to live in balance with Mother Earth.

WE WILL NOT BE SILENCED: THE IMPORTANCE OF INTERNATIONAL SOLIDARITY

In 2019 Global Witness documented "164 killings of land and environmental defenders—ordinary people murdered for defending their homes, forests and rivers against destructive industries. Countless more were silenced through violent attacks, arrests, death threats or lawsuits." The Philippines had become, under President Duterte, the deadliest place in the world for environmentalists.[40] One survivor of this brutality is Brandon Lee, a volunteer with the Chinese Progressive Association, whose commitment to democracy and liberation took him from San Francisco to the Philippines. His passion for the people's struggles for democracy and liberation took root during an exposure trip to the Philippines, where he met with Indigenous people, environmental activists, farmers, peasants, and human rights defenders.[41] He returned to the States and volunteered with BAYAN USA Northern California, but for him this was not enough. Despite the dangers for activists, he relocated to the Philippines in 2010 and volunteered as a paralegal for the Cordillera Human Rights Alliance and as provincial human rights officer for the Ifugao Peasant Movement and the Justice and Peace Advocates of Ifugao. In 2015 a death threat was mailed to him and nine others. Even after the killing of movement leader and farmer leader Ricardo Mayumi in 2018, Brandon stepped forward as an activist journalist campaigning against the Quad River Hydropower Project.

Beverly Longid, chair of the Indigenous People's Movement for Self-Determination and Liberation, testified before a US congressional hearing about the human rights situation in the Philippines: "We have been facing intensified incursion into our ancestral lands because of the government's 'Build Build Build' policy that would bring in destructive projects like mining, corporate energy projects and plantations. Alongside the 'Build Build Build' policy is Duterte's 'kill kill kill' policy against people who are resisting, dissenting, or critical to his policy or programs."[42] Nine days later, on August 6, 2019, Brandon was shot multiple times in the back by unidentified men whom he believes were state security forces or agents. Brandon Lee represents the kinds of courageous international and interethnic solidarities that are necessary if we are to transform our world. We must not be silent because our voices and acts of solidarity can make a difference.

It's been fifty years since I was criticized by my family for becoming a radical activist. Twenty years ago, over lunch with my then seventy-year-old parents, the topic of the war in Vietnam came up. My dad, who worked as an engineer as part of the US military complex, leaned over and asked, "Mama, what side was I on?" Mom looked at him and with a firm voice said, "The wrong side." Dad turned to me and said, "I'm proud of you." My heart swelled with joy. For me it was an affirmation that being radically "different" and acting on my views for peace was not a bad thing. I was lucky to have learned that over time my parents understood where I was coming from and that they were proud. So to all the Asians out there worried about advocating for a better world, my advice is to own it and trust yourself and your family.

For me organizing starts with the "ask." I was twenty years old when I gave my first public speech. I was attending a student antiwar rally planning meeting when Floyd Huen recommended that I deliver the Asian Coalition speech. Though I knew very little about the situation and was new to the movement, accepting that ask pushed me to study up on the war, understand why the United States was in Asia, and analyze why we as Asian Americans were taking a stand in opposition to the war. That ask was key for me in transforming my personal fear of public speaking into taking responsibility so my speech could bring clarity, tell the truth, uplift solidarity, and help to grow the greater radical "we." It was the organizing insight of people like Floyd who supported my development and pushed me to step up.

Radical love has sustained me throughout these years. In 2017, when I was invited to go on an exploratory trip to the Philippines, I hesitantly expressed concern for my husband's health and welfare. Ben's support and encouragement have been crucial in my ability to stay engaged, and he would now be home alone for two weeks. Almost immediately, Armael Malinis developed a spreadsheet. Friends and community stepped up, and each day for Ben was filled with visits, phone calls, shared meals, walks, and lively conversation. To this day Ben and I look back at how everyday situations can become transformative organizing moments that strengthen our love for the movement.

So many times the work of being in the journey toward liberation and environmental and economic justice can be overwhelming. During these moments I have learned not to internalize it but to reach out, instead, and ask my friends who worry about me, "What do you think I need to do?" I have learned that there is a difference between burnout and fatigue. With fatigue one should rest and recover. Burnout is when you no longer want to be a part of the movement. I have been blessed to be in the struggle alongside room attendants, community residents, and frontline environmental justice communities. I have been inspired by the grassroots leaders and freedom fighters and environmental defenders from around the world. These experiences and relationships have kept me grounded and engaged. When in the course of organizing, if a community resident, room cleaner, or ally invited me to go to their home for dinner or tea, I went. These were moments when we got to learn about and from each other. These were spaces where trust and authentic friendships evolved and we became each other's support and cheerleader. These are the spaces in which the real work of growing the greater we is done and where, instead of burnout, our personal commitment to the work becomes more grounded.

It is my hope that the radical love stories can provide some guidance on the crisis of "what can we do about the climate?" For me it has been about growing the greater we and not relying on the system that got us into this crisis to get us out. For me the root cause for this crisis is the system of capitalism that has evolved into imperialism, the hetero-patriarchial violence and militarization of our communities, and the brutal extraction of resources from the land and unbridled consumption. Dismantling this system needs to go hand in hand with a just transition away from capitalism and guided by a vision that a "better world is possible," one with a clean and healthy environment for all. This vision for the future is grounded in my firm belief that what happens in the world will be determined by working-class people. My own work as an environmental justice activist started with and will always be grounded in my family's roots in Chinatown, and I believe that our work and visions for a better world must necessarily emerge from and be rooted in place, class consciousness, and the experiences and visions of working-class people.

I also believe that the youth of today bring their own ideas about what we must do about the climate to make a better world possible and, through their visions, will continue to advance and grow in new ways the work that my generation and those before me began. Happy Lim, another elder mentor for many of us Chinese radical 1960s youths, inspired his generation of 1930s radical Chinese youths and believed in the power of young people to move liberation forward. In an interview for *East Wind* magazine, he said: "Only if we take reality as it is, do mass work, persist in the correct line, and struggle relentlessly will a free, just, and equal society become a reality. I will follow the advanced youth of today and keep fighting." For me, in the words of Happy Lim, I will follow the advanced youth and will strive to keep on fighting.

NOTES

This chapter is an expanded version of Pam Tau Lee's keynote address for the Contemporary Asian American Activism symposium, held at UCSB, January 24–25, 2019. Thank you, Monica Chan, Diane Fujino, and Robyn Rodriguez, for this invitation to document and reflect on the past, present, and the future. I also want to thank everyone who supported me in writing this chapter, including Katherine Lee, Ben Lee, Cassandra Smithies, and those whose stories I've included in it.

1 Red Guard Political Program, Point 11, *Aion Magazine* 1, no. 1 (1970): 30–31. The Red Guard Political Platform is modeled after the Black Panther Party's Ten-Point Platform. It is Asian focused and includes the additional demand on environment.

2 Indians of All Tribes, "The Alcatraz Proclamation, 1969," in *Environmental Justice in Postwar America: A Documentary Reader*, ed. Christopher W. Wells (Seattle: University of Washington Press, 2018), 93–94.

3 Vida Kuang, email message to author, November 10, 2018.

4 George Murray and Joudon Major Ford, "Black Panthers: The Afro-Americans' Challenge," *Tricontinental* 10 (January–February 1969): 96–111.

5 Murray and Ford, "Black Panthers."

6 Bobby Seale, Alex Hing, Sadie Lum, and Irwin Lum, in discussion with the author, July 2009; Fred Ho, ed., *Legacy to Liberation: Politics and Culture of Revolutionary Asian Pacific America* (San Francisco: AK Press, 2000), 396.

7 "I Wor Kuen 12 Point Platform and Program," in *Roots: An Asian American Reader*, ed. Amy Tachiki et al. (Los Angeles: UCLA Asian American Studies Center, 1971).

8 Angela Zhao argues that IWK was a feminist organization; this meant that the core leadership group was led by women and half the membership was women. For more about IWK as a feminist organization, see Angela Zhao, "The Righteous Fists of Harmony: Asian American Revolutionaries in the Radical Minority and Third World Liberation Movements, 1960–1978" (bachelor's thesis, University of Chicago, April 6, 2018), https://www.marxists.org/history/erol/ncm -1a/zhao.pdf. I found IWK women to be down-to-earth, responsible, and politically clear. They practiced methods of work that facilitated our personal and political growth and development, including study and discussion. Point 4 of the IWK platform reads: "The thousands of years of oppression under feudalism and capitalism have created institutions and myths of male supremacy over women. Men must fight along with sisters in the struggle for economic and social equality and must recognize that sisters make up over half of the revolutionary army. Sisters and brothers are equals fighting for our people."

   The IWK platform also emphasized mutual support and acceptance: "Asian people in Amerika have been continually oppressed by greedy and traitorous people in our own communities and wider racist exploitative society. We want an end to male chauvinism and sexual exploitation. We are working for a world of peace, where the needs of the people come first, which is without class distinctions and is based upon the love and unity of all peoples" ("I Wor Kuen 12 Point Platform and Program").

9 "I Wor Kuen 12 Point Platform and Program."

10 On the Chicano Moratorium Committee, see Lorena Oropeza, *Raza Si, Guerra No: Chicano Protest and Patriotism during the Viet Nam War Era* (Berkeley: University of California Press, 2005).

11 On the Bay Area Asian Coalition Against the War, see Daryl J. Maeda, *Chains of Babylon: The Rise of Asian America* (Minneapolis: University of Minnesota Press, 2009), 120–25.

12 Michael Liu, Kim Geron, and Tracy Lai, *The Snake Dance of Asian American Activism: Community, Vision, and Power* (Lanham, MD: Lexington Books, 2008), 66; Maeda, *Chains of Babylon*, 123.

13 "In the Belly of the Monster: Asian American Opposition to the
    Vietnam War," *Densho Blog*, November 15, 2017, https://densho.org
    /asian-american-opposition-vietnam-war; Maeda, *Chains of Babylon*,
    123.

14 United Church of Christ Commission for Racial Justice, "Toxic Wastes
    and Race in the United States: A National Report on the Racial and
    Socio-Economic Characteristics of Communities with Hazardous
    Waste Sites" (New York: Public Data Access, 1987); Christopher
    W. Wells, introduction to Wells, *Environmental Justice in Postwar
    American*, 3–21; World Rainforest Movement, "'For a Change of
    Paradigm': Interview with Tom Goldtooth from the Indigenous
    Environmental Network, 2016," in Wells, *Environmental Justice in
    Postwar America*, 286–90.

15 Charles Lee, ed., *The First National People of Color Environmental
    Leadership Summit, Proceedings* (New York: United Church of Christ,
    1992); Pamela Tau Lee, "Policy Group Workshop: Occupational Health
    and Safety Issues," First National People of Color Environmental
    Leadership Summit, October 24–27, 1991, Washington, DC; Rose Marie
    Augustine et al., "First National People of Color Environmental
    Leadership Summit Press Conference, October 24, 1991," in Wells,
    Environmental Justice in Postwar America, 171–77. On Charles Lee's
    career, see Dianne See Morrison, "Rallying Point: Charles Lee's Long-
    standing Career in Public Health," *American Journal of Public Health*
    99, no. S3 (November 1, 2009): S508–S510.

16 Press conference statements by Tom Goldtooth, Rose Marie Augustine,
    Benjamin Chavis Jr., Gail Small, Toney Anaya, Pat Bryant, Robert
    Bullard, Donna Chavis, and Richard Moore affirmed these experiences.
    See Augustine et al., "First National People of Color Environmental
    Leadership Summit Press Conference," 171–77.

17 Dana Alston, speech, First National People of Color Environmental
    Leadership Summit, Washington, DC, October 24–27, 1991.

18 On Dana Alston's work, see "In Memory of Sister Dana Alston," from
    the archives of Dr. Robert Bullard and reprinted in *Equitable & Just
    National Climate Platform*, https://ajustclimate.org/dana.html; Dana
    Alston, "The Summit: Transforming a Movement," *Race, Poverty, and
    the Environment* 2, nos. 3–4 (1991); Giovanna Di Chiro, "Defining
    Environmental Justice," *Socialist Review* 22, no. 4 (October 1992):
    93–131; Dana Alston and Nicole Brown, "Global Threats to People of
    Color," in *Confronting Environmental Racism: Voices from the Grassroots*,
    ed. Robert D. Bullard (Cambridge, MA: South End Press, 1993),
    179–94.

19 "The Principles of Environmental Justice, 1991," in Wells, *Environmen-
    tal Justice in Postwar America*, 180–82.

20 Executive Order 12898—Federal Actions to Address Environmental
    Justice in Minority Populations and Low-Income Populations, issued by

President William J. Clinton, February 11, 1994, https://www.archives
.gov/files/federal-register/executive-orders/pdf/12898.pdf.

21 Grace Lee Boggs, conversation with author, San Francisco, June 3,
1998.

22 Asian Americans held a special event to honor Grace Lee Boggs at the
2010 US Social Forum in Detroit.

23 Richard L. Rashke, *The Killing of Karen Silkwood: The Story behind the
Kerr-McGee Plutonium Case* (Ithaca, NY: Cornell University Press,
2000).

24 In Oklahoma residents from the local Ponca Tribe met with OCAW
carbon black factory workers. The workers learned about environmental racism, and members from the tribe learned about worker injuries
and illness, including cancer and job fear (unfair choice between
unsafe work and a job). See PACE International Union, "Ponca Tribe
and PACE Union Hold Protest March Condemning Environmental
Pollution and Employee Lockout," *Corporate Social Responsibility
Newswire*, August 25, 2003, https://www.csrwire.com/press_releases
/20966-Ponca-Tribe-and-PACE-Union-Hold-Protest-March-Condemning
-Environmental-Pollution-and-Employee-Lockout.

25 Public Health Institute and the Labor Institute, "Joint Statement on
Just Transition," *A Just Transition for Jobs and the Environment*,
July 2000, https://tools.niehs.nih.gov/wetp/public/Course_download2
.cfm?tranid=2569. This Just Transition community and worker
workbook was the main tool used to facilitate discussion.

26 I wish to acknowledge and appreciate OCAW union members Joe
Anderson and Paul Renner, who were strong allies in their support for
the environmental justice community in this process, and to Jenice
View, Jose Bravo, Richard Moore, Tom Goldtooth, Ruben Solis-Garcia,
and the late Connie Tucker for their dedication to keeping the concept
of a Just Transition grounded in the struggles of workers and grassroots work and centered around abolishing environmental racism.

27 Saul Elbein, "The Youth Group That Launched a Movement at Standing
Rock," *New York Times*, January 31, 2017; Daniel A. Medina, "Standing
Rock Sioux Takes Pipeline Fight to UN Human Rights Council in
Geneva," *NBC News*, September 20, 2016; Catherine Thorbecke,
"Leader of the Standing Rock Sioux Tribe Calls on Obama to Halt
Pipeline after Violent Clash," *ABC News*, November 21, 2016.

28 Delegates included Thuỳ Trang Nguyen, Pam Tau Lee, Leon Sun,
Rachel Gonzales-Vernon, Linda Lee, Shina Robinson, Armael Malinis,
Rachel Vernon, Cerise Palmanteer, Sammie Ablaza Wills, Alvina Wong,
Ellen Choy, Sarah Lee, Cynthia Fong, Vivian Huang, Sunshine Velasco,
Robin Castel, Eutene Kang, Cheuk-Ning Li, Yin Yu, Liz Mak, Leon
Morimoto, and Helena Wong. For coverage of the Berta Vive Delega-
tion from San Francisco Chinatown to Standing Rock, see *AppleDaily*,
October 9, 2016, http://hk.apple.nextmedia.com/international/art

/20161009/19795710 (Cantonese); and *AppleDaily*, October 8, 2016, www.appledaily.com.tw/realtimenews/article/new/20161008 /964227 (Mandarin).

29 The full beginning of the delegation statement reads: "We travel as the Berta Vive Delegation to join the actions to protect the water, life, and community from being destroyed by the Dakota Access Pipeline. We travel also to honor the life of Berta Caceres who was murdered for protecting her community's land and water in Honduras. We are humbled yet proud to be a part of this historic moment and contribute towards building international vigilance and solidarity with the Water Protectors at Standing Rock. While our group comes in solidarity under the organizational banner of the Chinese Progressive Association, we are of Hmong, Vietnamese, Chinese, and Yaqui/Apache/Mexican heritage. For many of us, the history and violence of US Imperialism and wars of aggression in our homelands capture the roots for the arrival of our people to America. This violence included the use of chemical warfare (Agent Orange and napalm), the dropping of bombs, the infusion of drugs and other acts of control and domination."

30 Oil pipeline construction crew "man camps" are linked to the sexual abuse of, violence against, and disappearance of Native women. See Nick Estes, "Prologue: Prophets," *Our History Is the Future: Standing Rock versus the Dakota Access Pipeline and the Long Tradition of Indigenous Resistance* (Brooklyn, NY: Verso Books, 2019), 8.

31 Press conference speakers were Gloria Ushigua Santi, Sapara Women's Association of Ecuador (ASHINWAKA); Corrina Gould, Indian People Organized for Change; Leila Salazar-Lopez, Amazon Watch; Metzali Andrade, PODER; Pam Tau Lee, Chinese Progressive Association.

32 The letter includes this statement: "The Sapara Nation of the Amazon . . . write to . . . request that you act to prevent the genocide of the Sapara Nation and of the Indigenous Peoples in Isolation and that the contracts . . . to explore and exploit oil be immediately and definitively canceled. The survival of the Sapara Nation and Indigenous Peoples in Isolation depends on the health of our rainforests, rivers, mountains and biodiversity, where our spirits are born. The Sapara Nation was never consulted. Nor did the Nation grant its free, prior and informed consent, as stipulated by the Constitution of Ecuador, international human rights treaties and the UN Guiding Principles on Business and Human Rights. . . . There are precedents of genocides caused by the exploration, extraction, exploitation and transportation of oil in the Amazon. The operations of Texaco caused grave destruction of the environment. Both the Tetetes and the Sanshauri who inhabited the region exploited by Texaco were wiped out." For Chinese TV and print coverage on the contents of the letter, see *AppleDaily*, July 16, 2017, https://hk.news.appledaily.com/international/daily /article/20170716/20091501.

33   For Chinese coverage of the delivery of the Sapara letter to the Chinese consulate, see *AppleDaily*, July 16, 2017, http://hk.apple.nextmedia .com/international/art/20170716/20091501 (Cantonese); and *Apple-Daily*, July 15, 2017, https://tw.appledaily.com/international/20170715 /3YOZYR75LWEUASKHKYKA6PK6HY (Mandarin).

34   See "Resolution Nro. MERNNR-MERNNR-2019-0013-RM—Ministerio de Energía y Recursos Naturales No Renovables," printed resolution, in possession of author, October 10, 2019.

35   Organizing the action at the consulate, translating the letter from the Sapara Nation to the Chinese oil company into Chinese, organizing the Chinese-language press conference, pulling together an Asians in Solidarity statement, mobilizing supporters to the consulate, and getting international coverage on Chinese TV were some of the tasks that this struggle entailed.

36   Sophie Maes, "Climate Protesters Created Largest Street Mural Thanks to Some Fearless Grandmas," *Global Citizen*, September 11, 2018, https://www.globalcitizen.org/en/content/climate-protest-mural -grandmas-san-francisco.

37   Asians Rise for Climate Justice, "From Our Homelands to Our Frontlines—Asians Rise for Climate Justice," printed informational flyer, in possession of author, September 8, 2018.

38   Asians Rise for Climate Justice, "From Our Homelands to Our Frontlines."

39   "Open Letter by the Swift Foundation Rejects REDD and Carbon Trading as False Solutions to Climate Change," *REDD-Monitor*, March 12, 2019, https://redd-monitor.org/2019/03/12/open-letter-by -the-swift-foundation-rejects-redd-and-carbon-trading-as-false -solutions-to-climate-change.

40   "Enemies of the State? How Governments and Businesses Silence Land and Environmental Defenders," *Global Witness*, July 2019, 8, https:// www.globalwitness.org/en/campaigns/environmental-activists /enemies-state.

41   On BAYAN's exposure trips, see Jessica Antonio's chapter in this volume, "BAYAN USA: Filipino Transnational Radical Activism in the United States in the Twenty-First Century."

42   "US Congressional Hearing: An Important First Step Forward," *ICHRP-US*, July 31, 2019, https://ichrpus.org/2019/07/31/us -congressional-hearing-an-important-first-step-forward.

RADICAL LOVE FOR A
NEW GENERATION

ROBYN MAGALIT RODRIGUEZ

> Be Love, Be Loved, Be Amado
> Amado Khaya Canham Rodriguez
> May 9, 1998–August 4, 2020

> Let's lift up his memory and remember his legacy.
> He is the new ancestor that has carved out a new path and
>   way of being.
> He is the success story we need to celebrate.
> He is the epitome of humanity.
> —EHGOSA HAMILTON, TEACHER AND BLACK STUDENT
>   UNION ADVISOR, CALIFORNIA HIGH SCHOOL

WE WERE IN THE MIDST OF FINALIZING THE REVISIONS TO this anthology when I received the tragic news that my son, Amado Khaya Canham Rodriguez, suddenly passed away on August 4, 2020, in Mindoro, Philippines. He was twenty-two. For two years he had been living and working alongside Indigenous peoples of the Philippines in their struggle for self-determination and national democracy. For the past few months Amado lived among the Mangyan people, supporting relief efforts in the wake of two successive typhoons and the onset of COVID-19.

FIGURE E.1. Amado Khaya Canham Rodriguez speaking at anti-gentrification rally in Oakland, California, in fall 2017. Photo courtesy of Robyn Rodriguez.

Amado Khaya, descended from the peoples of the Philippines and South Africa. His Filipino name, Amado, means "beloved." He was named after Amado V. Hernandez, the anticolonial poet whose words were considered treasonous by the American colonial government of the Philippines. His South African name, Khaya, means "home." Amado Khaya lived up to his name and committed himself to putting radical love into the world and creating spaces of liberatory hope—and thus a sense of home—wherever he went. In many ways Amado Khaya's life as a young activist deeply reflects many of the key themes of this anthology: intergenerational connections, solidarity, radicalism, internationalism, and the importance of ethnic studies and Asian American studies. As a member of the so-called Gen Z, what we anticipate will be a major readership for this book, Amado Khaya's life and legacy as an activist and organizer can offer vital lessons for his generation and beyond.

Amado—as he was mostly known by his friends and family in the United States—was the son of activist-organizers. His father, David Canham, was a student leader in the South African liberation struggle through the 1980s. One could say that cross-racial solidarity and internationalism were in Amado's very DNA. Yet his DNA is not what gave rise to his activism. His life experiences as a biracial Afro-Asian youth, especially as he shuttled between Oakland and the suburbs of the East Bay (where he attended high school in his maternal grandparents' community), prompted him to ask hard questions of his own about the world. The emergence of the Black Lives Matter movement and the rise of a more flagrant form of white supremacism with the ascendance of Donald Trump further radicalized him. His activism began with the simple act of standing up to his teachers. He walked out of a European History class when he felt the histories of his people were being denigrated and denied. He then proceeded to organize with other Black students in his high school to revitalize the Black Student Union.

Though we as parents shared stories of our activist experiences with Amado throughout his life, he took his own initiative in seeking counsel from earlier generations of lovers of justice and freedom to understand their best practices and to take heed of their warnings about what had failed in the past. As a resident of Oakland, he was inspired by the struggles of the Black Panther Party and wanted to build on the legacy left by them, so he actively sought out the mentorship of elders such as Bobby Seale and Emory Douglas. At the same time, he was inspired by Asian American Movement leaders like Greg Morozumi and others, taking time to listen to their perspectives, often asking hard questions of all of us and even pushing back. What he didn't get from people he got in books. Amado was an ardent student of history who wanted to understand the root causes of the oppression people suffer. He wanted to discover the wisdom of those who fought against oppression. He read both activist and academic texts on his ancestors' struggles in South Africa and the Philippines but also about the struggles of people of color in this country and, because he was a true internationalist, others around the world, including Latin America and the Middle East. In addition to self-study, he participated in informal and formal collective study. He took advantage of what he could learn while a student at Laney College, studying with progressive faculty. Indeed, as a student organizer, he became a passionate advocate for ethnic studies—a struggle first popularized by the Black Power movement and advanced by Filipino American activists—because he knew it helps our struggle if we are successful in carving out space in the institution for critical perspectives.

Amado often felt frustrated by his peers' reticence to do the work of face-to-face organizing and their dependence, instead, on social media to engage in activist discourse. Amado's social media profile, as compared to many of his Gen Z counterparts, was sparse. For Amado there was a clear distinction between being an activist and an organizer: while an activist might be an individual who responds to issues of the day through conscientious action or outspoken critique, an organizer is one with a longer view of radical social change, one who is embedded in broader collectivities of struggle with whom one grows and builds toward genuine liberation for all. There was always a vital difference between activism and organizing for Amado. He valued both yet ultimately believed that deep-rooted transformation comes from organizing. As a student at Laney Community College in Oakland, he was among the young leaders in a fight against gentrification. He helped to stop the building of an A's (baseball team) ballpark at the Peralta Community College Headquarters District, which for Amado and many others would unleash even more displacements in the city of Oakland. One former professor is convinced that Amado was vital to the campaign and is a major reason it succeeded. Indeed, in all his endeavors Amado fought to win. Yes, the A's campaign may have been only a small victory in the struggle against capitalism, a system that requires complete overhauling, but these wins, these moments when we accomplish liberation—even on a small scale—are what fuel our passion and energy for the longer fight. Amado understood that. Amado knew we need to build our capacity to win. We need to whet people's appetite for liberation. He knew that wins, however localized, lift us up with the joy that comes from exercising our collective power. He believed that we have to fight to win and thus propel ourselves forward, inch by inch, closer to genuine liberation.

During the second semester of his second year at Laney, in December 2016, Amado took advantage of an opportunity to learn directly from different marginalized communities organized by the International

Committee for Human Rights in the Philippines (ICHRP), a group currently headed by Pam Tau Lee, an Asian American Movement elder and contributor to this anthology. The program was not unlike the "exposure/integration" programs organized by BAYAN as discussed in this anthology. Amado spent several weeks in intensive learning from college student organizers fighting the increasing privatization of higher education; he tilled land alongside peasant farmers who struggle just to feed themselves yet who produce immense profits for brutal landlords; he witnessed both the trauma and resilience of "Lumad" communities (Indigenous peoples of the Southern Philippine region of Mindanao) as they fight to preserve their cultural traditions and retain their ancestral domain amid the constant rain of bullets fired from the private armies of multinational corporations supported by the US-backed Philippine police and military. After nearly three months of learning, Amado came back from the Philippines completely transformed. He was moved not only by the gravity of the situation facing many Filipino people—but most acutely by the Indigenous—but even more inspired by the fierceness of their resistance. By the following summer, in June 2018, Amado took the initiative to reconnect with people he had met during his 2016–17 trip to the Philippines. What was supposed to be a short-term trip ended up being a commitment to remain in the Philippines to deepen his learning and praxis. Two years later he died serving Indigenous communities.

Losing Amado was devastating to so many across several continents. Amado has emerged as a new activist-organizer icon for a new generation. Within weeks after his passing, a mural was painted in the streets of Oakland, and numerous artists produced songs and other visual art in his honor. Music inspired by his art, words, and actions has been composed and performed. Teachers have been sharing the lessons of his life, and students have found new inspiration. It was his unique biography, the important advances he pushed forward in different Bay Area struggles, as well as his bold commitment to give up his first-world privileges to struggle alongside the Philippines' Indigenous peoples that have touched thousands of people's hearts. Many of those who have taken to honoring Amado's legacy do not know him personally, but it is largely because of the deep love he inspired in those he did know that his story is being so widely shared.

For Amado organizing was about relationship building in struggle; it meant being fully present with fellow organizers; it meant treating them with gentleness, patience, kindness, and love. Amado was intentional about his time with "kasamas" (Tagalog for "comrades" or "companions") new and old, whether it was walking someone to class, sharing a meal, picking up the phone to talk, planning a hike, or singing karaoke. Amado wrote in his journal, "Smile kasama," to remind himself to always strive to embody love and to bring joy into organizing work.

Amado Khaya was his name; he was a "beloved home." He died doing the work of literally building homes for the poorest of the poor in the Philippines. That was preceded by work fighting to preserve affordable housing in his city of birth. And all along the way he worked

FIGURE E.2. Mural of Amado Khaya Canham Rodriguez in Oakland, California, produced within months of his passing in August 2020. Photo courtesy of Robyn Rodriguez.

to create and build community on a daily basis through his deep love of his family, friends, and comrades.

It is in the different lessons Amado offers from his short yet meaningful life as an organizer—in his commitment to study, in his courage in fighting to win, in his intentional and joyful approach to organizing—that I hope readers of this book will hold onto when they think of the hashtag BE LOVE, BE LOVED, BE AMADO, which we as a family have been propagating since his passing. Amado loved defiantly. He loved his heritage, his family, his friends, his community. Indeed, for Amado the whole of humanity were his people, and it was in service of humanity that he committed himself, and he committed himself body and soul.

CONTRIBUTORS

JESSICA ANTONIO was first elected as the national secretary-general of BAYAN USA at the Fourth National Congress held in Chicago in 2012 and was elected as the propaganda officer at the Sixth National Congress in 2018. She was first introduced to the National Democratic movement in Seattle in 2004 and has been part of this movement since joining the League of Filipino Students at San Francisco State University in 2007. Experiencing Philippine exposure programs in 2008, 2010, and 2017 solidified her commitment to human rights and activism on a local, national, and international level.

ANGELICA CABANDE was born in the Philippines and immigrated to the United States at the age of eight. She has been an organizer for over twenty-two years, combining art and organizing. She has supported the development of San Francisco immigrant residents in becoming engaged in issues of social justice, equity, and community planning and has educated, organized, and mobilized residents in local and national issues. She started with the South of Market Community Action Network (SOMCAN) in 2004 as a community organizer and became SOMCAN's organizational director in 2010.

GA YOUNG CHUNG is an assistant professor in the Department of Asian American Studies at the University of California, Davis. In her research she examines the surge of dislocation, precarity, and (im)mobility in the era of uneven globalization. Centering on political activism and resistance of undocumented migrants, she unpacks how the meaning of citizenship is dismantled, rearticulated, and reassembled in the Asia-Pacific.

MAY C. FU is associate professor and former chair of the Department of Ethnic Studies at the University of San Diego. She teaches classes on the comparative histories of communities of color, social movements, Asian American grassroots organizing, and women of color feminisms. Drawing on oral histories with movement activists, her research examines the political praxis of Asian American community organizing from the 1960s to the present. She has participated in grassroots movements for educational equity, transformative justice and community accountability, affordable housing, and cross-racial solidarity.

DIANE C. FUJINO is a professor and former chair of Asian American Studies at UC Santa Barbara and former director of the Center for Black Studies Research. Her research examines Japanese and Asian American activism, 1940s to the present, and the influences of Black Power and Third World anti-imperialism. She is author or editor of several books, including *Nisei Radicals: The Feminist Poetics and Transformative Ministry of Mitsuye Yamada and Michael Yasutake*, *Black Power Afterlives: The Enduring Significance of the Black Panther Party*, and *Heartbeat of Struggle: The Revolutionary Life of Yuri Kochiyama*. She serves as co-editor-in-chief of the *Journal of Asian American Studies* and is a core organizer or board member of Ethnic Studies Now! Santa Barbara, Fund for Santa Barbara, UCSB MultiCultural Center, and Cooperation Santa Barbara.

WAYNE JOPANDA is a doctoral student in cultural studies at University of California, Davis, researching Filipino student experiences with burnout, trafficked Filipino teachers, and the neoliberal university's commodification of Filipinos as bodies of labor. Wayne also studies how current Filipino students at US universities respond to these histories of Westernized colonial education in the Philippines through community building, collective activisms, and creating spaces of belonging. Wayne is a founding member of the Bulosan Center for Filipinx Studies and currently serves as its associate director and the founding director of the center's Internship Program. He aims to support and uplift critical Filipinx studies through his community organizing and academic work at the Bulosan Center.

SOYA JUNG has been active in the progressive movement since the early 1990s. She has worked in various sectors, including direct service, community organizing, government, and philanthropy, addressing issues such as immigration, police accountability, welfare, gender justice, and resource rights. She is cofounder and senior partner at ChangeLab, a grassroots think tank that uses research, convening, training, and communications to advance racial justice in an era of rising authoritarianism, with a strategic focus on Asian American racial politics.

KATHERINE H. LEE is the program coordinator of the Teaching & Learning Center at Foothill College in Northern California. Her research examines the history of writing instruction in ethnic studies programs and analyzes how these programs have reconceptualized the work and politics of academic writing. She previously taught in the writing programs at the University of California, Berkeley and Merced, and is the founding director of the Center for Writing & Scholarship at the California Institute of Integral Studies. She received her PhD degree in education at the University of California, Santa Barbara, in 2021.

PAM TAU LEE is an Asian radical elder whose working-class and San Francisco Chinatown roots led her to a lifelong journey dedicated to environmental justice. She is a cofounder of the Chinese Progressive Association–SF, Bay Area Asians for Nuclear Disarmament, Asian Pacific Environmental Network, Just Transition Alliance and the International Coalition for Human Rights in the Philippines–US, and a contributor to the Principles of Environmental Justice. In her nearly five decades of organizing and mentorship, she strives to uplift an ideology of radical love and resistance grounded in the practice of All Power to the People, Serve the People, internationalism, and women whose presence has taught her to act with generosity and courage.

KATHERINE NASOL is a PhD student in the University of California, Davis, Cultural Studies Graduate Group. She is a founding member and policy director of the Bulosan Center for Filipinx Studies, one of the first centers of its kind devoted to studying the issues of Filipinos in the diaspora.

ROBYN MAGALIT RODRIGUEZ is a scholar-activist/organizer who has been committed to advancing social justice through her writing and teaching as well as on the streets for over half her life. She currently serves as professor and is the former chair of Asian American Studies at the University of California, Davis. She is also the founding director of the Bulosan Center for Filipinx Studies, the first of its kind in the University of California system focused on the Filipinx experience in the

United States and diaspora. Among the organizations and movements that Dr. Rodriguez is working closely with are the Asian American Liberation Network (based in the Sacramento region) and the Malaya Movement, which advances human rights in the Philippines.

JAVAID TARIQ was born in Pakpattan, in Punjab, Pakistan. As a college student, he was active in the student movement against the military dictatorship. He migrated to Germany and later to the United States in 1990. He is a cofounder and senior staff member of New York Taxi Workers Alliance and treasurer of the National Taxi Workers' Alliance. Over the years he has organized numerous successful strikes, campaigns, and actions to promote economic and social justice for taxi drivers, a workforce that is 94 percent immigrant and primarily people of color.

ALEX T. TOM is the former executive director of the Chinese Progressive Association in San Francisco and cofounder of Seeding Change. Currently, he is the executive director of the Center for Empowered Politics, a project that trains and develops new leaders of color and grows movement building infrastructure at the intersection of racial justice, organizing, and power building. In 2019 Alex received the Open Society Foundations Racial Justice Fellowship to develop a toolkit to counter the rise of the new Chinese American right wing in the United States.

KAREN UMEMOTO is professor of Urban Planning and Asian American Studies at UCLA. She currently serves as the director and the Helen and Morgan Chu chair at the Asian American Studies Center. She engaged in community-based planning and research as a professor of urban and regional planning at the University of Hawai'i at Mānoa for twenty-two years.

EDDY ZHENG is the president and founder of New Breath Foundation and works to mobilize resources to support Asian American and Pacific Islanders harmed by violence and the unjust immigration and criminal justice systems. A 2019–21 Rosenberg Foundation Leading Edge Fellow and a 2015–17 Open Society Foundations Soros Justice Fellow, he served as codirector of the Asian Prisoner Support Committee and cofounded ROOTS, the first ever ethnic studies program in San Quentin State Prison.

INDEX

Page numbers in *italic* refer to illustrations.

Nisei Soldiers Break Their Silence: Coming Home to Hood River,
by Linda Tamura

A Principled Stand: The Story of Hirabayashi v. United States,
by Gordon K. Hirabayashi, with James A. Hirabayashi and
Lane Ryo Hirabayashi

Cities of Others: Reimagining Urban Spaces in Asian American Literature,
by Xiaojing Zhou

Enduring Conviction: Fred Korematsu and His Quest for Justice,
by Lorraine K. Bannai

*Asians in Colorado: A History of Persecution and Perseverance in the
Centennial State,* by William Wei

The Hope of Another Spring: Takuichi Fujii, Artist and Wartime Witness,
by Barbara Johns

John Okada: The Life and Rediscovered Work of the Author of No-No Boy,
edited by Frank Abe, Greg Robinson, and Floyd Cheung

The Unsung Great: Stories of Extraordinary Japanese Americans,
by Greg Robinson

Becoming Nisei: Japanese American Urban Lives in Prewar Tacoma,
by Lisa M. Hoffman and Mary L. Hanneman

*Contemporary Asian American Activism: Building Movements for
Liberation,* edited by Diane C. Fujino and Robyn Magalit Rodriguez